Steve [signature]

Science Studies Unit
Univ. of Edinburgh
June 2001

HEALTH AND MEDICINE IN BRITAIN
SINCE 1860

Social History in Perspective
General Editor: Jeremy Black

Social History in Perspective is a new series of in-depth studies of the many topics in social, cultural and religious history for students. They also give the student clear surveys of the subject and present the most recent research in an accessible way.

PUBLISHED

John Belchem *Popular Radicalism in Nineteenth-Century Britain*
Sue Bruley *Women in Britain Since 1900*
Simon Dentith *Society and Cultural Forms in Nineteenth-Century England*
Harry Goulbourne *Race Relations in Britain since 1945*
Anne Hardy *Health and Medicine in Britain since 1860*
Tim Hitchcock *English Sexualities, 1700–1800*
Sybil M. Jack *Towns in Tudor and Stuart Britain*
Helen M. Jewell *Education in Early Modern Britain*
Alan Kidd *State, Society and the Poor in Nineteenth-Century England*
Arthur J. McIvor *A History of Work in Britain, 1880–1950*
Hugh McLeod *Religion and Society in England, 1850–1914*
Donald M. MacRaild *Irish Migrants in Modern Britain, 1750–1922*
Donald M. MacRaild and David E. Martin *Labour in Britain, 1830–1914*
Christopher Marsh *Popular Religion in the Sixteenth Century*
Michael A. Mullett *Catholics in Britain and Ireland, 1558–1829*
R. Malsolm Smuts *Culture and Power in England, 1585–1685*
Heather Swanson *Medieval British Towns*
John Spurr *English Puritanism, 1603–1689*
W.B. Stephens *Education in Britain, 1750–1914*
David Taylor *Crime, Policing and Punishment in England, 1750–1914*
N.L. Tranter *British Population in the Twentieth Century*
Ian D. Whyte *Migration and Society in Britain, 1550–1830*
Ian D. Whyte *Scotland's Society and Economy in Transition, c.1500–c.1760*

Please note that a sister series, *British History in Perspective*, is available which covers all the key topics in British political history.

Social History in Perspective
Series Standing Order
ISBN 0–333–71694–9 hardcover
ISBN 0–333–69336–1 paperback
(outside North America only)
You can receive future titles in this series as they are published by placing a standing order. Please contact your bookseller or in case of difficulty, write to us at the address below with your name and address, the title of the series and the ISBN quoted above.

Customer Services Department, Macmillan Distribution Ltd
Houndmills, Basingstoke, Hampshire RG21 6XS England

HEALTH AND MEDICINE IN BRITAIN SINCE 1860

ANNE HARDY

palgrave

First published 2001 by
PALGRAVE
Houndmills, Basingstoke, Hampshire RG21 6XS and
175 Fifth Avenue, New York, N.Y. 10010
Companies and representatives throughout the world

PALGRAVE is the new global academic imprint of
St. Martin's Press LLC Scholarly and Reference Division and
Palgrave Publishers Ltd (formerly Macmillan Press Ltd).

ISBN 0–333–60010–X hardback
ISBN 0–333–60011–8 paperback

This book is printed on paper suitable for recycling and
made from fully managed and sustained forest sources.

A catalogue record for this book is available
from the British Library.

Library of Congress Cataloging-in-Publication Data

Hardy, Anne, Dr.
Health and medicine in Britain since 1860 / Anne Hardy.
p. cm. – (Social history in perspective)
Includes bibliographical references and index.
ISBN 0–333–60010–X (cloth)
1. Medicine—Great Britain—History—20th century. 2. Medical
care—Great Britain—History—20th century. 3. Social
medicine—Great Britain—History—20th century. 4. Public
health—Great Britain—History—20th century.
I. Title. II. Series.

RA485 .H324 2000
362.1'0941—dc21   00–030890

Editing and origination by
Aardvark Editorial, Mendham, Suffolk

10 9 8 7 6 5 4 3 2 1
10 09 08 07 06 05 04 03 02 01

Printed in China

In memory of Richard Hardy
General Practitioner, Casualty Surgeon
1921–1999

CONTENTS

Contents

LIST OF TABLES

ACKNOWLEDGEMENTS

My first debt in writing this book is to successive generations of medical students reading for the Intercalated BSc degree in the History of Medicine at University College London. Over some ten years, their curiosity, and the wide range of their research dissertations, has challenged and educated me. As great, perhaps, is my indebtedness to the many scholars working in the fields of the history of medicine and historical demography, whose publications have made this book possible. I am fortunate to have been on the staff of the Wellcome Institute for the History of Medicine, where colleagues, visitors and the Wellcome Library provided a uniquely favourable environment for teaching and research. I am grateful to the Wellcome Trust for their support. Veronica Gosling and Simon Szreter were generous in their encouragement, and I have benefited from conversations with Andrew Wear. I am deeply grateful to Jeremy Black, Graham Mooney and Michael Neve, who read through the whole manuscript and made valuable suggestions. Any errors are my own. My family were wonderfully unselfish in allowing me the time to finish the book. Henry went without his summer break, and Ruth Sutton and Ellen and Michael tolerated without complaint my near continuous daytime seclusion with a word processor during the summer holidays.

LIST OF ABBREVIATIONS

AIDS	Acquired Immune Deficiency Syndrome
BMA	British Medical Association
EHS	Emergency Hospital Scheme
EMS	Emergency Medical Service
GP	General Practitioner
GRO	General Register Office
HIV	Human Immunodeficiency Virus
IMR	Infant Mortality Rate
MH	Ministry of Health
MMR	Maternal Mortality Rate
MOH	Medical Officer of Health
MRC	Medical Research Council
NHS	National Health Service
PHLS	Public Health Laboratory Service
STD	Sexually Transmitted Disease
VD	Venereal Disease

INTRODUCTION

To return to Britain in the 1860s from the perspective of 2000 is to return to a society divided between now almost unimaginable extremes. It was a world in which town and country were still clearly demarcated, in which agriculture and industry remained distinct, and in which the well-to-do and the poor lived out their lives at either end of a spectrum of extreme wealth and opulence and of extreme poverty and deprivation. As industrial growth accelerated, and as towns and cities expanded to accommodate the new working populations, so environmental conditions deteriorated. Unregulated urban growth and the domestic overcrowding generated by poverty facilitated the spread of infectious disease, while the new concentrations of population revealed to medical men that a whole range of pathological conditions previously thought rare were much more common than had been believed.

From the early decades of the century, issues of poverty, environment and ill-health began to concern medical men.[1] In 1837, the establishment of the General Register Office (GRO), and provision for the registration of births, marriages, deaths and causes of death, opened the way for interested observers to study, to compare and to describe in precise, statistical terms the patterns of life events experienced by the people of England and Wales. Similar offices were established for Scotland and Ireland in 1855 and 1864 respectively. By 1851, when the GRO analysed the data collected in its first full decade of operation, a staggering variation in life expectancy and health experience between different parts of the country was clear. In the years that followed, from the 1860s right through to the end of the twentieth century and beyond, the registration data for the different parts of the kingdom provided social observers and reformers of many kinds with the material for shaping policies and critiques.[2]

The registration data have also provided historians with the means to study health and disease in the past. In the case of England and Wales, the materials furnished by the GRO have been well, if not extensively, exploited for the nineteenth century, and less so for the twentieth. The data for England in particular, especially for London, have received more or less detailed historical scrutiny, and it is not difficult to build up a picture of mortality patterns for England from the secondary literature.[3] Far less historical attention has been given to the other parts of the United Kingdom, and a great deal of that has been essentially antiquarian. The history of physical health in Wales remains obscure, and that of Scotland has barely been broached.[4] Beyond the registration data, however, both Wales and Scotland have been better served by historians interested in mental health.[5] Although an overall history of health in Ireland is as yet lacking, the burgeoning school of Irish historical studies has already yielded several valuable contributions on health, especially in relation to the famine, but also in respect of post-famine Ireland.[6] The same pattern of historical interest can be seen in the historiography of medicine itself, whether in respect of the professionalisation of medicine, the history of hospitals or the experiences of war. The current volume, inevitably, follows the inherent bias of the existing historiography by focusing on England and Wales.

One of the earliest observations made possible by the new statistics was of the difference in death-rates and in life expectancy between country and town. Health, and the chance of death, depended very much on where you lived in the mid-nineteenth century, as it does today. Then, as now, health in these terms was statistically defined – by death-rate and by illness rate. Already in 1860 it was clear that Britain was a divided nation, that people who lived south of a line drawn between the Wash and the Severn Estuary lived longer than those who lived north of that line. Pockets of health and wealth existed in the North, as did pockets of poverty and ill-health in the South, but, in general terms, the characterisation held good. There was also a clear difference in life expectancy between different social classes, and, as the Black Report demonstrated in 1980, that differential still held good at the end of the twentieth century.

For the later nineteenth century sickness records show a different divide: working people were more likely to fall sick in the west of the country than in the east. This pattern was probably the result of the concentration of industry and urban development on the western side of the country. Until the First World War, life was very much more hazardous in the great cities, London apart, than it was in the countryside: indeed, it was the cities that upheld the national death-rate into the 1880s.[7] Life chances were improving for children and young adults in these decades, but for infants aged under one year they did not improve until the early years of the twentieth century, when the infant mortality rate, which had long hovered about 150 per thousand live births, began to fall sharply. Again, infants suffered much more severely in towns.[8] For both sickness and death, Scotland, and especially Wales, were black spots: in Wales in the first decade of this century, the death-rate in even the rural districts exceeded that of England's urban counties for the age group 10–35, while the decline of infant mortality in Scotland lagged appreciably behind that of England in the years before the Second World War.[9]

The establishment of registration provided one way of measuring health: the analysis of death records. Despite the limitations of such data – which do not, for example, describe illness that exists during life – the mortality figure remains one of the most common and simplest ways of measuring the well-being of communities. The analysis of other types of demographic record, of friendly society, commercial insurance company and, from 1913, National Insurance data, provide a valuable insight into the incidence and experience of illness, of morbidity as opposed to mortality, and of the ways in which the use and practice of medicine related to that experience.[10] The relationship between health and medicine is ancient and complex: from the healers of the very earliest human societies who used vegetable drugs, plants, animal parts and excrement in their preparations, to modern practitioners of scientific medicine, the effectiveness of medical treatment has often lain not in the treatment alone, but in the nature of the relationship between patient, treatment and healer. The beneficial therapeutic influence of this relationship – known as the placebo effect – was and is an important component of successful medical practice.[11] For many centuries medicine was virtually powerless to improve health, or to alleviate or cure disease, yet medicine and its practitioners remained participants in the process of managing human distress.

It was in the 1860s, however, that a number of critical developments took place that were in the ensuing century radically to change the power and potential of medicine to influence human health. The nature and philosophy of medicine and medical practice had already changed. At the end of the eighteenth century a new emphasis on the study of morbid anatomy, and the association of the physical lesions found in the body after death with the symptoms experienced by the patient in life, focused medical attention increasingly on disease processes rather than on the personal reactions of the patient. Physical examination of the patient, previously rare, formed the basis of this new medical approach, which was practised at the bedside, in hospital and in the post-mortem room.[12] In this change of medical focus lay the essence of a powerful model for understanding illness that still survives, and which became known as biomedicine.

By 1860 another powerful model that was to place the physical concerns of medicine in a wider context had emerged: the concept of evolution. The year 1859 saw the publication of Charles Darwin's *On the Origin of Species*, after which existing concern about the impact of urban environments, and of personal behaviour, on human health and physique took on a new edge. Already in 1861 the sociologist Herbert Spencer noted the 'remarks of a suggestive writer' that 'the first requisite to success in life is to be a good animal', and declared, 'To be a nation of good animals is the first condition of national prosperity.'[13] Although Spencer derived his ideas from the early French evolutionist Lamarck, who believed that evolution was a process of improvement by adaption towards perfection, the Darwinian concept of evolution as survival of the fittest came to dominate late Victorian thinking. By the end of the century, concepts of evolution and degeneration, and of the breeding of 'good animals', had come to exert a powerful influence among Britain's educated classes.[14]

Against this background of a growing emphasis on the body of the patient, and the realisation of the ideal of the good animal, several specifically medical developments broadened the prospects for constructive medical intervention in problems of health and disease. Chloroform anaesthesia was discovered by James Young Simpson in 1849, and its application in surgical practice set in place the first important brick in the edifice of modern surgical competence: the invention of artery clamps and the elaboration of antiseptic and aseptic techniques subsequently helped to transform the range, and improve the effectiveness, of surgery by the end of the century. In 1864 Louis Pasteur announced his germ theory of disease and finally refuted the idea that diseases were able to generate spontaneously given the right circumstances, and by 1880 Robert Koch had demonstrated the existence of specific disease-causing organisms. In 1865 the great French physiologist Claude Bernard published his *Introduction to the Study of Experimental Medicine*, describing the principles and methods of experimental medical science and boosting the core research discipline of experimental physiology. Then in 1868 Carl Wunderlich published his manual of thermometry, which guided the physician in distinguishing between different febrile diseases through the use of the thermometer.

The 1860s were also a critical decade in the history of health in Britain. Although the public health movement had been active since the 1840s with the efforts of Edwin Chadwick and his associates to improve health and reduce the death-rate in the name of efficiency, it had not, in the intervening years, notched up any notable success in the reduction of the death-rate or the control of disease. The crude death-rate for England and Wales had stood at 22.4 per thousand living in 1841–50; between 1861 and 1870 it stood at 22.5. Recent research has, indeed, argued that Britain's standard of living deteriorated sharply in the second quarter of the nineteenth century, and although the decline was halted in the later 1850s and 60s, it was not until the 1870s and 80s that the trend was significantly reversed.[15]

The 1860s were a particularly turbulent decade in the country's health history. Beginning in 1861 and lasting until 1869, London was swept by a severe epidemic of typhus. In December 1861 the Prince Consort died of typhoid. With the coming of the cotton famine in 1862, typhus appeared in the Lancashire textile districts, where the operatives and their families had been reduced to a state of extreme misery through unemployment. Smallpox seemed to be increasing in virulence, measles was going through one of its cycles of enhanced fatality, and in 1869 scarlet fever became severely epidemic across the country. Cholera and cattle plague had been epidemic in 1866, and the army was deeply concerned by the impact of venereal disease (VD) on its manpower. There was also a worrying epidemic of wound infections in British hospitals.[16] Surveyed from the vantage points of the GRO and central government Medical Department, Britain appeared to be under siege from infectious disease. Nor did the 1870s open auspiciously: the century's severest epidemic of smallpox broke in the autumn of 1870, raging through 1871, and in December 1871, the Prince of Wales fell ill with typhoid.

In fact, the climacteric had been reached. The national death-rate fell steadily, if unevenly, in the 1870s. By 1900 it stood at 18.2 per thousand, and by 1939 it had stabilised at around 12. Whereas life expectancy for adult males in 1860 was a mere 40 years, in the 1990s it reached 74 years. Death-rate and life expectancy, however, present only one aspect of Britain's health between 1860 and 2000, that which can be measured in statistical terms. They tell us little about the health experiences of ordinary people, and still less about the ways in which they managed their health, or how medicine, whether orthodox or alternative, influenced their personal well-being. It is now commonly accepted that a generally high level of health has made people much more intolerant of minor physical and mental discomforts.

Yet the Victorians too were very conscious of their own state of health. As Bruce Haley has noted, Victorian intellectuals were afflicted with an extreme valetudinarianism and worried constantly about their own physical and mental condition.[17] Among the lower classes also, the awareness of bodily condition and the hazards of disease was sharp, but perhaps less of a consuming passion. Joseph Turrill, market gardener, of the village of Garsington near Oxford in the 1860s, was very health conscious. His diary survives in testimony of the constant presence and awareness of illness and death in the village communities of the past. Garsington endured a smallpox outbreak in February 1864, and heard with apprehension rumours of cholera in 1866, but Turrill's life was by no means dominated by the spectres of illness and death. Indeed, he appears to have held a quite specific framework of reference in regard to health: there was 'illness', which was severe, probably incapacitating, and required a doctor; there was sickness (English cholera); there were conditions of more or less discomfort, described as being 'middling' (as in 'I have had the diarrhoea very badly this day or two, and I feel very middling altogether'); and there was wellness ('They all appear to be got quite well now, and their relief is stopped'). Death was certainly more constantly present in the local community than it is today, but the impression is of a vigorous working community that remained active and positive in the face of human frailty.[18]

Perceptions of health and ill-health have perhaps changed less over time than is sometimes suggested, although the nature of illness may also have changed. Health itself has been variously defined: simply, by Haley, as 'a state of being which is free from discomfort or, more positively, which produces comfort'; or more elaborately, by the World Health Organization, as 'a state of complete physical, mental, and social well-being, and not merely the absence of disease or infirmity'.[19] The condition of health involves minor as well as major illness and discomfort, James Riley having emphasised that the Victorians counted minor as well as grave ailments as sickness and called upon their doctors to treat them. The picture that Riley draws from the records of the friendly societies (the popular working-class, self-help insurance organisations) endorses that reflected in Joseph Turrill's diary, that the common image of sickness in the nineteenth century was dominated not by the great infectious diseases but by the daily discomforts of colds, headaches and diarrhoea. The health preoccupations of the Victorians were remarkably similar to those of the New Elizabethans – those living in the reign of Elizabeth II – in being largely banal.[20] It is worth remembering that the dominance of infectious disease as a cause of death, and its prominence among the concerns of the public health authorities, masked a vast underlying reservoir of minor illness and discomfort that in many respects changed little in the years before the new millennium.

Making sense of social perceptions of health and illness and of the demographic patterns commonly used to describe them is a complicated task; relating them to medicine is a controversial one. The relationship between health and medicine exists on two or more levels – at the personal, between doctor and patient, and at community level, in what is generally termed 'public health'. Medicine can be defined as the science and art concerned with the cure, alleviation and prevention of disease, and with the restoration and preservation of health. Since 1858 medical practitioners in Britain have been effectively divided into two categories: the orthodox practitioners who were trained in recognised medical schools, and whose names appear on the Medical Register, and the alternative practitioners, who do not. Orthodox practitioners have been involved in personal and community health at many levels; until very recently alternative practitioners were excluded from involvement in state-sponsored community medicine.

Whether orthodox or alternative, however, medicine has for much of history been more concerned with the alleviation of illness and the maintenance of health than confident in its ability to prevent or to cure. Here the 1860s mark another watershed. In the years between 1870 and 1914, public health in Britain became increasingly well organised and systematically applied to the prevention of infectious disease, and from the 1880s the new possibilities of cure began gradually to emerge from a multiplicity of developments in medicine and surgery. New medical technologies – such as the X-ray (1895) and the electrocardiograph (1901) – offered medicine a new objectivity, a new science of diagnosis. In the twentieth century patients were increasingly to demand the use of the latest technologies from their medical attendants.[21] Within a hundred years popular expectations of orthodox medicine had been revolutionised in Britain as in other developed societies: by the 1960s people went to their doctors in the expectation that all minor, and a great many more serious, illnesses would be cured or alleviated.

Moreover, the diseases that brought about death changed radically between 1860 and 1960. Already in the 1880s the infectious diseases that had dominated the cause of death tables in the earlier nineteenth century were becoming less significant, to be replaced by the respiratory diseases; by 1914 it had become clear that chronic and degenerative diseases – cancer, heart disease and diabetes – were assuming a leading role among cause of death. Controversy has arisen over these changing patterns of disease and death and their relationship to the parallel changes in medicine.

Beginning in the interwar years, orthodox medical practitioners and historians began to attribute the revolution in the modern expectation of life and health to the public health movement and to the new scientific medicine, which had emerged in the nineteenth century.[22] Looking into the past, these observers saw that the decline in infectious disease paralleled the rise of the public health movement; that the introduction of anaesthesia and antisepsis in the 1860s had led to a transformation in the prospects and practice of surgery; and that the bacteriological revolution had permitted the development of new drugs and vaccines against infectious diseases such as syphilis and diphtheria. By the 1960s, in the context of a newly triumphant biomedicine, these conclusions seemed inescapable. At the same time Thomas McKeown, professor of social medicine at Birmingham University, was beginning with his colleagues to explore the behaviour of diseases in the eighteenth and nineteenth centuries. Their investigations, culminating in the publication of McKeown's *Modern Rise of Population* in 1976, destroyed the assumption that medicine had been directly responsible for the falling death-rate in England and Wales since 1870.[23]

McKeown demonstrated that many of the most important diseases contributing to the high death-rate in the past had all but disappeared as a cause of death before medical science had developed the techniques to control or to cure them. So why had these diseases become less fatal? McKeown argued that the main reason was a rising standard of living, more especially an improved diet, which had raised individual levels of resistance to infection and so reduced the number of deaths. With the exceptions of vaccination against smallpox, and the sanitary improvements that had reduced the impact of water-borne diseases such as typhoid and cholera, human intervention had, he suggested, remarkably little to do with the falling death-rate in Britain before the interwar years. In so far as the falling death-rate reflected better health, medicine had therefore had very little to do with improving the nation's well-being in the later nineteenth century. At a time when many people were beginning to question the motives and efficiency of

modern medicine, McKeown's thesis carried an attractive plausi-
bility, reinforced, ironically, by his authority as a medical specialist.

It was not long, however, before McKeown himself began to
come under attack. He had formulated his argument by elimina-
tion – if medicine were impotent, and public health of limited
impact, the reduced death-rate must be due to improved resistance – and on the basis of an unquestioning acceptance of the
accuracy of GRO's cause of death statistics. He had ignored the
rich and varied historical context of the question, including such
related issues as fertility, poverty, wages and expenditure, medical
provision, medical competence and statistical interpretation. The
historical behaviour of tuberculosis formed a crucial part of his
argument, but he managed to misread the statistical evidence for
that behaviour.[24] With the emergence of new and vigorous historical sub-disciplines – historical demography, urban history and the
social history of medicine – other scholars began to dispute
McKeown's interpretation of the decline in mortality. Since 1980
a growing body of literature has built up around McKeown's
thesis, both predating and postdating Simon Szreter's now-classic
polemic contesting the role of nutrition and instead stressing that
of social intervention, that is, the public health movement and its
locally administered preventive health measures.[25] A good deal of
this research, together with recent work on the history of medicine, has not been directly inspired by the McKeown debate but
touches on it tangentially, while scholars working in fields of
interest removed from that debate have also contributed to
furthering the understanding of the historical relationship
between health and medicine, and how this may have changed
over time.

The debate over the Mckeown thesis has relevance for the
history of health because the death-rate has been, and remains,
in the context of a general lack of sickness statistics, the principal
statistical tool for measuring the well-being of populations. It is
problematic, however, not least because it does not reflect health
during life, psychological fitness or social well-being, and because
there may be a difference in health experience between social or
income groups that diverge from the pattern of mortality.[26] Similarly, attempts made to measure the health of Britain's people by
analysing data on the heights and weights of children are useful

only in the limited sense that an improved height and weight reflect improving environmental conditions, not only of nutrition, but also of housing, disease insults and other conditions.[27] While such data are useful as a general indicator, and for comparison between different historical periods, regions and social classes, neither the mortality figure, nor data on heights and weights, can illuminate the minor underlying disturbances of physical well-being, or the greater or lesser mental stresses, that modify day-to-day health experience. Health itself, as well as the perception of health and of the relationship between health and medical intervention, is enmeshed in the wider social, cultural and economic context that determines the pattern of individual lives. Despite some fifty years of equal access to the National Health Service (NHS), the health experiences of the different social classes in Britain have not been equalised, and the death-rate remains higher in the north of England than in the south.

The relationship between health and medicine since 1860 has not been a straightforward one. There has been no simple progression between improving health and increasing medical expertise; instead, there has been a complex of fragmentary, overlapping and related developments. The years between 1860 and 1914 saw medicine acquire the apparent ability to control infectious disease as well as an enhanced ability to manage other disease processes and the potential for new techniques of disease management and control stemming from laboratory and clinical research. Between 1918 and 1939 that promise began to be fulfilled, and in the years after 1945 medical science appeared to realise its goal with revolutionary therapies across the range of medical intervention. Growing internationalisation, including not only the work of the World Health Organization but also the rapid expansion of global trade and communication networks and the establishment of international scientific and medical communities, meant that new discoveries were rapidly diffused. By the 1960s, for reasons far from those simply medical, Britain's people were healthier than they had ever been since 1860, yet a new popular sense of entitlement to perfect health and well-being served to maintain public demand on the national medical services.

1

AN AGE OF GREAT CITIES, 1860–1914

Introduction

Between 1860 and 1914 Britain became a definitively urban society. In 1851 half the county's population lived in towns; by 1901 four-fifths did so. At the same time the number and size of great cities rapidly increased. Whereas London was the only conurbation with a population of more than 100,000 souls in 1851, there were thirty-six such by 1911. These towns and cities held the key to the nation's health and well-being. While on the one hand they generated Britain's industrial wealth, on the other they exacted a terrible price from the people who worked within them. Already in the mid-1860s William Farr noted the relationship between population density and high death-rate: in places where there were no more than eighty-six persons to a square mile, the death-rate stood at between 14 and 16 per thousand people; where there more than a thousand persons to the square mile, the death-rate was between 24 and 25; and once there were more than 3,000 people packed into the same space, as was not unusual in the crowded poor districts of the great cities, the mortality rate soared to 26 and over.[1]

In straightforward terms this meant a significant difference in the death-rate between urban and rural areas: in the decade 1881–90, for example, the standardised death-rate for the urban districts of England and Wales was 22.3 and that for the rural districts just under 17.[2] Deaths from some of the most important infections, from smallpox, measles, scarlet fever, whooping cough and diarrhoea, were all markedly higher in the towns than in the countryside, and in the great cities than the smaller towns.[3] Although poverty, poor housing and disease were by no means absent from Britain's country areas, nineteenth-century towns were not a good place in which to live. Constructed at the whim of commercial developers, and in the first half of the century without building regulations of any kind, their environments had been devastated by the needs of the people who lived in them. Their skies were black with coal smoke, their streets strewn with horse manure; in summer they were alive with flies, in winter dank with damp and fog. If the country's cities powered the leading Western industrial economy and the world's greatest imperial power, they exacted a terrible price in terms of ill-health and premature death from their citizens.

The damaging impact of the urban environment on health was not reduced, in comparison with the countryside, before 1914, even though the death-rate in both was falling. Although real income was rising after 1870, there was little improvement in either urban housing conditions or urban atmospheric pollution. Respiratory disease remained a major source of ill-health and death throughout the period, but by 1914 the major infectious diseases had all but disappeared as a public health concern, and other diseases – cancer, heart disease and diabetes – were beginning to cause anxiety. Innovations in medical treatment had, as McKeown argued, little to do with this changing pattern of disease incidence and fatality. Yet at the same time, the influence of medicine on the pattern cannot be altogether dismissed. The urban populations of later nineteenth-century Britain had access to a wide and varied range of medical resources, and the evidence suggests that they made use of them. Medicine itself, while remaining restricted in its ability to cure, acquired a new professional authority that may have influenced patient response to treatment for the better.

Medical observation and research gradually increased the understanding of the behaviour of several important diseases, allowing doctors to manage them better, both in the community and at the bedside. A medically qualified public health organisation was put in place across the country in 1872, its concerns gradually widening from environmental pollution and infectious disease to encompass, by the turn of the century, issues of poverty, education and domestic management. By the early twentieth century, medical men had become influential in shaping new social policies. If medicine still had little power to cure before 1914, it was taking an increasingly confident part in the maintenance of the nation's health.

Medical Provision

It has become customary to speak of a medical marketplace when describing the range of treatment options available to eighteenth- and nineteenth-century patients, because of the number and variety of 'practitioners' of one kind or another who were competing for their custom. Orthodox medical practitioners had, by the 1860s, achieved the modern division between hospital consultants, with private practices on the one hand and general practitioners, or 'family doctors', on the other.[4] But although the referral system was beginning to emerge, there was still a sharp rivalry between the two groups and furious debate over 'outpatient abuse' – the use of charitable hospital facilities by patients who could well afford to pay private practitioners' fees.[5] This conflict well illustrates not only the strength of intraprofessional competition, but also the alertness of patients to treatment opportunities. Although the extent to which different families and different social classes called on medical advice depended to some degree on their individual financial circumstances, there were for most several different choices.

At the top of the scale were the consultants, who by 1900 had firmly established themselves as the elite of the profession. Operating private practices, often based in the Harley Street area of London but also in provincial towns and cities, both physicians and surgeons also acted as either general or specialist consultants in the hospital sector. Physicians, who possessed university degrees in medicine, and had long regarded themselves as a medical and social elite, treated elite patients: those belonging to the aristocracy, the gentry and the well-to-do middle classes – at most perhaps a tenth of the population.[6] They practised internal medicine and treated by management and prescription; in addition, although many remained wedded to the traditional medical ideal of general competence, there were those who had begun to specialise in, for example, respiratory medicine or the treatment of tuberculosis. The surgeons, in contrast, although they saw their upper-class patients privately, increasingly practised their art within the confines of the hospital. The development of anaesthesia and hygienic operating rituals, the requirement for a sterile operating environment and the need for numerous assistants meant that operations became more conveniently and safely performed in hospital. By the turn of the century, the specialised hospital operating theatre had become the surgeon's normal place of work. In their hospital practice both surgeons and physicians were available to the less affluent social groups who made up the inpatient number.[7]

The public image of the hospitals changed significantly in the later Victorian period. The voluntary hospitals' origin as charitable institutions catering to the poor was gradually replaced by a wider accessibility to their local communities. Subscribers' letters of recommendation, essential for admission in the eighteenth century, had virtually been dispensed with by 1900. From being institutions carrying the stigma of charity, the voluntary hospitals were transformed into popular medical institutions, the demand for whose services soared after 1860. A number of factors contributed to this change of image and function: the doctors' desire for medical control of cases, improvements in hygiene and nursing care, increasing respect for medical judgements, perhaps; the causes are probably complex.

Nonetheless, the demand for outpatient services in particular rose dramatically between 1860 and 1914. Between 1860 and 1900 the number of new inpatient admissions at the London Hospital alone increased from 4,000 to 12,000 a year, but the number of outpatient consultations soared from 25,000 to over 220,000. By 1910 there were some 1.75 million new attendances at outpatient clinics and casualty departments in London – an attendance rate of 280 per thousand population – and provincial hospitals experienced a similar surge in the number of applicants.[8] Such attendances put extreme pressure on medical staff, and by 1900 nearly all the voluntary hospitals in London had introduced measures intended to limit the number attending. Moreover, the services that hospitals could provide under this pressure were not of the best: on a contemporary estimate, the average consultation time was 1.3 minutes.

This new enthusiasm for outpatient facilities was therefore probably of limited medical effectiveness, but it does reflect the growing demand for medical attendance that characterised this period. These years also saw a significant extension in the range and type of hospital services available outside the voluntary sector. In the opening decade of the nineteenth century, a new kind of hospital, one specialising in a particular area of medicine, made its appearance. The first was Moorfields Eye Hospital in London (1805), but others quickly followed, catering for a wide range of special cases from children (who were usually excluded from the general hospitals), to tuberculosis and renal disease.[9] By 1860 there were sixty-six special hospitals in London and many more in the provinces. Apart from the specialist focus in treatment, which allowed them to sell themselves to patients as being at the cutting edge of expertise, these hospitals charged more modestly than the elite practitioners, and were free of the stigma of charity often still associated with the voluntary hospitals. They seem to have been especially popular with middle classes. In rural areas the 1860s saw the appearance of cottage hospitals, run by general practitioners (GPs) for the benefit of local communities, which were willing to treat the rural poor in return for a small fee. Some 300 cottage hospitals had been established across the country by 1900.[10]

Yet another dimension to hospital provision emerged with the creation of isolation hospitals for infectious diseases following the Sanitary Act 1866 and the Metropolitan Poor Act 1867. By 1900 London possessed a chain of more than a dozen infectious disease hospitals stretching across the outer suburbs, while most major provincial cities had also provided such a facility, sometimes with a separate provision for smallpox cases, and rural areas were coming under pressure to provide such accommodation too.[11] While the middle classes initially proved most reluctant to use these isolation facilities, and were indeed until 1887 debarred from the London hospitals, which were intended only for paupers, they had by the end of the century become widely accepted, both for the care they offered to patients, and to relieve households of the complex rituals of isolation and disinfection

on which the public health authorities insisted for such cases. In
the 1890s the London isolation hospitals were receiving an
average of 12,000 scarlet fever patients a year, an estimated 75 per
cent of all the capital's cases.

An increasing patient use of hospitals is relatively easy to document from the various statistics that the hospitals themselves
collected and recorded. It is not so easy to explore patient use of
GP services until after the introduction of National Insurance in
1913. The number of registered practitioners more than doubled
over the period, from some 20,000 in 1860 to nearer 45,000 by
1914, while the number of patients per qualified practitioner fluc-
tuated at around 1,500. Doctor availability, however, depended
very much on where one lived: doctors tended to prefer to practise in urban areas, and in the south of England rather than in the
north – south of that famous line between the Wash and the
Severn Estuary.[12] Medical attendance also cost money, on average
between 2/6 and 7/6 (one old shilling being equivalent to five
new pence) per visit. The scale of the charge usually related to the
social standing of the patient, and GPs commonly reduced their
charge to the poor. Inevitably, the well-to-do made use of their
doctors as they needed them, to attend minor ailments as well as
more serious illnesses, while the poor tended to leave summoning
the doctor until matters were desperate and the patient often past
hope of alleviation, let alone cure. Women and children in poor
families were especially vulnerable to neglected medical conditions, since available financial resources were generally concentrated on food, rent and the breadwinner's needs.

Working people's access to orthodox medicine was greatly
improved during the course of the nineteenth century by the
emergence of the insurance principle. Various forms of club practice appeared, ranging from sick clubs organised by doctors on a
subscription basis, to works clubs drawing on regular contributions out of wages, friendly societies, again operating on a
subscription basis, and medical aid societies linked to the life
assurance business.[13] Evidence from friendly society records indicates that working men, and even their dependants, were making
increasing use of medical services provided under insurance
schemes after 1860, and that by 1900 somewhere between two-
thirds and a half of all friendly society members had undertaken

17

to pay the ½–1d a week required for contract medical services. Indeed, it has been estimated that at least a third of adult males and more than 45 per cent of all working-class men obtained medical attendance through the friendly societies by 1900.[14] The nature of the illnesses treated under these schemes naturally varied, but besides more serious incapacitating illness, colds, headaches and minor abrasions all frequently feature in the records as a reason for taking more than three days off work. Between 1864 and 1883, for example, the most common recorded diagnosis noted among the members of the Eversholt Friendly Society was a cold.[15] Friendly society members were not passively health conscious: they took active measures to protect their health and to look after themselves as best they might in illness.

Beyond the availability of GP care through the friendly societies, working people also had the possibility of treatment and advice from a variety of dispensaries, some charitable, some provident, some under the auspices of the Poor Law. Again, dispensaries tended to be an urban facility, but within their often limited catchment area they offered a useful resource, each treating, on average, several thousand patients a year. The establishment of charitable dispensaries had essentially been an eighteenth-century movement, and they were especially numerous in the manufacturing towns of Lancashire and the West Riding. They generally refused to treat paupers, but aimed to help those just above destitution. The Poor Law briefly engaged in a programme of providing dispensaries in the 1870s. This was quickly curtailed by moral and financial considerations, but it did result in the establishment of forty-four dispensaries in London between 1871 and 1888, although many fewer in the provinces.[16]

At much the same time, provident dispensaries, operating on the friendly society model of subscription, began to appear. Local GPs served here, sometimes on a voluntary basis, sometimes salaried, so that the dispensaries offered professional diagnosis and prescription services, as well as dispensing medicines. Subscriptions, as with the friendly society medical contracts, were small at around a penny a week, and concern was often expressed with the quality of medicines provided, but there can be little doubt that these dispensaries provided a very real service to the urban working classes.[17] Local authorities were sometimes persuaded by urgent local problems to open dispensaries directed at special needs: both Manchester and Leicester, which were plagued by a high infant mortality rate (around 200 per thousand births), arranged to supply diarrhoea medicines free to the artisan and poorer classes during the 1870s, in the hope of reducing the toll of deaths. Between 10 July and 30 September 1878, for example, more than 3,000 people, half of them children, were treated for diarrhoea in Leicester.

For those who, through illness or inability to find work, found themselves without the resources to pay for medical treatment, there was the Poor Law. Sickness was, indeed, the great contributor to the need for such a social support system: it has been estimated that, in 1871, 72 per cent of pauperism resulted from sickness. Most typically, the severe illness, disablement or death of a bread-winner cast whole families upon the Poor Law. By the 1890s, however, the institutional facilities of the Poor Law had become the last resort of the chronically sick and aged poor. The organisa-tion and ethos of the Poor Law in the later nineteenth century altered sharply in 1871, when the old Poor Law Board was abol-ished and responsibility for the service was transferred to the Local Government Board, which also carried the brief for public health. Where the Poor Law Board had practised deterrence, under the principles of the 1834 Poor Law Act, with a view to discouraging the undeserving poor, the Local Government Board gradually extended the principle of public responsibility for medical treat-ment by developing infirmary and dispensary facilities.[18]

Hampered almost throughout the period by Treasury constraints on spending, the Board nonetheless managed some-what to raise medical standards in the Poor Law institutions. In the last decades of the century, the staffing, equipment and treat-ment offered in the Poor Law hospitals of London and other large cities gradually improved, notably where ambitious medical officers sought to raise the medical profile of their institution. Nursing services in these hospitals also improved, with the founding of the Workhouse Nurses' Association in 1879, which began to train nurses wishing to care for the sick poor. In general, however, urban hospital services under the Poor Law differed in quality and generosity, and in the countryside the situation was even more variable and unsatisfactory. In rural Wales, for example, it was noted in the mid-1890s that the workhouses were very small and their inmates very few, 'accustomed to an exceedingly simple and primitive style of life'. In these areas Poor Law guardians saw no reason to indulge paupers with trained nurses and up-to-date medical equipment.[19]

Outdoor medical relief, which had been a great standby earlier in the century, and which supported more than 300,000 persons in 1860, was phased out after 1871, forcing greater self-reliance and increasing the number of calls on voluntary hospitals, dispensaries and medical clubs. Moreover, Poor Law relief of any kind carried a social stigma – the stigma of pauperism – which led the poor to avoid calling on it until absolutely necessary. As a result, many were already destitute by the time they applied for help, or so broken in health that it was beyond the powers of nineteenth-century medicine to restore them. Nor could the quality of attention and treatment be guaranteed: although the duties of Poor Law doctors, including a minimum daily attendance of one hour at the dispensary for district medical officers, were prescribed, the regulations were permissive and were not subject to any systematic supervision. It was inevitable, therefore, that the services on offer varied and in some places were neglected. Poor Law medical officers were also expected to pay for medicine and medical supplies out of their stipends, and they had to apply to the guardians if they wished to supply their patients with 'medical extras' such as beef tea or brandy. Medical extras were a continuing source of tension between guardians and medical officers.[20] The suspicion was also frequently voiced, despite the medical officers' denials, that they provided their pauper patients with cheap and inferior medicine.

The medical services provided under the Poor Law were thus far from universally satisfactory, more particularly as they could by the 1890s be compared with new government-sponsored social insurance schemes, which, initiated in Germany in the 1880s, were being widely established across Europe.[21] A Royal Commission on the Poor Laws, reporting in 1909, undertook an extensive review of the services on offer. Although the Commissioners were unable to agree on their recommendations and could not agree to accept any substantive revision of established British Poor Law practice, its very existence was indicative of a new consciousness

in recipe

of social responsibility among Britain's ruling class, and of a growing debate over the nature and extent of such responsibility.

Whatever medical services were available, medication was a constant resort at all levels of nineteenth-century society, whether urban or rural. As in past centuries, families still kept medicine cupboards and receipt books, and sought advice from friends or reputed popular healers. The 1858 Medical Act had made no attempt to outlaw irregular practitioners, so that quacks continued to peddle their wares, whether in person or by post. The pharmaceutical trade, which had expanded greatly in the latter part of the eighteenth century, had begun to organise and professionalise in the 1840s, and chemists and druggists had become familiar among the retail traders of towns and cities.

Pharmacy was another varied trade, ranging from companies such as Allen and Hanbury, which imported and manufactured drugs, medical supplies and equipment, to those like Beechams' that supplied patent medicines (that is, medicines with a proprietary name), to local druggists' and grocers' stores, which dispensed, or sold on, commercial preparations to customers. Jesse Boot, founder of Boots the Chemist and pioneer of the chain store, began as an unqualified local retailer in Nottingham in the 1870s. The number of such local retailers increased dramatically in this period: in 1865 there were about 10,000 shops licensed to sell patent medicines; by 1905 there were more than 40,000.[22] This ballooning of the chemists' business was suggestive not only of the demand for medical products, but also of an enhanced purchasing power among ordinary people, and their willingness to spend money on the pursuit of health.

Controls on the content and quality of drugs and patent medicines were, however, minimal. The Sale of Food and Drugs Act, 1875 provided workable measures against adulteration, as well as obliging local authorities to appoint public analysts, but in other respects there was little regulation of the drug trade. Nostrums were frequently sold that claimed to cure a fantastic spectrum of ills – tuberculosis, cancer and syphilis at once, for example – while a wide range of drugs were available over the counter and without prescription. It was still commonplace for families to take their traditional receipts to the local chemist to be made up, while those alert to the latest products of scientific research could experiment more widely. When new substances of practical value began to appear on the pharmaceutical scene in the 1880s as byproducts of the German chemical industry, they were taken up by both practitioners and self-medicating patients. Phenacetin and phenazone, for example, were being widely used among the laity by the 1890s to relieve fever and pain, and doctors had begun to complain of being summoned to counteract the effects of 'domestic drugging', calling for controls on the sale of such drugs.[23] The medical contribution to patients' health already involved not only advice and the management of illness, but also advice on the maintenance of health by refraining from self-treatment.

Methods and Management in Medicine

In the years between 1860 and 1914, orthodox medicine became professional. Although doctors still had little to offer in the way of treatment that guaranteed a cure, developments in medical science, in the education and organisation of medical practitioners, and in the practice of hospital medicine all helped to establish the identity of a distinct profession, possessing specialist knowledge that set it apart from ordinary people. Laymen and women had in the past discussed their problems with the doctor on equal terms but by the end of the nineteenth century this was no longer the case.[24]

The impetus towards this new exclusivity came from within the profession itself, driven by financial pressure, by overcrowding within the profession and by competition from chemists, druggists and unqualified practitioners. Throughout the first half of the century, ordinary GPs struggled for reforms in the profession that would improve their social standing and financial security. When reforming legislation was finally achieved, in 1858, the GPs were disappointed, especially so because it did not make unqualified practice illegal.[25] The Medical Act did, however, mark a new era for medical practice in Britain. It established a compendium of properly qualified practitioners (the Medical Register), defined proper qualification as being obtained from recognised medical schools, and provided a supervisory body responsible for keeping the Medical Register and policing the doctors' professional and ethical behaviour: the General Medical Council.[26] After 1858 it was possible to confirm whether or not a practitioner was a 'proper' doctor by looking him up in the Medical Register, and a large number of official posts were restricted to properly qualified men: hospital consultancies, public vaccinator posts and medical officerships in insane asylums, prisons, the colonies, the Poor Law and the public health service were all open only to properly qualified applicants.

The knowledge that doctors qualifying after 1858 acquired through their education was also changing. During the early part of the century, medical schools, notably in London but also in the provinces, had become attached to many general hospitals, and the hospital had become the dominating experience of a medical student's life. The time-honoured system of qualification by apprenticeship had all but disappeared by 1860, replaced by an education that emphasised not only the doctor's participation in a distinct professional cadre, but also, increasingly, the exclusivity of his knowledge.[27] Clinical medicine, which encapsulated a system of diagnosis based mainly on the interpretation of physical signs, had developed in France at the end of the eighteenth century. Rooted in the study of morbid pathology, clinical medicine epitomised for ordinary practitioners a new scientific approach that broadened after 1860 with such additions to the curriculum as histology, clinical physiology, chemistry and bacteriology. Instead of attempting to correct the balance of humours within the body, clinical medicine sought to identify and counteract the physical causes of disease.

The study of anatomy became the foundation of medical training, medical students being initiated into this world of arcane knowledge through the dissecting room. Moreover, the practice of medicine was being given a new and visible specialist authority by new technologies. The stethoscope, invented by René Laennec in 1819, and the thermometer, whose usefulness as a guide to the nature and course of the various 'fevers' was confirmed by the publication of Karl Wunderlich's research in the 1860s, had by the 1920s become an accepted part of the practitioner's armoury. Quite how quickly these new technologies spread into nineteenth-century general practice is uncertain, but medical students certainly acquired a familiarity with their use during their hospital training.[28]

The new medicine and the new educational system also extended the student's familiarity – in theory at least – with an increasingly wide range of diseases. With professionalisation, a new formality entered medical education in the form of lectures, a syllabus and written examinations. These changes generated a profusion of new student textbooks, while the emergence of the new medical specialties seeking to affirm their status within the firmament of nineteenth-century medicine contributed further to this flow. Through these textbooks, if not in the hospital ward, students could learn about diseases that had recently been identified or confirmed – diseases such as diabetes, poliomyelitis, muscular dystrophy and multiple sclerosis – and current ideas on treating them. How far ordinary GPs, or their patients, benefitted in practice from these diagnostic guides is debatable. The GRO, which recorded all causes of death as given on death certificates, made strenuous efforts to force GPs into precise, scientific diagnoses, but John Tatham, Supervisor of Statistics at the GRO at the turn of the century, was still far from satisfied with their performance, estimating about 4 per cent of returns to be worthless for the purpose of classification. This was, however, a considerable improvement on performance in the 1860s, when some 20 per cent of recorded deaths were not certified at all.

There were nevertheless problems in the reporting of death from childbirth, tuberculosis, heart disease, cancer and 'dropsy'.[29] Significant social problems surrounded some of these deaths (many doctors being, for example, reluctant to admit to losing patients to puerperal fever), but it is clear that other conditions, such as internal cancer and dropsy, did present continuing difficulties in diagnosis, and presumably therefore in treatment, for practitioners. Of course, the wider picture of medical competence, as regards both diagnosis and management, was gradually changing as younger, more scientifically trained men moved into practice: 'a situation obtained where there were overlapping layers of practice but with some interaction between conservative and progressive elements'.[30]

New methods of studying disease emerged during the nineteenth century and led to a significant refinement in the diagnosis and recognition of different conditions. The new clinical medicine taught observation at the bedside and the association of symptoms with the physiological condition of the body. Epidemiology, which made use of statistics, especially those generated by the new GRO, and observed disease in the field, helped to clarify behavioural differences between the various infections. Physiology, which made use of animal models and experiments to explore the innermost workings of the living body, emerged as a powerful research tool and was regarded by its practitioners as the means of making medicine truly scientific. Finally, in the 1880s, the new bacteriology began the process of identifying the specific agents of different diseases in the laboratory.

Each of these methods of studying disease contributed towards an improved medical understanding of the identities and characteristics of individual diseases. In the early decades of the nineteenth century, for example, clinical methods enabled René Laennec in 1823 to distinguish between various respiratory afflictions, including bronchitis, pneumonia, pleurisy and emphysema. Pierre Bretonneau published his description of the individual features of diphtheria in 1826, and William Gerhard in America and William Jenner in London demonstrated the diagnostic differences between typhoid and typhus (in 1837 and 1849 respectively). Thomas Addison, William Bright, James Parkinson and Thomas Hodgkin described the diseases to which they gave their names. Epidemiological observation enabled John Snow and William Budd respectively to unravel the water-borne nature of cholera and typhoid epidemics. Claude Bernard established the connection between diabetes and glucose through his physiological studies of digestion, while David Ferrier's work in the 1870s on the functions of the brain paved the way for the first successful removal of a brain tumour in 1879.[31] Robert Koch's laboratory identification of the causal organism of anthrax in 1876 was followed by his identification of the bacilli of tuberculosis in 1882 and cholera in 1883. By the end of the century, the causative organisms of some twenty-one other diseases had been identified in the laboratory.[32]

For the most part, however, the burgeoning of medical research in the nineteenth century resulted in little practical extension of the healing powers of medicine itself. In the years before 1914 medicine was still concerned with managing diseases rather than curing them. Such, for example, was the message of John Syer Bristowe's highly successful *Theory and Practice of Medicine*, which went through seven editions between 1870 and 1890.[33] Not until the end of the nineteenth century did scientific medicine begin to deliver recognisable therapeutic benefits, although research and experiment led to the introduction of several useful new drugs as the German chemical industry began to seek uses for its numerous byproducts in the 1870s and 80s. A number of effective antipyretics and analgesics became available in the 1880s, to be followed in 1899 by aspirin, the most immensely successful domestic painkiller of all time.[34]

Before 1914, the elaboration of germ theory, the identification of the bacterial causes of a large number of diseases, and the arrival of the laboratory as the frontier of medical research and development proved disappointing in therapeutic terms. Only a very limited number of cures or preventive agents had emerged from the new bacteriological discipline to extend the power of medicine against disease. The introduction of antitoxin therapy for diphtheria in 1894–95, initially with most effect in hospital practice, and of Salvarsan, the first of the 'magic bullets', for the treatment of syphilis in 1910, were the only results of any immediate clinical importance. The first decade of the new century saw the formulation of new vaccines against diphtheria and typhoid, but the former made no impact on British medicine in this period, and the latter was of limited value in civilian practice, given that typhoid was already in steep decline. Pasteur's rabies vaccine, first used on a human subject in 1885, while of immense value to affected individuals, was also of limited public health significance: in that year there were sixty rabies deaths in England and Wales, compared with over 4,000 from diphtheria.[35]

For the entire period from its conception in 1796 to the implementation of immunisation against typhoid in Western armies after 1906, vaccination against smallpox remained the sole specifically preventive medical measure of any importance against disease in Britain, as elsewhere. Effective in preventing the development of smallpox, one of the most unpleasant infectious diseases known to man, if administered shortly after exposure to the virus or at intervals of around 10–15 years, vaccination had been adopted on a more or less compulsory basis in most European states in the early nineteenth century.[36] (Smallpox was declared by the World Health Organization in 1977 to have been eradicated.) In Britain, compulsory infant vaccination was enacted by the legislature in 1853, and measures to enforce it through inspection were enacted in 1871. Despite vehement opposition from principled anti-vaccinationists (with moral, ethical and intuitive objections to the procedure), which eventually achieved the effective repeal of compulsion in 1907, the use of vaccination, together with the preventive strategies of notification, isolation and disinfection, succeeded in eradicating smallpox as an indigenous disease in Britain after 1885.[37] It was the combination of such preventive techniques with voluntary vaccination that was successfully used to eradicate smallpox from the global community in the twentieth century.[38]

With the exception of the new painkilling and fever-reducing drugs, however, most of the medical innovations introduced at the turn of the century were of limited influence in general practice, and the 'art' of medicine continued to be extensively practised by doctors who relied on an understanding of their patients and their needs, as well as on familiar prescriptions, to alleviate suffering. The old heroic medicine of bleeding and purging had largely vanished by 1860, to be replaced by supportive treatment. Joseph Turrill's old mother, intermittently ill throughout almost the whole period of his diary (and dying in 1871), was described by her doctor in July 1864 as 'a very weakly subject and wanted a great deal of care and good living', but she improved under his care. Among the medicaments he prescribed for her, cod liver oil was specified in July 1866. Good medical management increasingly helped to prolong life after 1860 when patients had died more quickly in earlier decades. Even with damaging chronic diseases such as tuberculosis, the evidence suggests that many sufferers were surviving longer by the 1890s. Ironically, this could in health terms be seen as a negative outcome: people did not die, and they were sick – in the sense of incapacity for work – less often, but their illnesses lasted longer.[39]

While general practice and internal medicine remained constricted in their curative endeavour and often traditional in their medical approach, hospital medicine had, in the area of surgery, recognisably moved towards a modern, scientific and dynamic mode by the end of the century. Indeed, developments in surgery began in this period to emerge as the public, progressive face of medicine. Chloroform anaesthesia introduced in the 1850s, the invention of the artery clamp (which enabled surgeons to work in 'dry' operating sites), and the application of antiseptic and aseptic techniques, which greatly reduced the chance of wound infection, transformed the prospects of surgery. Before 1860 surgery was essentially an emergency measure, carried out, usually as amputation, after an accident or when conditions such as tumours became unbearable. After 1860 the character of surgery changed: it became increasingly constructive.

By 1900 surgeons were regularly performing operations that greatly enhanced the quality of life for their patients. Compound fractures no longer commanded amputation, and diseased joints could be excised rather than removed. Hernias, a significant cause of nineteenth-century pauperism, had long been managed by wearing a truss, but after 1870 they began to be treated surgically. Hernia repairs constituted 2 per cent of the operations performed by Joseph Lister between 1877 and 1893, but nearly 12 per cent of Watson Cheyne's between 1902 and 1912.[40] When, on 24 June 1902, the surgeon Frederick Treves successfully removed King Edward VII's appendix shortly before his scheduled coronation, he demonstrated the new confidence and the new skills of surgery in the most public possible fashion.

In therapeutic terms, the achievements of the new scientific medicine of the nineteenth century were limited before 1914, and McKeown was right to dismiss it as a direct causal factor in the decline in mortality. He may, however, have been wrong to dismiss medicine's contribution to general health and greater longevity after 1860. For many patients with many different diseases, including the infectious killers of childhood as well as tuberculosis, a more supportive style of disease management might have contributed to a longer survival time or to a reduction in the incidence or severity of chronic sequelae after infection. The improvement in life expectancy seen among older children and young adults may, for example, relate to the decline of smallpox, which often had serious respiratory sequelae, and of scarlet fever, which can permanently damage the hearing, heart and kidneys. It is difficult to assess the impact on general and even hospital practice of the young specialty of paediatrics, but one of its main exponents, Charles West, founder of the Hospital for Sick Children in Great Ormond Street, was a leading proponent of supportive treatment for childhood illness.[41]

It is also probable that people increasingly sought medical care for illness in the years after 1860, partly because more medical services became available and partly because the rising real income allowed them to spend money on medicine and medical treatment. Ordinary working people were taking more care of themselves by 1900, and in this endeavour they were increasingly assisted by medical practitioners. The new clinical medicine, professional training and, after 1870, the exciting new specialism of bacteriology helped to raise the professional authority of medicine. Doctors became more confident of their diagnoses and their management of disease, and patients became more confident of their doctors' expertise. In the 1860s, as James Riley's investigation of friendly society records has shown, working-class patients frequently disputed the doctor's management and questioned his professional authority. By the 1890s that expression of equal status had disappeared, perhaps dissipated by the doctors' 'specialised and arcane knowledge'.[42] A growing acceptance of doctors' special knowledge may have enhanced the effectiveness of the placebo dimension in later nineteenth-century medicine.

Health, Environment and Medicine

During the course of the nineteenth century, the British state began to move towards the management of public health. Where health had previously been considered a wholly private matter, the pressure of unregulated urban growth, together with an increasing interest on the part of the medical profession, combined to drive government action on health issues. In contrast to the tentative, permissive beginnings of public health legislation in the 1840s, the years after 1850 saw an increasing commitment by central and local government to public health reform, as medical men began to make their influence felt, especially in local government.[43] This influence was particularly clear in the progression towards the compulsory vaccination against smallpox for infants between 1840 and 1871, but extended more widely with the establishment in 1858 of the Medical Department of the Privy Council (after 1871 of the Local Government Board), whose first Medical Officer, John Simon, played a significant part in the development of public health legislation in the 1860s.[44] Simon's tenure of office saw the new concept of 'state medicine' evolve as a specific, scientific and medical approach to public health, in contrast to the environmental engineering policies of earlier Chadwickian reformers. Epidemiological surveys, disease surveillance and statistical analyses all became an integral part of the new management of public health, which aimed to monitor the national disease picture, to discover ways and means of controlling disease, and to encourage local administrations to perform their health duties effectively.[45]

New administrative structures for the supervision of public health were, however, already being put into place by the time of Simon's appointment. Whereas the Public Health Act 1848 had made the appointment of Medical Officers of Health (MOHs) compulsory only in cities with a death-rate of over 25 per thousand, the Metropolis Local Management Act 1855 set a precedent by making their appointment compulsory in all London's administrative districts. This provision was extended to all urban and rural districts under the Public Health Act 1872, and the sanitary enforcement powers of local government were redefined and made explicit in 1875. If the appointment of an MOH testified a commitment to sanitary reform, some of the great cities, such as Leicester and Liverpool, joined the movement early; others, like Birmingham and Wolverhampton, waited until obliged to by legislation. As with all other aspects of medical provision in the Victorian period, local circumstances and provision differed radically. The year 1872, however, rather than 1848, marks the serious beginning of national public health reform in England and Wales at the level of *local* effort in the municipalities and rural districts, rather than as a concern of central government expressed in permissive legislation. A year earlier, central government had taken the final step towards compulsory vaccination against smallpox for infants, by providing for inspectors to enforce the law.

The searing disease experiences that the country had undergone in the 1860s and early 1870s proved to be the last chapter in the high-mortality infectious disease regime that had ruled Britain's expanding cities since the 1830s. In the last three decades of the century, the new public health organisation, supported by local administrations, began to chip away at the environmental problems that nineteenth-century sanitary orthodoxy since Chadwick had pinpointed as the root causes of a high death-rate and ill-health. In this effort, the local authorities were increasingly imbued with a spirit of civic pride and civic competition, rather than of rate-payer-protective parsimony.[46] Sewage systems, clean water supplies, the control of infectious diseases, cleaner air, decent housing conditions, better quality food supplies and tolerable working conditions all became, in one degree or another, and with greater or less success, the focus of attention and remedial action. All these areas were in 1870 related to poor health and illness, either by directly disseminating infection, or by reducing individual resistance to it or simply by inducing permanent weariness and ill-defined misery. As one London MOH remarked in 1861, insanitary conditions produced in many people a state of ill-health that made life irksome but which did not necessarily end in death. It was, however, in the areas where direct links with disease could be made by medical men, and where action could be taken by local authorities, that most progress was made in securing better conditions.

The beneficial impact on nineteenth-century populations of improved sewage systems and water supplies was not disputed, even by McKeown. The two principal water-borne diseases of the period were cholera and typhoid, the former imported, the latter indigenous. Their transmissibility through water contaminated with infected faecal material had been known since the 1850s, when John Snow and William Budd respectively had demonstrated their modes of transmission. Although this remained a matter of medical dispute, many practitioners acted safe: the medical officer of Millbank Gaol was delighted when, as a result of Snow's work, he restricted the prison's water supply to a local well, rather than drawing it from the Thames, and found that the rate of diarrhoea and gastritis among prisoners dropped dramatically. In London, legislation improving the quality of water supply by insisting that it be taken from beyond the limits of the city's self-pollution, and that it be properly rested and filtered, had been in place since 1855; in the years after 1870 these precautions were gradually extended countrywide, in towns at least.[47] Originally run as private commercial enterprises, the Public Health (Waterworks) Act 1878 made it financially possible for local authorities to buy up the private waterworks. In 1879, only 415 urban local authorities controlled their water supply, whereas by 1905 more than two-thirds of the existing 1,138 authorities had taken over the local waterworks.[48]

Local authority control tended to improve not only the quality of the water supplied, but also its quantity. Before 1870 most water companies supplied water for only two or three hours a day, perhaps two or three times a week. Interim supplies, often stored in unsatisfactory domestic conditions, were liable to various types of contamination, and health officers were adamant that water should be freely available for the preservation of health and cleanliness. In London the extension of a continuous supply began around 1870, and as other urban authorities acquired control over their water, so continuous supplies gradually became commonplace in Britain's towns and cities. It was, however, a slow process. Even at the end of the century, piped water was not available everywhere, and even where it was it was not necessarily laid on to every house. In Manchester, for example, a dozen or more houses shared every street standpipe.[49]

The same uneven pattern of improvement characterised the provision of drains and sewers, and of water-carriage systems of sewage disposal. Massive urbanisation created a massive problem of sewage disposal, which was far from solved by 1914: river pollution was appalling and an issue that Victorian sanitary reformers had barely begun to tackle. The development of the flush toilet, and its widespread adoption by the well-to-do in the early decades of the century, had the advantage of carrying the problem out of built-up areas, although at the expense of local water courses. Where water carriage systems were not adopted, the problem of disposal remained. In the north and east of England, where privy midden and pail systems were the norm, vast quantities of solid faecal matter were disposed of to farmers for manure: in the 1890s, Nottingham had to rid itself of more than a thousand tons of nightsoil a week. Nottingham's nightsoil was removed by boat; Huddersfield and Sheffield sent theirs by train into the country-side, where it was spread on the land. It was by no means remark-able that typhoid lingered longest as a public health problem in the north and east, where the water supply remained constantly at risk of sewage contamination where filtration systems were inadequate, and where the presence of middens, pails, or ash-pits in and near houses increased the danger of infection through careless personal and domestic hygiene.[50] It was the scientific discovery of healthy carriers of typhoid around 1905–6 that gave the final stimulus to the eventual replacement of these 'dry' conservancy systems by water closets and water carriage.

Typhoid and cholera were, moreover, only the most visible consequence of a contaminated water supply and unhygienic practices. The faecal contamination of foodstuffs by flies and through dirty handling practices was commonplace, and transmis-sion of the various food-poisoning bacteria was inevitable. Diar-rhoea was a constant affliction for people of all ages and all social classes, especially during the summer months, while infant diar-rhoea (not always distinguishable as a distinct infant disease) killed many thousands of babies every year. As was inevitable in a horse-drawn society, flies swarmed in their millions between June and October, and the problem of disposing of horse manure in the cities was almost as urgent as that of disposing of the human kind. The coming of the motor car in the early twentieth century marked the beginning of the end of this particular environmental problem, but not before MOHs had identified flies as a significant public health hazard.

Another perennial problem was that of domestic refuse, often stored in unsightly and unsavoury dumps before it was sorted and recycled or otherwise disposed of. Raised levels of infant diar-rhoea, and no doubt of other gastric illness, had been associated with such dumps in proximity to domestic housing.[51] The collec-tion and domestic storage of refuse was another problem. Again, the private companies generally contracted for the business of removal proved unsatisfactory, and more and more local authori-ties took refuse removal into their own control. The moveable dustbin, invented in 1884 by Eugène Poubelle, prefect of the Seine, only made its appearance in Britain after 1900, when its introduction met some resistance. Fixed refuse receptacles, difficult to clean and an ideal harbour for flies, were a standard urban fixture until at least 1914.

Although at their peak in the summer months, gastric illnesses occurred all the year around and must have been a constantly recurring shadow on health for children and adults alike, to an extent that cannot be measured by mortality data for typhoid and infant diarrhoea. The declining incidence and fatality of infant diarrhoea after 1900 (typhoid deaths remaining stable between about 1885 and 1904, after their initial fall from 1870 to 1885) suggest that gastric illness in general became less frequent, although this – like the cause of the decline in infant diarrhoea – remains speculative. For typhoid, however, it is clear that sanitary interventions adopted on the basis of medical knowledge, first of its transmission by the faecal–oral route, and second of the healthy human carrier, made a substantial contribution to its virtual eradication as a public health problem before 1914.

Less obvious as a health hazard, and far more complex as a public health problem, air pollution exerted a largely undefinable effect on the health of urban populations in this period. As with river pollution, this was an area in which attempts at reform were fruitless, partly because it was so difficult to establish a causal link with any specific illnesses. It was well known to medical men that the spectacular London particulars (the dense, often orange-hued fogs, which reduced visibility in the capital to a couple of feet) were associated with a dramatically raised death-rate from bronchitis, asthma and other respiratory diseases, but equally that these diseases had been well established in individual patients before the event of the fog. Many argued for the generally deleterious effects of pollution, however, pointing to nausea, poor digestion and lack of appetite, general malaise and sleeplessness as other consequences of the inhalation of the smoke, stench and gas that comprised the air in British cities.[52] Industrial activity was partly to blame, more especially so for the rich variety of unpleasant smells that loitered in localities accommodating, for example, tar works, breweries, glue, pickle or jam factories, slaughter houses and tripe- or bone-boilers, but smoke pollution was at least as much the result of the domestic fires burned in every home to provide heat, hot water and cooking. It was estimated that 2.5 million tons of soot were produced annually by domestic fires, the country as a whole burning over 100 million tons of coal a year. For individual towns and cities, the density of soot of course varied, but in Oldham before 1915, 960 tons were said to have fallen on every square mile of the city each year.[53]

Respiratory diseases apart, smoke pollution also contributed to a specific nutritional deficiency disease: rickets. Rickets, which manifests itself in softened bones, bow legs and a pigeon chest, occurs partly as a result of a lack of vitamin D in the diet, but also when the skin is exposed to insufficient sunlight as sunlight stimulates the skin to release calciferol, without which the body cannot synthesise vitamin D. The pall of smoke that overhung Victorian cities resulted in rickets for almost all urban children. When John Snow arrived in London in the 1840s, he was shocked by its presence in all social classes; in 1884 every child examined on Clydeside was found to have the disease. A study by the British Medical Association (BMA) showed it to be prevalent throughout the country, even in rural areas, but most heavily concentrated in London, the industrial areas of Wales, the Black Country, Tyneside and the Tees cities, as well as in the towns of Durham, Lancashire, Yorkshire, Cheshire, Derbyshire and Nottingham. The association with smoke pollution rather than diet is clear and probably also connects with the higher urban mortality from measles and whooping cough among small children whose reduced chest capacity left them less able to cope with the secondary respiratory infections that were so frequently the killers in these diseases.

The black skies over Britain's nineteenth-century cities, and the endless fall of smut on all surfaces exposed to the weather, probably aggravated the adverse health effects of poor and insanitary housing conditions. MOHs were obsessed with the need for improved ventilation in the homes of all social classes. Even for the well-to-do, the well-shuttered windows intended to exclude smoke from domestic interiors meant rooms unhealthily deprived of fresh air. Women and children were particularly noted to be living mostly indoors, thus being overexposed to tuberculosis and infectious diseases, the seriousness of many of which is related to the intensity of exposure to the infectious agent. In poorer homes, these conditions were greatly aggravated by overcrowding, especially where whole families lived in one room. Middle-class observers frequently reported with nausea the stench generated by unwashed people crowded together in airless rooms, in which all domestic functions – cooking, washing, sleeping, and so on – took place. Too often, domestic vermin seethed behind the wallpapers and in the beds; the fires necessary to provide heating and cooking made rooms stifling; and the need to dry washing indoors contributed an overwhelming atmosphere of damp. Respiratory diseases such as bronchitis and the secondary infections following on childhood diseases, chronic infections such as tuberculosis, and serious attacks of dose-related infections like whooping cough were all generated in such surroundings.

With wages low, and a need to live close to their place of work, the working classes were, throughout this period, seriously disadvantaged in a competitive, commercial private housing market. Although the great cities embarked on considerable programmes of slum clearance, which swept away the most fantastic slum areas, vast tracts of urban housing continued below any reasonable standard. Housing conditions were another area of public health concern in which action was slow to take effect, despite such legislative efforts such as the Torrens (1879) and Cross (1875) Acts, and the Housing of the Working Classes Act 1890. MOHs were very conscious that, in enforcing regulations against overcrowding in their own districts, they were simply displacing people to similar situations elsewhere. In 1911 an estimated six million people – about one-fifth of the entire population – were still living in overcrowded accommodation.[54]

The deleterious health effects of overcrowded, poor-quality housing were, for working people, too often compounded by the conditions they were obliged to endure at work. A whole range of adverse health effects can be traced to nineteenth-century working conditions. Examples include the notorious phossy jaw of the match industry; the grinder's lung of the Birmingham and Sheffield cutlery trades; silicosis among miners and potters; mercury poisoning in hatters, furriers and mirror-makers; anthrax among skin and fur workers; and inflated tuberculosis death-rates among highly paid print workers, and among shoe and bootmakers in new, mass production factories at the turn of the century. Women were especially at risk of lead poisoning in white lead and pottery manufacture, and from insanitary conditions in a wide variety industrial situations.[55] Factory legislation was often ignored, and workplaces were hot, humid, badly ventilated and overcrowded, as the young Beatrice Webb discovered when investigating the working conditions of London seamstresses in the 1880s. For both men and women, the damage wrought by specific industrial processes was only one end of the spectrum of industrially associated disease. At the other stood a wide variety of respiratory, digestive, urinary and nervous conditions that, although not clearly causally linked to occupation, still demonstrated a clear occupational association in simple statistical analyses; file-makers, for example, had a death-rate almost double the national average for gout.[56]

Government attempts to tackle the manifold problems of industrial disease were largely piecemeal before 1900, and loopholes in the law were many. Reluctant to tamper with the freedom of industry to operate according to its own financial criteria, using such raw materials as it saw fit, Victorian governments tried to manage the health aspects of industrial practice by persuasion, sanitary regulation and inspection, but with a conspicuous lack of success. A reluctance to intervene in the mechanisms of economic activity also marked attitude to food supply in this period. Issues of quantity and pricing apart, Britain's urban food supplies were in a qualitatively parlous condition by the 1860s. Although the medical community had been alert to the dangers of adulterated food, and suspicious of the health implications of rotting food and meat from diseased animals since the 1830s at least, government made little attempt to regulate for improved food hygiene or agricultural practice in this period. Chemical adulteration alone commanded any kind of government concern: all social classes were at risk from the addition of poisonous chemical additives to food and drugs, and such regulations did not impinge on powerful agricultural vested interests. It was not, however, until the 1870s that measures began to be taken against adulteration, notably with the Food, Drink and Drugs Act 1872. Under this legislation local authorities were permitted but not required to appoint public analysts, while medical officers were empowered to order analyses without waiting for the public to complain. In 1875, the government sought to impose uniformity of practice by establishing standards of purity with a further Food and Drugs Act. Despite these endeavours, the permissive nature of crucial sections of the acts, commercial pressure and the complexities of central government supervision in an era of financial retrench-ment meant that the situation with regards to the deliberate adul-teration of foodstuffs remained unsatisfactory. Although many large firms took pride in working with the spirit of the law, the multiplicity of tiny operations that characterised the British food industry at this period ensured that standards of composition and production remained highly variable.[57]

The adulteration of foodstuffs undoubtedly had an adverse effect on health in the years before the First World War. Dramatic fatal poisonings were not common, but indigestion was a wide-spread complaint among all social classes, adulteration also reducing the nutritional value of foods eaten. Recent research provides little substantial evidence for McKeown's assertion that improved nutrition helped to reduce the fatality of infectious disease, but instead reinforces the conclusion that, for a signifi-cant proportion of Britain's population, rising real income had little direct impact on improving nutritional standards. This was in part because of the vagaries of the economy. Although it appears that real wages did rise significantly in the 1880s, as more intensive farming and cheap imports brought down prices, the value of the pound declined between 1896 and 1914, and prices rose again while wages were not increased.[58]

Family income, moreover, was often not distributed for the equal benefit of all the family . It was customary in working-class households for the husband to hand over part of his wage to the wife but to keep back part for his own uses. Long-established dietary habits within families also limited the impact of rising wages. In working-class families, men customarily received the greatest share of the food resources, their diets generally including meat, potatoes, milk and porridge, which together adequately supplied their needs. Women and children, on the other hand, survived on a diet largely consisting of bread, jam and tea. In households where the woman worked, there was little difference, probably because these were the very poorest families, in which the wife's earnings were sufficient only to bring the total income up to survival level. A low intake of milk, dairy products, fruit and vegetables meant that deficiencies of calcium, as well as of essential vitamins and trace elements, were commonplace in late nineteenth-century diets. A family income in the average working-class range of 20–40 shillings a week was simply not sufficient to permit a nutritionally adequate diet in the years before 1914.[59] It seems unlikely indeed that the debilitating conditions endured by many nineteenth-century working people at home, in the workplace and in the very streets of their cities were significantly counterbalanced by nutritional improvements in the years after 1870.

Poverty, Hygiene and National Degeneration

At the end of the nineteenth century, public health concern took a fresh turn. With the reduction in the number of deaths from infectious disease, some MOHs had already in the 1890s begun to pay increased attention to private hygiene, especially in connection with worries over the continuing high level of infant mortality. In the early 1890s progressive local health authorities such as Glasgow, Manchester and Brighton began to appoint women health inspectors specifically to supervise domestic hygiene and to instruct new mothers in childcare, other authorities following their example. A high level of infant mortality was especially worrying when seen in conjunction with a falling birth-rate (although the latter might, in fact, testify to an improvment in health for both women and children). Moreover, the physical condition of the country's working population was causing increasing concern and was an integral part of that wide range of secular and spiritual fears that made up the social crisis of the *fin-de-siècle*.[60] Fears about the effect of city life on the physique of town-dwellers dated from at least the 1830s, when the visiting Scottish physician John Hogg described with dismay the physical decrepitude of the average Londoner, and increased as the century wore on. Charles Darwin's theory of evolution and natural selection, published in 1859, was seen by many to have direct, and sinister, applications to Victorian society.

Darwin's cousin, Sir Francis Galton, was the first to formulate the concept of 'eugenics', which advocated, at its most extreme, the selective breeding of human beings and the sterilisation of the 'unfit'.[61] In the 1890s, a movement for 'National Efficiency' emerged among the politically concerned upper middle class, which included such diverse figures as R. B. Haldane, Sydney and Beatrice Webb and H. G. Wells.[62] The crunch came in 1899–1900, when, with the outbreak of the Boer War, the British Army went recruiting for volunteers for the first time since the Napoleonic Wars. To the consternation of senior army personnel, politicians and the educated public alike, men meeting up to the army's physical requirements were hard to find in the great cities: in Manchester alone, 8,000 men out of a total of 11,000 volunteers were not fit for active service. In all, nearly 35 per cent of would-be recruits were rejected as being unfit for service, clear evidence, it seemed, of the reality of physical degeneration in the British people.

The issue of physical degeneration put the public health administration on the defensive. Public health reform and the resultant reduction in the number of deaths from infectious disease had, eugenicists argued, contributed to the degeneration of the race by allowing the unfit to survive and reproduce themselves. It was an accusation not only that the public health service found wounding, but also which it explicitly resisted for reasons of both ideology and professional pride.[63] Wider social issues began to open in the general national anxiety over health – issues of poverty and nutrition, and of education and childcare – behind which lay the ever-present concern that Britain should maintain the manpower capacity to hold her own on the world stage and to defend her empire and her naval supremacy against the ambitions of other powers, in particular Germany.[64] Here were public health problems that, in their nature and dimension, required medical officers and their administrations to develop new strategies of health management in a political context that forbade any attempt to reach out for the real roots of these problems.

While Sir Francis Galton was developing his theory of eugenics, and the Webbs were pondering the shortfalls of social administration in the last decades of the century, a new school of social investigator had begun to investigate the problems of poverty.

Poverty was the bottom line of a great many public health problems, but the importance of poverty was, if not denied, then at least avoided by nineteenth-century politicians and health administrators.[65] Because the bottom line of poverty was wages, and any mandatory improvement in wages meant interference with the independence of industry and employers, solutions to poverty were evaded by policy-makers, being abandoned to philanthropists and voluntary societies.

Political and economic changes in the 1880s led, however, to the emergence of more organised, vociferous working-class demands for social improvement, and to a growing middle-class recognition of poverty as a political problem.[66] This recognition was not confined to the medical officers and local government officials who observed its impact on the ground and who were to be influential in instigating remedial legislation. Where the public health service had organised investigations into, for example, typhoid outbreaks, industrial diseases and the causes of infant mortality, a new type of social investigation developed from the concern over poverty. In the early 1880s Charles Booth, a well-to-do Liverpool ship-owner, was so dismayed by the claim that a quarter of London's population lived in poverty that he initiated his own extensive investigation to prove the claim wrong. Seventeen years and ten published volumes of detailed evidence later, Booth had demonstrated that more than one third of the city's population lived in poverty.[67]

Booth's investigation, which ranged from wages and domestic living conditions, to conditions of work and the privations of old age, initiated a new type of independent, social investigation. Another such survey, by the Quaker industrialist Seebohm Rowntree of York, in the 1890s confirmed that a third of that city's population also lived in poverty or below subsistence level.[68] An original feature of Rowntree's investigation was his attempt to use scientific standards of nutrition to assess how far the standard working-class diet contributed towards maintaining physical efficiency. Nutritional science was then very much in its infancy, the emphasis of investigation being on proteins, calories and fats, and scientific disagreement was to the fore.[69] Rowntree, however, was adamant that his evidence showed that the working classes received on average about 25 per cent less food than nutritional

science recommended for physical efficiency. Rowntree's introduction of nutritional issues to the problem of poverty was
prescient. With his survey begins a line of concern and social
inquiry, increasingly influential between the wars, that was to
escalate out of all proportion as nutritional science and the
epidemiological investigation of the dietary causes of disease
developed in the later twentieth century.

The revelations of the Boer War recruitment drive resulted in
the appointment of a civil service committee – the Interdepartmental Committee on Physical Deterioration – that reported in
1904. The Committee's brief was three-fold: to establish, with the
help of the medical profession, methods for measuring the
health and physique of the people; to suggest the general causes
of such physical deterioration as did exist; and to point out the
most effective means of diminishing it. The minutes of evidence
constituted a battle ground between the deteriorationist/eugeni-
cists and the public health service, which insisted on the essentially 'environmental' causes of poor physique, including
inadequate diet, a lack of physical exercise, air pollution and
under-age smoking. The nutritional inadequacy that Rowntree
had detected at York was underscored by the evidence presented
to the Interdepartmental Committee, more especially in respect
of children, whose pitiful performance at school, breakfastless
and on a regular diet of tea, bread and margarine from which
milk and meat were standardly omitted, spoke only too clearly
of deprivation.

It was, indeed, widely acknowledged that the women and
children in working-class families were desperately malnourished,
the lion's share of food resources being devoted to the breadwinner, on whose strength the whole family depended. The
medical evidence presented to the Committee, especially that from
Alfred Eichholz, an inspector of schools with extensive experience
of institutions for children with physical and mental problems, was
decisive in persuading them of the primary importance of deprivation rather than degeneration in producing a physically damaged
population. Among more than fifty recommendations for action to
improve the national physique were proposals for the medical
inspection of schoolchildren, the feeding of children in elementary schools, physical exercise for all schoolchildren, the instruc-

tion of girls in infant feeding, milk depots in all towns and measures to ensure its purity of supply, stricter measures against smoke pollution and the banning of tobacco sales to children.[70]

A legislative response to the Interdepartmental Committee's findings was implemented within a few years. The Conservative government that had been in power since 1895 fell in 1905, and a new Liberal government took office, with a renewed mandate for social reform. Legislation introduced in 1906 and 1907 established a system of medical inspection of schoolchildren, permitted the provision of free school meals for children in state elementary schools, and required the notification of births to local health departments, in order to enable the first days of a child's life to be supervised by trained health visitors.[71] Initially permissive, the Notification of Births Act was made mandatory under the shadow of war in 1915. The new legislation established frameworks of public health surveillance that, although initially neither extensive nor effective, were attuned to the more broadly educational approach that was developing in the public health services at this time.

Despite the new consciousness of a need for health interventions at the level of the individual rather than essentially through environmental management, both central government and health reformers were constrained by contemporary social attitudes. By directing their efforts at social amelioration through the schools and at vulnerable young mothers, the state avoided trespassing directly on domestic ground and on the independence of the family – trespass that might still have been unacceptable in many British homes.[72] And while government and society remained deeply reluctant to tackle the issue of wages and poverty, public health education appeared to be a relatively inexpensive and potentially effective alternative to interference with the economic and political *status quo*. While the Interdepartmental Committee's recommendation of a national system of milk depots was never implemented, local authorities began slowly to establish milk depots and mother and child clinics, and to increase the numbers of health visitors, in a further extension of the principle of managing domestic health reform through education.[73]

In fact the early twentieth-century adoption by central and local government of education as a tool of health improvement borrowed from well-established traditions in the voluntary sector, as well as in private and public health medicine. How far these efforts were effective in improving domestic standards of health and hygiene in the later nineteenth century is entirely a matter of guesswork, but there is no doubt that the efforts made were extensive, and certain indicators do suggest at least a degree of effectiveness. Private doctors had, of course, long been involved in advising patients on how to manage their health, but they did so with increasing certainty in the Victorian period as ideas about contagion and the mechanisms of infection became clearer. GPs, as well as MOHs, became involved in educating the public in hygiene by giving lectures and writing pamphlets on such subjects as running a healthy home, cleanliness, cooking and infant care.

Voluntary organisations also joined in. The great explosion of philanthropic activity and enthusiasm among middle-class women after 1860 centred to a considerable degree on the domestic lives of their poorer sisters and on the enhancement of health and hygiene in the home.[74] The Ladies Sanitary Association, founded in 1857 and with branches in nearly a dozen cities by 1865, was convinced that the secret of reducing infant mortality lay in educating working-class mothers in domestic management, and issued millions of tracts, supervised hundreds of voluntary workers among the poor, and distributed quantities of soap, washing powder, disinfectant and cleansing equipment before the century's end when, its activities largely taken over by municipal efforts, it was wound up. Similar associations sprang up in other cities – in Liverpool, Manchester and Salford, for example – while throughout the nation countless Bible Societies and other women's organisations laboured similarly to educate and sanitise the working classes and the poor.[75]

While these middle-class labours had little evident effect on infant mortality, there are indications that women were profiting from new medical and hygiene lessons. In particular, the death-rate from typhoid and respiratory tuberculosis fell faster among women than it did among men in the years after 1870 (although, again, the local pattern varied).[76] Once typhoid's faecal–oral transmission route had been established by William Budd in the 1850s, and Villemin's researches in the 1860s had indicated that tuberculosis was infectious, hygienic practices based on such knowledge were gradually (although by no means universally) diffused. The theory that rebreathed air was a contributory factor in tuberculosis would also have had a beneficial effect on domestic practice with respect to the disease. It is unclear, for example, which medical theory lay behind a Welsh GP's advice to a 'patient' in 1872 not to sleep with her sister who had tuberculosis; the important point is that he did give her that advice.

There is a good deal of evidence that health consciousness increased substantially among middle-class Victorian women, while the enormous popularity of Florence Nightingale's *Notes on Nursing* (1859), which was in fact intended for the domestic rather than the hospital sick-room, may well have effected a considerable improvement in the management of sick-rooms and the sick, and of domestic hygiene in general, across the nation.[77] Following the introduction of compulsory notification for many of the common infectious diseases in 1889, working-class families were inundated with advice on the recognition and management of sickness. The fall in death-rate among children beyond infancy may be one indication of the better domestic management of potentially damaging illnesses in this period.

The importance of medical management in the preservation of health was officially recognised in 1911 with the passing of the National Insurance Act, to come into effect in 1913. It was the first time a British government had directly intervened with positive intent in the personal health provision of some of the most vulnerable groups in society, and marked a transition in policy that has traditionally been regarded as a first step towards the NHS. Copied in part from the pioneering social insurance schemes that had been implemented in Germany since the 1880s, the national insurance scheme also borrowed from the well-established tradition of friendly society sickness provision. The British scheme was designed to protect the classes just above the poverty line from tipping below it through illness. It was a contributory scheme, workers earning under £160 a year putting in 4d a week, a sum topped up to 10d by employer and government contributions. The sums so raised funded GP services for insured persons – but not for their dependents – as well as tuberculosis sanatoria and a Medical Research Committee (now the Medical Research Council [MRC]), which was to sponsor research into problems affecting the health of the British people. Given a mixed reception by those whom it was supposed to benefit, the scheme had barely come into operation when the outbreak of war dramatically altered the social context within which it operated.

Conclusion

Any survey of health and medicine in the years 1860 to 1914 must end with the conclusion that, despite the gain in mortality and life expectancy registered in the vital statistics of the period, the overall gain in health – as opposed to the reduction in the number of infectious disease deaths – was probably small, especially among the poorer classes. Medicine had certainly contributed to reducing death from infectious disease, by pointing the way to controlling typhoid and cholera, by supporting the immunisation programme against smallpox and by offering supportive treatment to countless thousands of patients suffering from infectious disease in the urban isolation hospitals. While the fear of infectious disease had been significantly reduced by 1914, these infections were essentially acute illnesses that initially took patients unaware and which, while they might affect subsequent quality of life, stood apart from the miserable run of chronic respiratory, rheumatic and digestive illness, and nutritional inadequacy that dominated the health experience of the majority of British people in the Victorian and Edwardian periods. If we accept, as so many authorities do, that the infant mortality rate (IMR) is a sensitive indicator of the general health of a nation, it was not until the early years of the twentieth century that Britain's health began to improve.

2
ARMAGEDDON, 1914–18

Introduction

The impact of the Great War on health and medicine in Britain is still a matter of debate. The war was traditionally regarded as bad for civilian health and good for medicine: for the nutrition specialists Jack Drummond and Anne Wilbraham, there was 'clear evidence' that the general state of health declined, while for the eminent clinician Sir Clifford Allbutt, the war transformed medicine from 'an observational and empirical craft' to a scientific calling.[1] These judgments have been called into question by more recent scholars: J. M. Winter has argued that the paradox of the Great War was that civilian health actually improved, while new research has begun to consider the mixed benefits that war conferred on medicine itself, in both the short and the longer term.[2] The tragedy of the battlefields in France, and the trauma of soldiers continually exposed to senseless carnage, has overshadowed the experience of the home front. For many civilians war brought new liberties (as well as the loss of some old ones), new employments and raised income. The pattern of mortality decline established in the years before the war was not significantly disrupted and, with the sole and singular exception of influenza in 1918, the country suffered no major epidemic outbreaks resulting from war-related social deprivation or dislocation.

Civilian Health

The Great War should be viewed above all as an immense psychological trauma for both soldiers and civilians. It was a hundred years since Britain had been involved in a major European war, but it was an event for which the country had been preparing, emotionally and culturally, for many decades. The cult of chivalry, pervasive among the upper and middle classes for much of the Victorian period, had produced an elite culture that believed nothing more glorious than to die for one's country, and that a fight in a just cause was both honourable and desirable. This culture was engrained in the public schools, but was spread more widely through society by organisations such as the Boy Scouts, boys' clubs and brigades, and popular literature. The Boer War added edge to the promotion of military values. Baden-Powell, for example, was led to found the Boy Scouts at least in part from the determination that the lack of fitness and practical training evident among would-be recruits to the fighting in South Africa should not be repeated.[3] Painting, sculpture, architecture and decoration were all influenced by these martial ideals, while women found their own role within the mythology, exalting the supportive role of womanhood, especially in the vital task of nursing. Just as Victorian and Edwardian women campaigned for the vote, for education and for the right to work, so they began to move into the hitherto exclusively male domain of war. And in the years after around 1900, the prospect of war became increasingly real, Germany clearly being identified as the potential enemy.[4]

The Boer War of 1899–1902 provided a salutary – if unfortunate – prelude to the conflict in Europe. It involved some 450,000 British and Imperial soldiers, of whom about 22,000 died, in a faraway theatre of war. It was not long before the mismanagements and failures of the campaign faded in popular memory while some glorious images – the reliefs of Mafeking and Kimberley, for example – remained. The real military lessons of the war, that modern rifles and machine guns combined with trench warfare were likely to produce a stalemate, went unrecognised. In military and medical terms, the lessons of the war were that antiseptic techniques were effective in treating gunshot wounds, and that disease was as significant a killer as war itself: 68,000 men fell ill with enteric fever (the generic term for typhoid and the paratyphoids) during the course of the war. By 1914 intensive campaigns of sanitary training in the army, together with an improvement in the prevention of enteric fever – from immunisation and an awareness of the danger of the healthy carrier (an individual who continued to be infectious after recovering from the disease) – resulting from advances in bacteriology, contributed to a sense of improved efficiency and modernisation in the medical conduct of war.

The outbreak of war in August 1914 was greeted with euphoria, as fulfilling a long-awaited expectation, and with foreboding among the educated classes for whom it betokened the end of civilisation as they had known it.[5] In personal and economic terms, the early months of the war were for many devastating. An immense wave of chivalric and patriotic fervour swept a million male volunteers to the front: 750,000 in September 1914 and a further 125,000 a month until June 1915. The domestic market for luxury goods and consumables collapsed, casting the many women working in these trades into unemployment. It was esti-mated that nearly half of all women workers were briefly unem-ployed that September, and in London the number of schoolchildren fed by the London County Council increased from 35,000 to 75,000.[6]

Early expectations had been that the war would be over in six months, but, with the establishment of trench warfare in October, that expectation receded, increasing the pressure on civilian workers and families with men at the front. By mid-November the probable scale of casualties was becoming clear – more than half the British Expeditionary Force had been killed or wounded – and by the end of 1914 some 30,000 had died. By the end of the war, more than six million men had been mobilised, 723,000 had died, and 1.2 million were sufficiently maimed to qualify for a disability pension. More than 500,000 young men in the age group 15–30 lost their lives, and the privileged social groups who made up the officer corps suffered disproportionately.[7] Although the great majority of those who served in the war returned, the sense of grief and loss was felt throughout British society, sharp-ened by the months and years of continuing acute anxiety.[8]

Almost every family in the country, it has been calculated, lost one or more of its young men in the conflict.

Despite the immense tragedy of the war, to which the culture of chivalry had so contributed, that culture, and the sense of service and patriotism, that accompanied it, may have been significant in sustaining morale on the home front. If the tension of war for civilians should not be underestimated, reasonable physical health was maintained for the duration of the conflict. One long-term effect of the war was the rapid spread of the habit of cigarette smoking through British society, among both combatant and non-combatant men, and among middle-class girls. Stress almost certainly played a great part in this. As Andrew Clark, Rector of Great Leas in Essex, noted, one cold January morning in 1917, one indirect result of the war was a great increase in cigarette smoking among both sexes. Since his own servant had been called up, and he had been left alone to manage all the outdoor and indoor work of his establishment, 'I have smoked in each week more cigarettes than I used to do in any whole year before the war.'[9]

In part also, the rise in cigarette smoking occurred in compensation for the wartime controls on the drink trade, introduced when, early in 1915, the failure of the munitions industry to keep pace with army requirements was blamed on absenteeism among munitions workers as a result of excessive drinking.[10] Alcohol had been the great standby of the Victorians, accounting for 18 per cent of total consumer expenditure in 1900. From March 1915, however, the British government mounted an energetic campaign against drink, and in May it set up the Central Liquor Control Board for the sole purpose of regulating trade. By the end of the war, the British people had been broken of their drink habit (for the temporary space of some thirty years at least). The displacement of alcohol by tobacco was, however, to have a long-term health implication that had begun to become apparent by the outbreak of the Second World War.[11]

The essential stability of civilian health in wartime Britain is measurable by the death-rate for women and babies, whose downward trend continued in line with prewar figures. Women's death-rate in particular stands in sharp contrast to that of Germany, where there was a moderate increase in female mortality in the first two years of the war and a sharp increase in the crisis year 1917 (Table 2.1).[12] (The figures for both countries for 1918 were distorted by the influenza epidemic.) Several factors lay behind this continuing pattern. In the first place, there was Britain's success in the management of food supplies and their distribution throughout the course of the war. The country was heavily dependent on imported supplies of foodstuffs and raw materials. At the outbreak of war, 60 per cent of Britain's foodstuffs and 80 per cent of her wheat came from abroad. Although there had for at least a decade been considerable discussion of the management of supplies in the event of war, the government remained reluctant to impose food controls.

It was not until more than two million tons of shipping had been sunk by enemy naval operations that a Food Controller was appointed in December 1916 and controls were introduced on the distribution of wheat, flour and sugar. By October 1917 prices were rising, distribution becoming increasingly chaotic and profiteering starting to become noticeable. Under pressure from the trades unions, and with the energetic action of the new Food Controller Lord Rhondda (his predecessor Lord Devonport

Table 2.1   Female mortality in Germany
and in England and Wales, 1913–23

| | Deaths per 1,000 women | |
Year	Germany	England
1913	14.3	12.2
1914	15.2	12.4
1915	15.3	13.2
1916	15.2	11.7
1917	17.6	11.4
1918	21.6	14.6
1919	16.7	11.9
1920	15.3	10.9
1921	13.6	10.2
1922	13.9	10.5
1923	13.6	9.3

Source: Avner Offer, *The First World War: An Agrarian Interpretation* (Oxford, 1991, corrected edn), p. 35.

having retired because of ill-health), controls were gradually extended on meat and fats (butter and margarine).[13] By the summer of 1918, all important foodstuffs were under government control, remaining so until well after the Armistice. Meat rationing ended on 15 December 1919, butter rationing on 30 May 1920 and that of sugar on 29 November 1920. Controls on the production of flour did not end until 31 March 1921. Nonetheless, despite problems in the earlier years of the war, food supplies were successfully maintained throughout the country.

A change in family circumstances and in diet in many cases worked further to benefit living standards. There was a sharp fall in the birth-rate (from 23.8 per thousand population in 1914 to under 18 in 1917 and 1918), which reduced the call on family budgets. The absence of menfolk almost certainly resulted in a more equal distribution of rations within family groups, while the re-entry after 1916 of women into employment in place of their menfolk helped to maintain the family income. The strict wartime control on the production and consumption of alcohol also had a beneficial effect on the family budget: Andrew Clark noted that whereas middle-class working women indulged in cigarettes, working-class girls preferred alcohol. Controls on alcohol consumption may have significantly improved working-class family budgets. The beneficial effect of alcohol limitation on health was noted particularly in certain age groups: survival rates for men over the age of forty-five, for example, improved, with a reduction in the number of deaths from cirrhosis of the liver; the death-rates from late-onset diabetes and cardiovascular disease, which are associated more generally with the overconsumption of food, also improved.

There were three exceptions to the stable or still-improving picture. The first, an ominous but transient development, was the outbreak early in 1915 of the worst epidemic yet seen in Britain of meningitis, then known as 'cerebrospinal fever'. Beginning among troops still on the home front, the outbreak spread to civilians and caused some 2,000 deaths; the previous highest recorded total, in spring 1914, having been 194. The incidence in London and the south of England was much heavier than elsewhere, a clear indication that the infection had been spread by military movement.[14] Yet although this outbreak caused some alarm, it was not repeated in the subsequent years of the war. In terms of the wider destruction of life being caused by epidemic diseases at home, and by warfare abroad, the outbreak was of limited significance: in the same year more than 16,000 young people died of measles, some 6,000 from whooping cough, 5,000 from diptheria and over 2,000 of scarlet fever.

A more important regression of mortality lay in the rise in death-rate from respiratory disease, notably from respiratory tuberculosis among young women, which rose year by year until 1918, registering an overall increase of 25 per cent on the prewar level, and 35 per cent in the age group 20–25. Conditions at home and at work, stress and nutrition are all recognised contributory factors in the development of this very complex infectious disease, and the interplay of these factors in the tuberculosis history of English women during the First World War has been disputed by historians.[15]

As with so many questions about the behaviour of tuberculosis in the past, it is not clear that the precise determinants of the disease's behaviour in any given historical situation will ever be resolved. While recent research has emphasised the migration of non-immune rural women into work in tuberculosis-infested urban areas as a cause of the rise in mortality, there are problems with this interpretation for Britain.[16] Biopsy and post-mortem evidence, for example, indicated that 90 per cent of Britain's population in the early twentieth century had suffered primary tuberculosis infection by the time they reached adulthood, although only 1 per cent went on to develop the disease.[17]

The nutritional explanation offered by contemporary observers, and supported by Linda Bryder, appears to be belied by the abrupt fall of tuberculosis mortality in 1919, since normal conditions of food supply were not fully restored until 1920. It seems equally plausible to link women's adverse tuberculosis experience in the Great War with the rise in the tuberculosis death-rate during the first two years of the Second World War (see Chapter 4), and to link both with the level of stress in the community, rather than with nutrition or the standard of living in general. Great War diaries, letters and memoirs clearly reflect a rising level of tension and anxiety among civilians as the war dragged on without any apparent prospect of resolution. Young women in the

Table 2.2   Total deaths among people
aged over 60 in London, 1913–20

Year	London	Increase
1913	22,929	100
1914	23,219	101
1915	26,912	117
1916	25,236	110
1917	25,341	111
1918	25,857	108
1920	22,321	97

Source: J. Winter and Jean-Louis Robert (eds), *Capital Cities at War.*
Paris, London, Berlin 1914–1919 (Cambridge, 1997), p. 463.

worst affected age groups were those whose lives and prospects, like that of the young Vera Brittain, were most sharply transformed by the loss of brothers, friends, lovers and husbands on the battlefields.[18]

The stress factor probably also lay behind the second extraordinary mortality phenomenon, a raised death-rate among the elderly. This pattern was repeated in the Second World War. Catherine Rollet has described an 'unmistakable' demographic crisis among the over-60s in London, Paris and Berlin between 1914 and 1920 (Table 2.2), and has drawn attention to the deep suffering of older people who lost sons and grandsons in the conflict.[19] The effect of deep grief on the survival chances of the elderly is well known: the death of a partner significantly reduces the life chances of the survivor for at least six months after the bereavement. While many older people undoubtedly also suffered during the Great War from difficulties with food and fuel supplies, and from the stress of assisting the war effort by their labour (elderly men in London, for example, suffering a sharply increased rate of heart disease, perhaps as a result of their re-entry into active work late in life), their overall mortality pattern in these years must in great part be attributed to depression and despair.

The differing wartime mortality patterns of different age groups were, as always, masked by the pattern of the overall trend, as were local variations. Variations in adult mortality have

Table 2.3   Infant mortality in England and Wales, 1913–23

Year	Deaths per 1000 females aged 0–1	Year	Deaths per 1000 females aged 0–1
1913	96	1919	78
1914	93	1920	69
1915	96	1921	72
1916	80	1922	66
1917	85	1923	60
1918	86		

Source: Avner Offer, *The First World War. An Agrarian Interpretation* (Oxford, 1991, corrected edn) p. 36.

been neglected by historians, but the IMR, that generally well-regarded index of community health, continued its downward trend between 1914 and 1918 (Table 2.3). In a handful of areas, however, things were different: in Bradford, Leeds, Carlisle, Aberdeen and Aberdeenshire, levels rose in those years, for reasons that have still to be explored. While the fall in birth-rate probably meant that babies benefited from the better spacing of siblings, local circumstances clearly differed. The demands of war undeniably stimulated local authorities to look more closely at their provision of services to women and children, who were, after all, the source of future cannon fodder. The number of health visitors employed by local authorities increased from some 600 in 1914 to 2,557 in 1918, while the number of municipal and voluntary maternal and child welfare centres rose from 650 to 1,278. For the first time, municipal schemes began to outnumber voluntary ones. Much of this work focused on the poorest areas, but the indications are that social and economic factors such as overcrowding negated attempts to reduce local levels of infant mortality in the period 1900–30 as a whole.[20]

The increased provision of health services for mothers and babies apart, the continuation of the downward trend in general death-rate during the war took place in spite of a reduction in medical services to the civilian population as doctors were urged into military service. Ten per cent of the country's medical practitioners enlisted during the first few months of the war, and by July

1915 a quarter of the profession had joined up. By 1918, 12,284 doctors were enrolled in the army, one to every 376 soldiers. At home, in contrast, the proportion was one GP to 3,000 civilians: 11,482 practitioners serving a population of 24.5 million, with the assistance of 3,236 physicians and hospital consultants. Many of these doctors were working 12–15 hours a day, and in some areas, notably in towns housing munitions factories, people queued at surgeries far into the night.

For many, the absence of adequate medical care probably had little real impact on health and fitness.[21] For some, the pressure on medical attention might even have been beneficial: the death-rate for women in childbirth, where medical intervention still held danger, declined during the war. For others, however, those who needed medical reassurance and those whose reliance on doctors for the management of their disease had grown with the growing authority of scientific medicine, scamped consulting times could make an adverse contribution to the effectiveness of any treatment. The reduction or absence of medical management may have been especially significant with respect to the rise in the number of deaths from tuberculosis among women, since the evidence suggests that increased medical management had contributed to prolonging life expectancy for tuberculosis sufferers in the later nineteenth century.

It is possible that some of the rise in women's tuberculosis deaths can be attributed to the return to the workforce of married women, who had become accustomed to putting their own physical and material needs below those of their families. In the early twentieth century, and indeed until after the Second World War, it was customary for women to give up work on marriage. After the introduction of conscription in January 1916, however, married women re-entered the workforce in an increasing number, most of the million and a half women who entered employment before April 1918 being married.[22] It was symbolic of wartime attitudes and pressures that the great London medical schools for the first time opened their doors to women. Those doors were firmly closed again soon after the war ended.[23]

Right up until the Great War, most working men and women had been exploited by their employers, working long hours in poor conditions under inadequate safety regulations. The circumstances of war excused even more ruthless exploitation, work in munitions factories often involving greater privations than such peacetime occupations as dressmaking: workers later recalled night shifts where getting a drink of water was impossible, meals eaten in the dust and fumes of workshops, and long walks to new factories in mud and darkness. Shifts were often outrageously long – twenty five or thirty hours was not uncommon. Such conditions were certain to have an adverse effect on health. Common minor ailments as indigestion and varicose veins were aggravated by hastily eaten meals and long hours of standing, while the stress inherent in such conditions undoubtedly contributed to activating latent tuberculosis infection.

Exploitation by employers apart, the new wartime industries carried their own particular hazards. Shell-filling, which involved handling the explosive trinitrotoluene (TNT), and the making of 'aircraft dope' (varnish), were positively dangerous, exposing workers to slow toxic poisoning. Symptoms experienced in advanced cases included nausea, anorexia, giddiness, drowsiness and swelling of the hands and feet; in such cases death invariably followed. Yet although thousands of women workers in these industries were exposed to some degree of TNT poisoning, only a tiny number, estimated at 0.1 per cent, died. Government and employers, well aware of the hazards, and anxious that workers should not be discouraged from undertaking the all-important work of munitions on that account, used factory medical inspectors to try to identify women at risk and to encourage those in danger of serious poisoning to work elsewhere. More importantly perhaps, the workers themselves were well aware of the early symptoms, and probably used the freedom of the wartime labour market and a newly discovered independence of thought and action to change jobs when they began to find their health affected by their work. The lure of munitions lay in high wages and an involvement in an important, direct contribution to the war effort, but good wages and different contributions could be made elsewhere.[24]

The health of women as workers, of mothers and children as the source of future soldiers and workers, and of men in reserved occupations essential to the war effort were a source of civil concern in the years 1914–18, attempts accordingly being made to safeguard their physical welfare. Other social groups – those on a fixed income, such as the elderly, or families whose bread-winners were fighting – may well have suffered from a poorer diet and a reduced living standard during the war. Those confined in institutions probably also suffered: the death-rate from tuberculosis rose in the lunatic asylums, where budgets were under pressure and medical staff had often been severely cut back. There is no satisfactory measure of morbidity to modify the impression given by the mortality figures that civilian health in Britain was not seriously affected by the relative privations of the war. Mortality data from other European countries support this interpretation. France and neutral Sweden essentially maintained their mortality status during the war years, but in Belgium the death-rate soared, and for Germany the years 1916–18 saw seriously deteriorating life chances as the wartime economy gradually lost the struggle to maintain food supplies and services to the home front.[25]

Behind these differing national experiences lay the success or failure of individual governments in handling their national economies, above all in maintaining an adequate food supply to their civilian populations. For the first time in history, the welfare of civilians was of profound military importance, because of the need to service and support the vast armies operating in entrenched positions away from home. Medicine played little direct part in sustaining the health of essential civilians during the Great War, and the strain on civilian medical services as a result of service demands for doctors and nurses may even have reduced the life chances of those whose welfare depended on medical management. The general continuation of the decline in mortality during the war does not, however, justify a conclusion of generally improved civilian health as a result of the circumstances of war. Instead, it reflects the extent to which Britain successfully maintained the complex social, economic, and environmental improvements that had contributed to the prewar fall in mortality, and that determined the further continuation of that demographic pattern in the unsettled postwar years.

Soldiers Abroad

The call for doctors to serve the army was relentless throughout the war and suggests the extent to which medicine had been identified by the military authorities, and indeed by the general public, as a necessary adjunct to war. Doctors, it was accepted, were integral to army morale, and their provision was an integral part of the army's duty to its men, not only for their potential to return the sick and wounded to fitness, but also for their power to sustain and support men whose lives were continually in danger.[26] To a greater extent than in any previous war, medicine was involved in selecting, preparing and maintaining Britain's war machine. Men were vetted for military fitness, immunised against infections and trained in camp sanitation; the sick and wounded were tended; disease incidence was monitored; and research into old and new military medical problems was actively conducted during the course of the war, sometimes on the battlefield itself. Among the allied armies, mobile bacteriological units investigated the potential of infections and devised methods for containing them. Medical procedures for the retrieval and treatment of the wounded were more sophisticated and better organised than in any previous war, while contingency arrangements for tackling new medical problems, such as that of shellshock, were effectively put into operation.

Although the terrible toll of deaths on the Western Front has to a great extent overshadowed the experience of the survivors of that carnage, medicine successfully demonstrated that it had a positive contribution to make to the military effort. The new preventive medicine kept the traditional predators of war at bay: for the first time in history, more men died of wounds than died of disease. Although typhus caused terrible losses in Serbia in 1914–15, and in Russia between 1917 and 1921, sanitary measures ensured that typhus, typhoid and smallpox, the classic diseases of war, were largely absent from the Western Front. Curative medicine, both of the mind and of the body, played its part: 82 per cent of the 'wounded' and 93 per cent of the 'sick and injured' were eventually returned to some form of military duty.[27]

While many of the effective treatments for the sick, injured and wounded were worked out during the course of the war, the prevention of infectious disease depended crucially on medical research carried out in the two decades immediately preceding it. Had the Great War begun in 1900, the toll of infectious disease on all combatant troops would have been unimaginable.

War and Infectious Disease

In each of the wars witnessed in Europe since the fall of Napoleon, disease had played a significant part. In the Crimea, fevers had been more fatal than wounds; smallpox wrought havoc among the French troops in the Franco-Prussian War of 1870–71; and British efforts in South Africa had been significantly inhibited by typhoid, which claimed some 60,000 sick and 8,000 dead among the 557,653 fighting strength. Typhoid was known to be a potential hazard on the Western Front, partly because of a British mistrust of French sanitary arrangements and also because it was recognised that healthy carriers of the disease would inevitably find their way into the army and, in the conditions of war, cause serious epidemic outbreaks.

The typhoid bacillus had been discovered by Carl Eberth and Edwin Klebs in 1880, their discovery opening the way for bacteriological methods of controlling the disease. The existence of healthy carriers of typhoid infection was uncovered around 1900, when the new bacteriological techniques led to the discovery that some 2 per cent of people who have recovered from the disease continue to excrete live typhoid bacilli in their faeces and/or urine. A knowledge of this condition resulted in greatly improved typhoid control among British troops stationed in India, where the disease had been a serious endemic problem.

In 1896 the British bacteriologist Almroth Wright, and the German researchers Richard Pfeiffer and Wilhelm Kolle, had almost simultaneously produced the first vaccines against typhoid. Despite initial troubles with severe, if temporary, side effects, these had by 1914 been successfully modified into a generally acceptable operation and could be extended to include protection against the paratyphoids as well. Typhoid-only vaccine was extensively used in the British army during the Great War. Immunisation against smallpox was already compulsory for men joining the British army, and the experience of the war demonstrated the effectiveness of the new vaccines not only through the prevention of typhoid outbreaks, but even more by a sharp reduction in case fatality: across all six fighting fronts, there were, among an average strength of two million men, just 20,000 cases of typhoid and paratyphoid, and some 200 deaths, between 1914 and 1918.[28]

The army had made concerted attempts since 1900 to educate its professional soldiers in the importance of hygiene in war conditions, and it did its best to instill sanitary discipline into the volunteers. Nonetheless, sanitary conditions in the camps and along the transit routes were appalling in the early months of the war, before the more settled conditions of trench warfare allowed by improved sanitary organisation. The typhoid vaccines undoubtedly played a large part in preventing an outbreak among British troops in these months, and their effectiveness continued to be demonstrated throughout the course of the war: whenever sanitary arrangements were disrupted by a period of military 'activity', there was a sharp increase in the number of bowel complaints such as bacillary dysentery but no corresponding increase in typhoid. These outbreaks of diarrhoea confirm that the sanitary precautions detailed in camp instructions were, in general, adequate to prevent the serious presence of bowel complaints, but also demonstrate the fragility of a system that depended on the boiling or sterilisation of all water, the incineration of excrement and the emptying of urine into suitable soakage pits.

The absence of typhoid's ancient companion, typhus, from the Western Front was all the more notable because of the serious epidemic outbreak experienced in Serbia in the early months of the war. The comings and goings of typhus had long been associated with the social disruptions brought about by famine and by war, but it was only in 1910 that the French bacteriologist Charles Nicolle discovered that the disease was carried by the human body louse. Once again, it seems likely that the sanitary organisation possible in the relatively settled conditions of trench warfare helped to keep the disease away from the Western Front, where the bathing of soldiers and the steam sterilisation of their clothes was regularly undertaken, and the men were instructed in the importance of admitting to lice. Important too was the freedom of France and Flanders from indigenous typhus infection. The

Serbian epidemic early in 1915 occurred because soldiers were allowed to fraternise freely with civilians in a typhus endemic area, the epidemic being brought under control only by the reimposition of rigorous military discipline, although not before 150,000 lives had been lost. But sanitary controls were not well enforced in general on the Eastern Front, and typhus remained a persistent problem, smouldering throughout the war among Russian troops and civilians, and culminating in the terrible epidemic of 1918–22, in which an estimated 2.5 million people died.[29]

A crucial contribution to the control of the Serbian typhus epidemic was made by a British mobile bacteriological unit, whose analysis of the epidemiological problem resulted in the adoption of successful measures to combat the spread of the disease. These units were a novel feature of the Great War organisation but proved invaluable in the assessment and solution of medical problems in the field. They were originally intended to function as special diagnostic and treatment facilities, for example in dealing with convalescent typhoid patients and ensuring that they were not returned to active service while still excreting typhoid bacteria. They came instead to perform a unique research function – resolving medical problems generated by the new methods of warfare. Trench fever (a non-fatal, louse-borne infection), trench foot (damage and infection resulting from prolonged exposure to cold or to cold water), gas gangrene (the invasion of dead tissue by gas-forming bacteria) and gas poisoning were all tackled more or less successfully by these units, sometimes with assistance from colleagues at home. Research into such problems helped to reduce the miseries suffered by men in the trenches, even if they did not extend to any degree the capabilities of medicine beyond the battlefields of the Great War.

Heroic histories of the medicine of war have often been framed in terms of the spur that war has provided to medical expertise and medical knowledge, but in reality many war-generated discoveries relate closely to wartime situations and have little bearing on civilian practice. This was certainly the case with much of the bacteriological research and practice of the First World War. In some areas it can, however, be shown that the experience of war provided a stimulus that led to an extended understanding of the phenomenon of disease. Among the bacteriological team investigating typhus in Serbia early in 1915 was William Whiteman Topley. A cellular pathologist before the war, Topley's experience of typhus in Serbia turned him towards epidemiology and the study of disease behaviour in herds of laboratory mice. That research led to the concept of herd immunity and a fuller understanding of the ways in which infectious disease operates in human communities. In the same way, the mass mobilisation of young men, many from relatively isolated country districts, brought outbreaks of meningitis among recruits and resulted in the first serious bacteriological and epidemiological studies of the disease. The problems of dysentery in all theatres of war also led to research that eventually revealed the variety and complexity of this group of diseases and enhanced the medical understanding of their behaviour among civilian populations in time of peace. The application and development of bacteriological and epidemiological techniques in the context, and as a consequence, of war was an important aspect of the 'scientific transformation' of medicine noted by Clifford Allbutt.

The Surgery of War

Much of the medical mythology of the Great War centres on the refinement of surgical techniques developed as a consequence of the terrible injuries inflicted on soldiers by shells and shrapnel. Yet within a decade the historian Fielding Garrison had concluded that the medical innovations of the war were 'clever, respectable, but not particularly brilliant'; for Garrison the real innovations had taken place in medical administration.[30] The medical record card, for example, was invented during the Great War and translated back into civilian practice by returning doctors who had discovered its utility in the circumstances of war. Discussion of the long-standing assumption that war is good for medicine has recently been opened by Roger Cooter, whose own research has shown that the transfer of knowledge gained from the military into the civilian sphere is often complex and slow.[31] The medical innovations developed for the maintenance and restoration of soldiers' health during the First World War did eventually feed back into civilian practice, but the process of translation sometimes took decades. Blood transfusion, for example, which had become the surgeons' preferred method of resuscitation by the end of the war, did not become an established part of the peacetime surgical regime until the Second World War precipitated the organisational changes necessary to secure a reliable supply of donated blood.

In any war, the treatment of wounds is critical both to soldiers themselves and to their military masters. Misled by their experience of the war in South Africa, the military authorities and their medical staff found themselves, in the autumn of 1914, confronted by entirely novel and unexpected types of wounds, for whose treatment they were quite unprepared. The experience was common to medical men on all sides of the conflict. The nature of warfare had changed significantly in the late 1880s with the introduction of small-calibre weapons into military use. The principal Boer weapon in South Africa had been the high-velocity Mauser rifle, which, usually fired at long range, inflicted clean, penetrating wounds. As long as they missed vital organs and blood vessels, the Mauser's long, slender bullets passed through body tissue, causing little peripheral damage. In the sun-baked, uncultivated landscape of the veld, such wounds remained clean, and army medical staff were convinced of the effectiveness of antiseptic techniques in preventing wound infection.

The situation in France, and later in Flanders, was quite different, both in terrain and in the technology of war. The Great War was fought over highly cultivated land, tended and manured for generations, whose soils were a haven for bacteria. The rifles that featured so dramatically in South Africa were useless in the stalemate of the trenches and were quickly replaced by high-explosive shells and shrapnel shot – ammunition that caused shattering, complex wounds invariably massively infected by the bacteria-laden soil and debris thrown up by the impact and explosion of the shell. In these circumstances, military surgeons soon discovered that antiseptics, however strong, were virtually useless in controlling infection, which was often well established by the time the wounded man reached the clearing stations. More drastic solutions were required, surgeons learning that damaged tissues are a breeding ground for bacteria and that cutting them out (debridement) before cleaning the wound was the best way to stop the spread of infection. Alternatively, as the Americans discovered by accident and the necessity of getting badly wounded boys home, the complete encasement of damaged limbs worked almost miraculously to kill off bacterial infection.[32]

These techniques were learnt on the job and through bitter experience, but they paid off. With an increasingly meticulous debridement of wounds, British surgeons achieved a case-fatality rate among the wounded of just 10 per cent; in the Crimea it had been 39 per cent and in the Franco-Prussian War 25 per cent.[33] The terrible affliction of tetanus, popularly known as 'lock-jaw', was one hazard at least that most wounded did not have to suffer in this war, since a prophylactic antitoxin had been developed following bacteriologists' elucidation of the causes of the condition around 1900. In the early months of the war, there were no specific regulations regarding the administration of antitoxin, and the incidence was eight per thousand wounded. From mid-October 1914, however, every wounded man was routinely given a dose, and the incidence of tetanus fell to an average of 1.5 per thousand by 1918.[34]

The enhanced survival chance of so many seriously wounded soldiers confronted medical men with the challenge of repairing shattered bodies to a level at which physical damage or handicap permitted, if at all possible, a bearable quality of life. A direct result of the type of wound experienced during this war was the emergence of several surgical specialties, notably orthopaedics and reconstructive surgery, which aimed to restore or improve physical function and appearance. While these specialties made a notable contribution to the lives of war-damaged soldiers, orthopaedics especially priding itself on its special importance in the surgery of this war, both had difficulty in maintaining independent specialty status once peace returned. The ethos of British hospital medicine remained strongly generalist during the interwar period, and the orthopaedic surgeons in particular found themselves continuing practice within a general surgical context rather than in specialist units or institutions.[35]

The problem of sheer physical damage to the wounded was compounded, as always after extensive injury, whether accidental or following surgery, by shock. Research into the nature and causes of shock continued throughout the war, with notable contributions to understanding the condition made through the co-operation of British, French and American surgeons. Especially important was the work of Ernest Cowell, of British Casualty Clearing Station 33, who after repeated forays into the trenches concluded that loss of body heat was a critical factor in the onset of secondary shock in the seriously injured. Although his observations were made towards the end of the war, and led to the effective training of resuscitation teams only in the closing months of the conflict, the lesson of shock prevention subsequently passed into civilian practice, becoming of ever-greater relevance as the use of motor cars, and the number of motoring accidents, burgeoned after the war.[36]

The Medicine of War

If wounds constitute the major emergency of war, problems of internal medicine are by no means absent, despite the medical audit of professional soldiers and recruits. Heart disease, or 'soldier's heart' as it became known, had first been recognised as a military problem in the 1860s, being characterised by chest pain, palpitations, breathlessness and exhaustion. Since then it had generally been considered to be caused by mechanical defects, the result of the army's training methods – of poorly designed drills or over-stylish uniforms. It began to appear with alarming frequency among British troops during 1915. Following research by a young physician, Thomas Lewis, who had already made use of the electrocardiogram in the study of heart disease, the condition was reconceptualised as 'effort syndrome'. Measured in terms of the heart's functional capacity, the symptoms of 'soldier's heart' were interpreted as an extreme manifestation of the normal response to effort. Put on a course of graduated exercises, half the affected soldiers were returned to duty within a couple of months.[37] As a result of this research, which carried an important financial implication in terms of invalidity pensions, the immediate postwar years saw government support for the institutionalisation of the new specialty of cardiology. It was a development of significance not only for the Ministry of Pensions, but also, in the long term, for patients with heart disease.

The military problem of heart disease clearly had its origins in the health of the ordinary working men recruited into the army, in part reflecting a level of unfitness or morbidity normally hidden in civilian society. The other significant medical problem of the Great War was, however, specifically related to the circumstances of the war. Gas poisoning was an unpleasant novelty in twentieth-century European warfare, one for which British troops and army medical staff alike were completely unprepared. Suggestions for the use of poison gas in warfare had been made from time to time during the nineteenth century but had invariably been rejected by the British military and naval authorities as unethical and unacceptable.[38] Faced with stalemate in the trenches, however, the German military authorities took advantage of the expertise of the national chemical industry. Early in the second battle of Ypres, on 22 April 1915, at 5.30 pm, lachrymator shells containing xylyl bromide were released towards the French lines at Langemarck. Initially seen as jets of white smoke rising above the German sector, a cloud of choking, poisonous, yellow-grey gas had within minutes engulfed the watching allied troops. Destructive of lung tissue when not almost immediately fatal, the various forms of gas used during the course of the war left a long-term legacy of chronic debility and respiratory problems among soldiers who survived exposure.

A research response was by now an almost inevitable reaction to a new military medical problem of this kind. In the years that followed, physiologists in laboratories at home developed the administration of oxygen as a therapy for acute gas poisoning. The treatment raised little enthusiasm among doctors in the field, who had been trained to think of oxygen as a dangerous irritant and who had little chance to study for themselves the beneficial effects of its long-term administration to men with damaged lungs. Medical attitudes towards oxygen therapy continued to be mixed long after the war was over, for the technique proved disappointing in rehabilitating the chronic effects of gas poisoning and as a treatment for industrial lung disease. It did, however, became established in medical practice, partly for non-medical reasons, but also because it proved helpful in a wide range of medical conditions such as pneumonia, severe bronchitis and heart failure, where poorly oxygenated blood, causing cyanosis (a blue tinge to the skin), is a potentially serious complication.[39]

The emergence of cardiology as a medical specialty and the integration of oxygen therapy into ordinary hospital practice are examples of the translation of wartime medical developments into civilian medicine. But many medical innovations generated by the Great War and provenly useful in restoring soldiers to the front or back into civilian life failed to transfer into civilian practice for either intellectual or practical reasons. The techniques of reconstructive surgery, for example, found very limited application between the wars, while the use of blood transfusion, explored and approved by military surgeons in the Great War, was used only to a very limited extent before the exigencies of the Second World War resulted in the creation of a nationally organised system of donor registration, storage and provision. In two special areas of military medical concern, however, the sexually transmitted diseases (STD) and mental health, the experience of the First World War meshed with problems of civilian welfare.

War, Sex and Disease

Since the sixteenth century at least, STD had constituted a largely hidden but probably significant cause of ill-health and death in British society. Until the beginning of the twentieth century, it was a taboo subject, both socially and medically, and could only be discussed in relation to prostitutes and the military. In the later nineteenth century, attempts by the army to control its spread became entangled with sensitive issues of public morality, individual liberty and feminism. The Contagious Diseases Acts, passed in the 1860s, aimed to impose medical inspection and regulation on prostitutes in specified garrison towns and provoked one of the first significant pressure-group responses in British politics. As a result, both medical and lay groups began to call for the provision of free treatment and for equality of treatment between men and women. They also began to emphasise the moral aspects of prevention. By the 1890s STD had become associated with concerns about degeneration and public health, as a cause of infertility, infant mortality and hereditary enfeeblement.

Bacteriology, meanwhile, identified the causative organism of gonorrhoea in 1879 and that of syphilis in 1905. The first diagnostic blood test (the Wasserman test) for syphilis became available in 1906, and four years later Paul Ehrlich announced his discovery of compound 606, known as Salvarsan, the first effective remedy for the disease. Medical interest in STD increased sharply as a result of these discoveries, and demands for a Royal Commission on VD became vociferous. As syphilis became medically treatable, so the profession moved to ensure its professional hold on the disease. Breaking the taboo surrounding the subject was one way of retrieving the management of the disease from unorthodox practitioners and encouraging possible sufferers to come forward for treatment. The Commission was duly appointed in November 1913, with a brief to inquire into the prevalence and prevention of STD in the United Kingdom.[40]

The outbreak of war, although it did not directly influence the result of the Commission, added urgency to its deliberations and eased the subsequent introduction of measures that might, in other circumstances, have provoked opposition: the establishment of treatment centres, the training of GPs in diagnosis and treatment, and the provision of free diagnostic services and supplies of Salvarsan. The monopoly of orthodox medicine and private practice over the condition was also made absolute. As John Eyler has noted, the central health authority had rarely acted so swiftly in implementing a major new policy, and rarely had the recommendations of a Royal Commission been enacted with so little change.[41] The 1917 Venereal Diseases Act made it illegal for state-funded and unqualified practitioners to treat, prescribe for or give advice about STD.[42] Between 1917 and 1920, a network of 190 treatment centres was set up across the country. Usually based in voluntary hospitals, these clinics offered a free, confidential service to all asking for treatment. In 1920 alone they recorded more than 100,000 new patients.

Deemed a success by their contemporaries, the impact of the treatment centres in the interwar years is difficult to evaluate. For obvious reasons, the diseases were made notifiable, and very few deaths were recorded under this heading. Despite efforts by the Ministry of Health (MH), the clinics were not particularly user-friendly and women in particular were reluctant to use them.

Many patients did not finish their course of treatment. Salvarsan had some unpleasant side effects, while gonorrhoea remained untreatable until the sulphonamide drugs became available in the later 1930s. There is some evidence that the incidence of gonorrhoea actually increased in the 1920s. While STD clinics represent a significant extension of state medical provision, and an excellent example of the medicalisation of a previously ignored condition, their effectiveness as a strategy for reducing the incidence of disease is more debateable.

In curious contrast to the growing civil determination to limit the ravages of VD, government authorities showed little resolution in tackling the problem of these diseases in the army during the Great War. It was a long-established military tradition that sex was a basic recreational need for soldiers. As in the 1860s, the military authorities therefore construed the rising problem of STD among its manpower during 1915 as a *civilian* problem: the troops must be protected against women infected with VD. The control of STD within the army inevitably became caught up with the issues of morality, individual liberty and feminism: the Home Office had no intention of taking action against civilian victims of the disease, and the War Office had no wish to penalise infected men beyond docking their pay while they were under treatment. Nor did they wish to appear to condone immorality by encouraging personal preventive measures. Although laboratory tests had shown that disinfection with permanganate of potash within hours of intercourse would arrest syphilis infection, it was not until late in the war that the prophylactic began to be issued to troops.[43] On the civilian side meanwhile, provision for soldiers' recreation went on unhampered. The police force, who were responsible for controlling the activities of prostitutes, had been seriously reduced in strength as a result of war recruiting, and many English cities became a virtual hot-bed of prostitution. By 1917, VD was a major military problem.

It was one of the ironies of the war that while wartime circumstances finally broke the taboo on the discussion of STD, eased the introduction of measures against them into civil life and accelerated the emergence of voluntary movements for educating the public on the dangers of disease and how to avoid them, military efforts at control were seriously limited by a reluctance to part with traditional values. Yet the epidemic of VD in the military was not without its positive consequences, since it sent military medical officers back to civilian practice familiar with the symptoms of venereal infection, accustomed to the new chemotherapy as demonstrated by Salvarsan and with new preventive procedures. Before the war, Salvarsan had been a German product, imported into Britain. The disappearance of trade with Germany galvanised the British pharmaceutical industry into the production of Salvarsan substitutes and other medicinal chemicals, which Germany's prewar strength in the production of finished synthetic drugs and fine chemicals had previously made unnecessary.[44] The postwar expansion of British pharmaceutical firms into medical and chemical research, with long-term consequences for civilian health and the country's balance of trade, can be directly linked to the wartime disruption of trade and the medical demands of war.

War and Madness

The Great War brought about a re-evaluation of the nature and treatment of mental illness. The Victorian period had seen the rise of the lunatic asylum and the emergence of psychiatry as a medical specialty in both Britain and the rest of Europe. In Britain asylum medicine had become a considerable industry by the early twentieth century, with over 100,000 asylum inmates and more in licensed houses and workhouse infirmaries.[45] With the rise of morbid pathology, older theories of insanity as being the result of psychological or psychosomatic factors amenable to special management gave way to an organicist theory, which linked mental illness to specific lesions in the brain. Among the explanations for the causes of such lesions, heredity inevitably found a place, and by 1900 mental illness too had become enmeshed in the spectrum of evidence for racial deterioration. Psychiatry – the medical treatment of diseases of the mind – dominated the British medical landscape of treatment for mental illness in this period. Although psychological methods, like Freudian analysis of the unconscious mind, were concurrently being developed in Europe, mainstream British psychiatry was strongly opposed to these new techniques as being morally corrupting and destructive of the clear distinction that existed between the sane and the insane in English law.[46]

Before 1914 mental illness was associated with the physical outcome of hereditary degeneration, and was treated by medical means. As with the surgeons' confidence in antisepsis, this concept was to be shattered by the soldiers' experiences on the Western Front. The shells that caused those lacerated, heavily infected wounds created in their passage through the air shock waves that could throw men 15 metres or more from their positions and 4–5 metres into the air. Men caught in the blast could be found dead without a mark or injury upon them. Yet the epidemic of 'shellshock' that beset the British army from 1915 onwards was the result not of physical shock from exploding shells but of the mental distress that conditions of war on the Western Front generated in men raised in an ethos of chivalry and in a world of ordered security and peace, in which violent destruction and damage to human life was rare. Continuous bombardment meant continuous noise and terrible environmental damage. The noise, the destruction, the dominance of machinery in the conduct of war, the horrible deaths and devastating wounds suffered by comrades, the stalemate and constriction of trench warfare, all contributed to creating an unprecedented epidemic of mental illness among officers and men on the Western Front.

The symptoms of shellshock were various, ranging from deep depression, compulsive shaking and nightmares to mutism and paralysis, but all involved a horrifying departure from the heroic ideal of stoicism in the face of danger. The historical novelist Jeffery Farnol was shown the 'mad ward' at a base hospital in France and described with pity the room full of men with:

A vagueness of gaze, a loose-lipped, too-ready smile, a vacancy of expression. Some there were who scowled sullenly enough, others who crouched apart, solitary souls who... felt themselves outcast; others who crouched in corners haunted by the dread of a pursuing vengeance always at hand.

These badly shellshocked boys, he noted, 'claw their mouths ceaselessly'.[47] For the army doctors, educated like the officer corps and so many of the volunteers, in the nineteenth-century cult of manliness, courage, honour and stoicism, these novel manifestations of male hysteria were both revelatory and deeply disturbing.[48]

The condition described as 'shellshock' was first described and named by Charles Myers, a Cambridge laboratory physiologist, in February 1915. In late 1916 it was said that up to 40 per cent of the casualties from the zones of heavy fighting arose from shellshock. Special arrangements had to be made to treat these cases at home. More than twenty military hospitals for mental patients were established, and by the end of the war some 80,000 cases had passed through them. At the return of peace the pensions authorities were confronted by more than 100,000 former servicemen suffering from nervous conditions. Reported cases peaked in 1922, but on the eve of the Second World War, two million pounds a year were still being paid out to the shock victims of the Great War.[49] Expensive in terms of manpower loss, treatment and pension payments, shellshock also had a serious effect on morale among the troops.

Shellshock had wide repercussions, not just on the psychiatric perception of mental illness, but also throughout British society and culture more generally. Among ex-combatants, it was one of the factors shaping the unique war experience that set them apart from non-combatants for the rest of their lives.[50] For society more generally, it forced a re-evaluation of standards, blurring the accepted distinctions between courage and cowardice.[51] Concern and sympathy for the shellshocked on the home front led to an increased public awareness of mental illness, as well as an increased medical awareness among the doctors who had to cope with it and who themselves often experienced forms of 'shock' during the war. Moreover, doctors involved in the treatment of shellshock cases faced a profound ethical dilemma. Their military duty consisted of sustaining morale, handling sickness and returning men to the fighting line. When it came to mental illness, it was the doctor's acceptance or rejection of disorder that decided a man's immediate fate, whether he was sent for treatment or shot for cowardice. And the act of restoring the sick man to soundness condemned him to return to the very conditions that had caused his illness.[52]

For psychiatrists, the specialists in mental illness, the study of shellshock had important implications. It was demonstrated that the condition could not be associated with any particular lesions in the brain, doubt thus being thrown on the prevailing organicist concept of mental illness, clearing the way for the acceptance of psychotherapy in the treatment of nervous disorders. The prevalence of shellshock among so many of those identified as belonging to the flower of the imperial race discredited eugenic interpretations of mental illness, while their undoubted masculinity assailed established ideas of mental illness as an especial burden on women and an indicator of effeminacy in men.[53]

In contrast, those practising the new psychotherapeutic methods had their prospects transformed by the problem of shellshock, for which their techniques seemed admirably tailored. Once again many British doctors were introduced to psychotherapeutic methods while serving with the army, subsequently translating that experience, and interest, back into civilian practice. Their wartime experience of shellshock further led them to question Sigmund Freud's theory of the sexual origin of mental illness, even while they adopted the concepts of the unconscious mind and repressed emotion. During the 1920s psychotherapy and psychoanalysis established themselves as moderately reputable medical interests in Britain, although the establishment of a specialist institutional basis proved elusive. While the Ministry of Pensions supported more than 100 treatment centres for former servicemen, there was no parallel expansion of facilities for civilians. Many regarded psychotherapeutic treatment as invasive and unsympathetic, acceptable in exorcising the horrors of war but less so as an intrusion into private life. Once again the impact of war-related medical development was reduced and diffused as prewar social and cultural values returned with peace.

Influenza, 1918

Overshadowed by the Great War, the influenza pandemic that swept the world in the closing months of 1918 was the worst ever experienced. The number of deaths has been estimated at anywhere between twenty and forty million worldwide: it was a demographic catastrophe on the scale of the Second World War.[54] In Britain some 225,000 lives were lost, mainly in October and November, as the war was drawing to a close. Although an earlier wave of the disease had passed through America almost unnoticed as she entered the European war in April, the autumn phase of the pandemic proved far more lethal.

Somehow, between April and September, the virus mutated into a killer. The virulent strain of the disease travelled across the Atlantic with troopships and merchantmen in the last week of September. The transport 'Olympic', for example, arrived at Southampton on 21 September after a six-day voyage during which 450 of her complement of 5,600 men had shown signs of flu. Ten days later 2,000 of them had been struck down with it. From the ports the disease spread out across the country, following the lines of railway communication, as typhus had done in Serbia early in the war.

Influenza, even in epidemic form, was not an unfamiliar disease in 1918. The most recent pandemic had occurred in 1890–91, while the Rector of Great Leas in Essex had recorded suffering several episodes earlier in the war. But the virus strain active in the autumn of 1918 was uniquely virulent, particularly to young adults. Many died quickly, sometimes within forty-eight hours of the onset of illness, literally drowning as their lungs filled with fluid. Then, as now, medicine offered no palliation, no cure (although a new generation of 'plug drugs' may soon change this long-standing reality). Medical services everywhere were virtually crippled by demand and by the incapacity of personnel through disease. In Britain, where half the country's doctors and nurses were serving abroad, medical effort was over-whelmingly concentrated on prevention and preservation of the stiff upper lip. British doctors generally advised their patients to ignore the disease, because fear itself increased vulnerability to infection. Where nursing and care facilities were provided, it was usually through local, lay initiative.[55]

Despite the swift and brutal impact of the epidemic, the staggering number of deaths, the disruption to local life and the additional loss mainly of young adults in so many families already scarred by war, the 1918 influenza epidemic had remarkably little long-term impact. As with so many devastating epidemics in the past, the immediate reaction of the damaged communities was to put the experience behind them, to try to forget. Preventive policies and emergency services were not reviewed with a view to meeting any such repeated emergency, and poetry and prose reflected little of the epidemic horror.

Conclusion

The influenza epidemic constituted perhaps a fitting civilian coda to the searing tragedy enacted on the battlefields of France and Flanders. Nonetheless, most flu victims recovered, while the lives mentally and physically maimed on the battlefields remained as a reminder of the past. In demographic terms, however, British society was remarkably unscarred by the Great War, the established trend of birth and death-rate being barely disturbed. While the contribution of medicine to civilian health remains debateable, there can be no doubt that the medical contribution to the health and welfare of the fighting forces was an integral component of the eventual successful outcome of the war. Nor was it only the surgeons, the traditional practitioners of war, who played a critical role. Research scientists, bacteriologists, physiologists, public health men, cardiologists, psychiatrists, specialists in physical rehabilitation, ordinary practitioners and many others all contributed to the war effort. Occurring as it did within a context of modernising scientific medicine, the Great War provided a means of utilising a range of new medical methods and a stimulus to the development of more. Although wartime innovations often took years to enter civilian practice, it was the breadth of the impact of this war on medical interests that fed Sir Clifford Allbutt's perception of a radical transformation in the ethos of medicine.

3

RENEWAL AND DEPRESSION, 1918–39

Introduction

In the decades after the Great War, infectious disease ceased to dominate British health concerns, the demand for medical services grew, and medical science began finally to deliver new and effective treatments for a number of previously incurable conditions. The National Insurance scheme, inaugurated in 1913, unfolded with the peace, its provisions being gradually extended. The establishment of the new Ministry of Health (MH) in 1919, successor to the Local Government Board, promised integrated, health-oriented policies at national level. The Ministry's first Chief Medical Officer, George Newman, came to office with a clear, holistic vision of the path the new Ministry should follow, a combination of the old environmental measures and a new emphasis on personal health and healthy living.[1]

Although in practice the orchestration of such policies proved difficult to achieve, the MRC, which had been established under the National Insurance Act, actively promoted the investigation of problems of health and disease that were more or less closely associated with the welfare of the insured working population. Projects examining the incidence and causation of rickets in children, for example, could be justified in terms of the probable adverse effect of childhood rickets on the adult physique. Work on nutrition and on the health of workers employed in industry developed following on the experience of war, and, if these researches generally had little immediate impact on welfare policy, they did help to establish fields of expertise. When conflict again rolled over Europe, specialists like the nutrition scientist Jack Drummond became prominent in advising government on critical aspects of domestic policy during the Second World War.

The prospects for reforming and improving the delivery of health care and environmental reform were clouded throughout the interwar years by economic depression and financial stringency. After a short postwar boom, the British economy lapsed into depression in 1921, after which social initiatives involving government expenditure were suspended or abandoned. The Great Depression that followed the collapse of the world's financial markets in 1929 initiated further retrenchment.

By 1931 three million British people were unemployed, largely in the old industrial areas of the North and in Wales, and government was struggling to contain welfare expenditure. Issues of nutrition and health became contentious during these years. Contemporary observers were divided on the connection between health, nutrition and unemployment, and much historical interest has since focused on the impact of the Depression on the health of people in the depressed areas. Government made no attempt at any disinterested assessment of conditions in these regions. Following the immense sacrifices made during the war, and with the spectre of Bolshevism and social revolution haunting the political elite, interwar governments tracked a cautious path through social appeasement and financial prudence.

In these circumstances, George Newman showed himself to be more of a politician than a reformer. Already by the mid-1920s, he was more concerned with providing political support to government than with developing new approaches to problems of health and social conditions, and in the early 1930s the Ministry continued to downplay evidence of distress. Newman continued in office until 1935, neither he nor his successor, Arthur MacNalty, showing any inclination to develop for their office judgement and leadership on issues of health and welfare beyond what seemed appropriate in the wider context of government. It was left to local authorities to take action within the law, and to individual medical men and MOHs, social commentators, voluntary organisations and independent medical agencies such as the MRC and the BMA to flag up the health issues surrounding unemployment and financial privation, as well as to explore the social and physiological factors determining the nation's health.

The National Insurance Scheme and Medical Services

The interwar years did, nonetheless, see an extension and consolidation of the welfare reforms initiated before the war, although the local implementation and execution of national policies remained inevitably uneven. The impetus to social reform generated by industrial competition from Germany, which had before the war made the offer of security against illness and unemployment to working people politically acceptable, was reinforced by the need to guard against social revolution and to build national strength against another war. Several of the new measures of social welfare that were enacted between 1905 and 1913 had barely come into effective operation before the Great War, and their impact is best assessed in terms of interwar performance.

Between 1918 and 1939 the British government added various further measures of health provision. Within a basic framework established by Lloyd George's National Insurance Act of 1911, a series of associated measures, some dating from before that Act, aimed to provide medical supervision and treatment for a range of social groups whose welfare was of concern to the state. These began with the Notification of Births Act 1906 and the establishment of the School Medical Service in 1907, continuing with the National Insurance Act (which included provision for a national tuberculosis service), the Venereal Diseases Act 1917, the Maternal and Child Welfare Act 1918, the Midwives Act 1922 and the Cancer Act 1939. The reform of the Poor Law in 1929, and the transfer of the Poor Law infirmaries and infectious disease hospitals to the municipal authorities, also falls within this package of modernising measures of health provision.

At the heart of this extension of health provision lay the National Insurance Act, which had barely come into effect in 1913 when its application was complicated, and its nature transformed, by the Great War. In essence the Act consolidated the work of the friendly societies and gave it government sponsorship.

It was a half-way house, in terms of provision, between the negative and deterrent Victorian Poor Law and the positive and democratic post-1945 National Health Service.

Originally designed to keep families from falling into poverty during the illness of a breadwinner, the perceived success of wartime medicine translated it into a means of access to clinical medicine.[2] It was a contributory scheme and has been described as a poll-tax. Insured persons contributed at the rate of 4d a week for men, and 3d for women, further contributions from the employer and the state bringing the weekly total to 10d. Manual workers aged over sixteen and earning under £160 a year were initially covered under the act; the income limit was subsequently raised to £250 in 1920 and £420 in 1942. Benefits to women workers were, however, cut on grounds of financial stringency in 1915 and again in 1932.

The income group covered was thus that just above the poorest, who were entitled under the scheme to medical, sickness, disablement, maternity and sanatorium benefits, but the provisions extended only to the insured person and not to his or her dependants. Most women and all children, together with the elderly and the self-employed, fell outside the scheme. It was a system that, although drawn from the model developed in Germany after 1880, still had much in common with the type of provision offered by its native predecessors, the friendly societies.[3] The importance of the societies' existing organisation was tacitly acknowledged by Lloyd George, who gave them the task of disbursing cash benefits, medical and sanatorium benefits being administered through local insurance committees.

Three types of health benefit were offered under the Act. First, there was sickness benefit, including a cash payment during illness, initially at 10/- a week for men and 7/6 for women, a one-off maternity payment to married women of 30/-, and a disablement pension of 5/- weekly. Second, specific medical benefits – GP services, drugs and appliances – were offered, and third there was a miscellaneous range of additional services, from consultant advice to ophthalmic and dental treatment, which could be provided at the discretion of the local insurance committees. Sanatorium care for the tuberculous was specially provided for. Hospital treatment and specialist care, however, fell outside the remit of the Act, a fact that caused increasing dissatisfaction, especially since GPs, paid on a capitation basis, had little financial incentive to cherish the long-term and chronic sick. Although doctors commonly had little time for their 'panel patients', as the insured were known, and the consultation time could be exceedingly brief, the services were well used. By 1938 some 54 per cent of the total population of England and Wales, some twenty million people, were covered by the scheme, of whom half became 'patients' in any one year.

The impact of health insurance on health is difficult to assess, because of the limited resources of medicine at the time and the restricted scope and nature of the services. To a great extent the services offered simply replaced those previously provided by friendly society arrangements, and an increasing number of people made use of them throughout the period. For some, the new arrangements meant a new security, removing the immediate financial anxieties brought by illness, and ensured a greater readiness to consult a doctor, perhaps at an earlier stage of illness, with the greater possibility of alleviation or cure that earlier consultation brings. The fact that contributions were levied from the wage packet meant that insured workers saw themselves as having paid for, and obtained a right to, medical services, despite their initial resentment at the reduction in their pay-packets. There was certainly the advantage that, unlike friendly society contributions, the payments were 'invisible' in the family budget. A measure of the effect of this sense of ownership was a novel readiness to complain: already in 1913, patients in the tuberculosis hospitals went on strike in protest at the quality of food and the requirement for domestic work.[4]

Another measure of confidence was an increased readiness to use the new services. It had been assumed that each panel patient would make fewer than two calls a year on the doctor's time, but by 1924 each patient was making three calls a year, and by 1939 more than five. Moreover, these figures relate to surgery attendance and home visits only and do not allow for the 2.3 extra or night visits, three minor operations, two injections and thirty-four signings of certificates (sick notes) that were included in the average panel doctor's weekly workload.[5] So working people included under the National Insurance scheme made increasingly generous use of the services available in the years to 1939. A computation of the nature of their illnesses by the insurance authorities cast new light on the causes of morbidity in Britain – and, incidentally, underscores the relative powerlessness of the medical profession significantly to relieve their patients' sufferings. In sharp contrast to the leading causes of mortality (heart disease, cancer and tuberculosis), panel patients visited their doctors most frequently for bronchitis, rheumatism, influenza and digestive troubles.

The quality of medical care offered to panel patients was said by some contemporary observers to be second class, an accusation that the medical profession strenuously denied. Nonetheless, because practitioners were paid on the capitation system (at around 9/- per patient), income being related to the size of the panel patient list rather than to the quality of service, a certain amount of scamping did occur. In 1920 the MH limited the number of panel patients on any one doctor's list to 3,000; it was further reduced to 2,500 in 1924. Most GPs combined their insurance work with private practice, and sometimes also with part-time work in welfare clinics, sanatoria, schools or the public health service. Surgeries were often poorly equipped; sterilising instruments, for example, were a dispensable luxury, while doctors had themselves to pay for laboratory services.

As Anne Digby and Nick Bosanquet point out, the interwar doctor rarely invested in new methods and new equipment, functioning more as a sorter of cases and issuer of certificates and prescriptions than as the classic family doctor.[6] Surgery consultations for insurance patients at this time averaged three-and-a-half minutes, and home visits four minutes, so there was little opportunity to engage in any systematic examination or diagnosis. Yet, as Anne Digby points out, this was not so very different from the average five minutes now spent under the NHS.[7] The 40–50 million prescriptions issued annually to panel patients provoked a discussion about over-prescribing among the profession, but not one of the health implications of such rapid processing for patients, or of the pressures that produced it.[8]

Against these shortcomings in the insurance system lay the growing authority of medicine, and the apparently increased willingness of patients to seek, accept and derive support from the doctor's opinion. The same pattern of increasing use of medical services that manifested itself among panel patients can also be found among private patients. Doctors' income from private practice rose substantially in these years, indicating an increased consultation rate as well as higher fees. Medicine, in fact, received a great deal of publicity during the interwar period, through the new medium of the radio, which the MH used as a means of health education, and through health columns in the new popular press and magazines. A growing health-consciousness was also fostered by mother and child clinics, the school health service and local authority health campaigns organised by progressive MOHs. Changing economic circumstances also helped. In the south and east, in particular, where new industries brought rising real income, families began to extend their sickness cover by subscribing to GP lists and hospital insurance schemes. By 1938 almost half the costs of the voluntary hospitals were being paid for by private patients, mainly through contributory insurance schemes.[9] Access to hospital care remained easier in the towns than in the countryside and in the south of England than in the north: the regional distribution of hospitals established by philanthropy and municipal enterprise in the nineteenth century remained little changed in the twentieth.

For the hospital authorities, national health insurance brought new problems and helped to change the role and function of hospitals within the community. With the re-organisation of the Poor Law in 1929, municipal authorities throughout the country began to take over the infirmaries and develop them into general hospitals. At the same time they often began to modernise both buildings and facilities, and to turn a facility that had essentially catered for the long-term sick into something more like an acute voluntary hospital. In the years 1931–38, the number of admissions to these hospitals grew by 5 per cent per annum, but the number of operations performed rose by 10 per cent and the number of outpatient attendances by 25 per cent.[10] The role of the voluntary hospitals also changed. These had come under increasing financial pressure since the 1870s, when falling agricultural income began to undermine the prosperity of their traditional subscriber base among the aristocracy and landed gentry. With some reason, the voluntary hospitals feared a further fall in subscriber income as a result of the introduction of National Insurance. While this did not happen immediately, from January 1913, when the Act came into operation, many hospitals refused to treat insured persons unless referred by their GP or in an emergency.

At a stroke, therefore, the old-established relationship between these hospitals and their local communities was radically altered. Outpatient clinics that had formerly functioned as alternative general surgeries found their patient base restricted largely to women, children and the elderly. Inpatient departments, however, began to take an increasing number of seriously ill patients referred by GPs who had neither the time, the expertise or the financial incentive to continue treating them in their own homes.[11] For these patients, the continuity of care offered by the old traditions of hospital and GP disappeared. It was a change that eased the voluntary hospitals into an increasingly specialised role, as the providers of services beyond the capability of the GP. It was a role into which their developing identity as the providers of capital-intensive services such as laboratory and X-ray facilities and serious surgical work was already directing them. By the 1920s the hospitals had less and less to do with the routine maintenance of health through minor medical services, and more and more to do with its restoration, or attempted restoration, in the seriously sick.

Although the growing specialist function of the general hospitals was an unplanned consequence of the insurance care system, provision within the National Insurance Act for the better care of tuberculosis patients set a precedent for government support for specialist services, which was developed in the subsequent establishment of the venereal disease centres and the encouragement of mother and baby clinics. The establishment of the tuberculosis service from 1913 was curiously poignant, in view of the history of the disease and the fact that it had passed its peak of demographic and economic significance. In 1911 tuberculosis was still the most statistically visible, as it was historically the most prominent, of the long-term chronic diseases, but the number of deaths had been falling since the 1880s. Nonetheless 75,000 lives a year were being lost to the disease, these being overwhelmingly of men and women in the most productive and socially responsible years of their lives. Not only did society lose the input of their labour, but it was often left picking up the bill under the Poor

Law both for treatment and for the maintenance of a young family left without other means of support. Lloyd George's own father had died of the disease, and he was well aware of the trauma that such deaths inflicted on the many families involved.[12] Although the new scientific medicine had not yet thrown up effective methods of medical treatment for the disease (Robert Koch's announcement of tuberculin as a cure in 1890 having been premature), methods of managing it had been developed in the Victorian period that offered greater hope of arresting or limiting the disease in its victims.

These new methods of treatment centred on a specialist institution – the tuberculosis sanatorium. The concept of the sanatorium evolved in both Germany and the United States, centring on seclusion, rest, fresh air and plentiful food. The aim was to restore the patient to a strength sufficient to return to normal life, sanatoria often undertaking to provide such care on a regular or continuous basis. Although a number of specialised tuberculosis hospitals had been established in the previous century, the government now took the initiative in establishing a system of sanatoria supported by tuberculosis dispensaries that would offer ongoing advice and treatment to sufferers still at home.

The service was to be free to all those diagnosed as suffering from tuberculosis by a registered medical practitioner. The capital costs of the programme were met by central government, the costs of treatment for individuals by a special fund in the case of those covered by the National Insurance Act, and jointly by central and local government for those not covered by that scheme. As a chronic infectious disease transmitted by close personal contact, tuberculosis had special public health status, so it was important that all affected individuals had access to treatment in the interests of the wider community. At the very least, sufferers could be educated in personal habits of cleanliness, which, it was hoped, would prevent them infecting others.

The rise in the number of tuberculosis deaths among young women during the war, and the return of some 58,000 tuberculous ex-servicemen in the immediate aftermath of war, justified the expansion of the tuberculosis service in the 1920s. There is little indication, however, that either the institutions themselves or the methods of treatment offered had any significant impact on the behaviour of the disease. The general trend in the number of deaths, downwards since the 1880s, continued at a steady decline into the mid-1940s.[13] The provision of the service may have been a mixed blessing for tuberculosis sufferers, since identification as a tuberculosis victim could mean a social stigma that made ordinary life more difficult. In the later decades of the previous century, many tuberculosis victims had spent their last months in workhouse infirmaries, and right up to 1939 the municipal hospitals continued to receive a large number of tuberculosis sufferers, a third of whom died while in their wards.[14]

Moreover, sanatorium treatment also could be a bleak experience under the enthusiastic experimental regimes of their managers, with more outdoor exercise and less food than patients perhaps had a right to expect. Many ex-patients had little desire to return.[15] Even the educational effectiveness of sanatorium and public health propaganda can be doubted: public spitting was a habit greatly discouraged in the belief that particles of dried sputum contained in dust acted as an effective means of transmitting the disease, but spitting remained a very common habit into the 1930s.[16]

The establishment of the tuberculosis services, like that of the VD treatment centres, the school medical service and the provisions for maternal and infant care, marked an overall significant extension of state involvement in the health of particular social or patient groups, which became effectively institutionalised in the interwar years. In every case, the effective delivery of services at local level was modified on the one hand by the attitudes and efficiency of service providers, and on the other by the social, cultural and economic circumstances of those who received, or were supposed to receive, them. Unsympathetic specialists in VD treatment centres, the fear of being identified as a sufferer from a socially unacceptable disease, a reluctance to invite middle-class patronage, an inability to implement medical recommendations because of adverse domestic circumstances – all of these were factors that could, and did, intervene to diffuse the intentions of the legislature.

The several separate sets of provisions were linked, and linked to the National Insurance scheme, by the common intention of preserving the economic and military strength of the country and its people. In gender terms, these priorities were essentially male, even while they had associated benefits for women, and in this respect they were part of the tradition of restricted public health concern that went back to the days of Edwin Chadwick.[17] The great majority of women, who fell outside the provisions of National Insurance, experienced little expansion in the facilities available for medical advice and treatment, and were often further discouraged from seeking advice and help by dismissive doctors and the expense of medication. Women doctors remained rare in general practice – most preferring to work directly with women and children in the clinics – and women patients were often shy of taking their troubles to a male doctor. The poignant personal accounts collected from working-class wives by Margaret Llewellyn Davies in the 1930s indicate widespread patient suffering among working-class women, from varicose veins, prolapsed wombs, anaemia and undernourishment, to sheer weariness, which rarely, if ever, reached doctors' surgeries.[18]

The extent to which the effectiveness of the several new specialist state services rested on a complex balance of factors is well illustrated by the case of maternal and infant welfare. Although womens' health was not the primary objective of this legislation, which was intended to secure the preservation of infant life, women may have been the main beneficiaries.[19] For women with young families, the maternal and infant welfare services could provide support and also fulfil a critical educational function. As we have seen, the number of such clinics increased sharply during the war, and in 1918 the Maternal and Infant Welfare Act permitted local authorities to develop a state-funded system. By 1935 local authority services to young mothers were attended by the great majority of women with young children. These clinics were not especially successful in reducing level of infant mortality, because of factors beyond their control in the home, but they could make an impact on maternal health. The medical management of pregnant women could thus preserve lives, but the uptake of medical assistance might be reduced or modified by a range of social factors.

The clinics appear to have been most been notably effective in poorer areas, where greater attention was paid to encouraging mothers to attend. Of the four London boroughs studied by Lara

Marks, working-class Stepney had a lower rate of maternal mortality in the years 1910–30 than did the wealthier boroughs of Hampstead and Kensington.[20] Other special campaigns, such as the Rochdale Experiment and work under the auspices of the National Birthday Trust Fund in mid-1930s Wales, also appeared to demonstrate that maternal mortality was reducible by special attention.[21] The critical factors in achieving a reduction in maternal death seem to have been two: service providers dedicated to the cause of maternal health, and the essentially medical nature of the problems associated with childbirth (even where, as in the Rhondda, the root of the problem appeared to lie in malnutrition). The primary causes of maternal death were medical – puerperal fever, toxaemia and haemorrhage. Medical management, in the sense of alert antenatal care and proper management during birth, was more likely to make an impact here, although it was not until the suphonamide drugs became available in the mid-1930s that medicine was able to exert any control over the biggest of those killers, puerperal fever.[22]

The principal causes of infant mortality, on the other hand, seem to have been social, and far less susceptible to medical or educational intervention through the medium of the clinic. Although the IMR continued overall to fall between 1919 and 1939, it seems clear that domestic factors such as overcrowding, poor sanitary facilities and cold and damp could limit the impact that welfare clinics made through maternal education. The London boroughs of Woolwich and Stepney, for example, relatively successful in reducing maternal deaths, were also successful in reducing the level of infant mortality, but the despite a considerable input of effort from numerous local welfare organisations, infant mortality continued to be extremely high in the poor district of North Kensington.[23] Poverty, both public and private, which prevented an increased expenditure to improve or rent better housing stock generally (despite the endeavours of the MH) reduced the effectiveness of municipal and voluntary efforts to save infant lives.

The influence of much the same domestic circumstances can also be seen in the health concerns associated with older children, for example bronchitis, septic infection and poor teeth. Although the school medical services were diligent in inspecting and observing older children, a lack of imagination and a reluctance to commit financial resources limited their ability to reach to the roots of child ill-health. Housing conditions, domestic cleanliness and food choice were all important factors in child health but remained beyond the reach of the school medical services. Although local authorities were allowed to provide children with free school meals, these were far from freely available. Only 2 per cent of the school population was receiving them in 1939, and they were too often of poor quality.[24]

Of the environmental factors that still operated to depress health and living standards among the working classes, housing was the focus of both central and local government activity between the wars. Although not a health provision in terms of the supply of a medical service or of clean water, housing had long been considered a public health issue, even if one fraught with complicated political questions of private property and personal liberty. In the context of the Great War, however, it became a critical issue. As the President of the Local Government Board, Walter Long, expressed it: 'To let them [the soldiers] come home from horrible, water-logged trenches to something little better than a pig-sty here would, indeed, be criminal... a negation of all we have said during the war.'[25] The phrase 'Homes Fit for Heroes' captured it perfectly and was incorporated into postwar government policy as a crucial plank of the bridge against social revolution.[26]

Although disrupted and modified by financial crisis, the central government's emphasis on housing reform, in which it was supported by the MH, resulted in the provision of nearly four million new homes between 1919 and 1939, in a greatly improved standard of working-class housing, and, in the 1930s, in a concerted attack on the old slum areas that by the outbreak of war, saw about half the officially recognised slum areas cleared and a further 439,000 houses made fit for habitation. Although continued population growth ensured that there was still a housing shortage in 1939, and around a third of all working-class housing remained well below acceptable 1930s standards, a quiet social revolution was accomplished for many thousands of working-class families in these years.

The raising of the standard of working-class housing was an especially important aspect of the interwar house building programme. Just after the war, a committee chaired by Sir John Tudor Walters produced recommended specifications for new working-class housing that, subsequently enshrined in legislation, transformed expectations of urban housing. The Tudor Walters recommendations included a minimum of three rooms on the ground floor and three bedrooms above (two capable of containing two beds), a bathroom and a larder. Frontages were to be generous, with side access and a garden behind and houses were to be built in blocks of no more than eight. On this plan, interwar working-class housing reached a standard previously achieved by the lower middle classes and paved the way for a great increase in standards and expectations of living.[27]

Initially, many working-class families had problems adjusting to their new conditions: the habit of sleeping all in a bed, for example, often translated into the new surroundings. MOHs, such as C. C. M. M'Gonigle of Stockton-on-Tees, were disconcerted to find that rehousing in modern stock could result in poorer health, and more disease, because a higher rent meant less money for food and fuel. The history of housing reform in these years presents something of a mixed record, and its impact on health was variable, especially in the wider context of depression and unemployment. In the long term, however, the raising of the standard of working-class housing was an important component of the changing social expectations of ordinary people that characterised the years 1919–39.

Health, Poverty and Medicine

The expansion in medical provision and its use that took place during the interwar years had little visible effect on the nation's health, although the downward trend of mortality continued. The most notable postwar change in health, as reflected in mortality statistics, lay in the definitive shift from the common infectious diseases to chronic and degenerative diseases as the principal cause of death, which became increasingly marked. It was a shift that had little apparent connection with medical intervention, but which initiated a gradual change of perception towards disease as a threat to human health.

With the retreat of the acute infectious killers, human life became more secure. The IMR had fallen from 151 per thousand live births in 1901 to 76 in 1921–25; by 1939 it had reached an all-time low at 51. The death-rates from measles, whooping cough and scarlet fever were all in sharp decline, although diphtheria was still troublesome, causing some 2,000 deaths a year. The major infections of adults, typhoid, typhus and virulent smallpox, all seemed to belong to the Victorian past, and tuberculosis, although still feared, was nevertheless a declining cause of death. The proportion of people aged over sixty-five in the population rose steadily: from 6 per cent in 1920 to 9.2 per cent in 1940.

As life expectancy increased, however, the chronic and degenerative diseases of middle and old age began to become more noticeable as killers. Although in 1922 George Newman noted cancer to be the only cause of death that had 'definitely and uniformly' increased, by 1931 the number of deaths by accidental crushing, as result of vehicle and railway accidents, had doubled since 1920, and in the following year Newman drew attention to the steady increase in the number of deaths from diabetes in the age groups over 55.[28] While the rise in accidental death was real, and definitely associated with the new technology of the motor car, any evaluation of the increase in the number of both cancer and diabetes deaths was complicated by known improvements in the efficiency of diagnosis. Both cancer and diabetes, however, received growing attention from both central and local health authorities and from the MRC.

The continuing downward trend of death from diseases associated with the past, and medical and public health interest in the diseases that were discovered to be newly important causes of illness and death, helped to set many doctors, as well as national public health policy, at a remove from the social emergencies of the interwar period. If the effects on the national health of the postwar depression of the early 1920s appear to have been minimal, those of the depression that followed the collapse of the world stock markets in 1929 were disputed both within and without the medical profession at the time, and have more recently caused dissension among historians. Charles Webster and Margaret Mitchell have seen the 1930s as a period of hunger and distress, with adverse health consequences for those caught up in it, while others, such as John Stevenson, have taken a more optimistic view.[29] Any assessment of the nation's health between the wars must take both sets of views into account, and they are not, as Keith Laybourn's thoughtful study makes plain, by any means irreconcilable.[30]

Difficulties of interpretation arise in this period partly because of a significant difference in the experience of the nation and of different individual localities, as measured by standardised death-rates, but also because perceptions of health and ill-health were often confused by individual memory and experience. The changes in cause of death and in life expectancy were marked enough by 1920 for the contrast with conditions around 1900 to be notable. In 1901–5, the average national death-rate had been 16 per thousand; in 1931–5 it was 12. Life expectancy averaged 50.4 years in 1901–5, but 60.8 by 1930.[31] Postwar surveys of social conditions by Arthur Bowley (1925) in southern England and Seebohm Rowntree in York (1935–36) confirmed a significant improvement over earlier surveys conducted in 1913 and 1899 respectively.[32]

It was estimated by Rowntree that the standard of living had improved by some 30 per cent between 1899 and 1936, although he admitted the survival of considerable poverty among working families with children, the chronically sick, the old and the low-paid. Neither York nor the towns surveyed by Bowley (Bolton, Warrington, Northampton and Reading) were seriously affected by the Depression and unemployment. No similar studies existed of such towns, but the Depression years spawned a critical literature that condemned the condition of Britain and criticised a capitalist economy that permitted hunger, bad housing and poverty.[33]

The change in social conditions and disease patterns inevitably affected the way in which many older medical men viewed contemporary problems of health and disease. George Newman's relentless insistence on the improving condition of the British people throughout the Depression years may, for example, have had its basis in part in his personal memories of conditions in Finsbury when he was MOH there in the first decade of the century. The experience of thirty years or so of practice in a greatly changed world thus influenced personal perspective, and made it possible to ignore or dispute the health consequences of unemployment and economic upheaval.

Moreover, many medical men, especially of the older generations, had been trained within a medical tradition that, at the least, played down links between poverty and disease, if not ill-health. The Victorian public health establishment, following the example of Edwin Chadwick, had first dismissed and later neglected the association of ill-health and poverty.[34] Reinforced in the interwar years by a declining death-rate and reduced infant mortality, and by the differing experience of depression between most of Britain and the old industrial areas, the legacy of the long preoccupation with sanitation and infectious disease, and with mortality figures as an indicator of health, blinded many to lower-profile indicators such as anaemia, debility and undernutrition. Already in the early 1920s, as the postwar economic boom collapsed, causing depression and unemployment in many areas of the country, MOHs in towns such as Birmingham and Northampton were unable to trace any resulting deterioration in general health.[35] Finally, MOHs and medical practitioners in poorer districts often became so accustomed to seeing patients in relatively poor health that they came to view them as being normal for their area.

In 1929, however, with the collapse of the Wall Street stock market, Western economies found themselves plunged into depression. Financial stringency had been operative within the British economy since the end of the war, and this had been reflected, within the MH, in the postponement of plans to widen the scope of National Insurance, and in the failure to extend the scope of Ministry action on health. The principal focus of public health activity in the interwar years remained improved housing.[36] The advent of depression put a further strain on the country's exchequer. Between 1929 and 1931 the number of unemployed in Britain rose from one to three million. Unemployment benefits were reduced, many married women were deprived of benefit, and new benefit scales, determined by means-testing, were introduced for the long-term unemployed. Between 1931 and 1935, in the worst years of the Depression, a married man with three children received a maximum of 29/3 a week.[37] The situation was not uniform across the country, however. In the south of England and in the Midlands, the new light industries, such as electricity, and car and radio set manufacturing, continued to prosper. The old industrial areas of the North-east, Scotland and South Wales, where coal mining, shipbuilding and steel were already weakened by postwar restructuring, experienced severe distress, unemployment in some areas of Wales rising to over 70 per cent of the working population.

It was in these circumstances that the average national mortality figure, used by George Newman as evidence of the nation's resilience, proved misleading, and that the inadequacy of the existing social provision was exposed. In fact, the death-rate for England and Wales rose to 66 per 1000 in 1931, against 60 in 1930. Nearly all the Lancashire county boroughs experienced a raised death-rate in that year. Local data from cities such as Jarrow, Bradford and Brynmawr, in the heart of the most depressed areas, revealed the bleak picture of a static or rising mortality level throughout the interwar years. In Bradford, for example, the standardised death-rate had been 15.5 in 1910–14, and 14.1 in 1921–25; it never fell below that level until 1938.[38] Recent research into National Insurance data has uncovered the downside of the Depression for working people and shown that unemployment carried a real risk of physical and mental illness. Increased competition in the job market, too, meant that people whose illnesses or disabilities had not previously barred them from obtaining work now found that they did so.[39]

Most debate on the issue of unemployment, low income and health has, however, crystallised around the health implications of malnutrition, and inevitably around the issues of infant mortality, child health and maternal mortality. The IMR, generally accepted as an important indicator of the general health of the community, nicely illustrates the complexities of the statistical debate. Standing at around 150 per thousand live births in the later nineteenth century, infant mortality had begun to tumble from 1901. By 1920 it stood at a national average of 88; in 1931–35 it was 62, and in 1936–40, 56. Yet these figures disguised significant annual, local, regional and class differences, and both England and Scotland had slipped in the international league tables by 1939. In 1930 the IMR had been 60 for England and Wales; by 1931, with the Depression well launched, it rose to 66.

The rate in Scotland was significantly above that for England and Wales throughout the period, as was that for the North-east in the early 1930s. The IMR continued to vary between and within towns, as well as between social classes: in Lancashire and Cheshire, as Webster has noted, the level ranged from around 93 per thousand in social class V to 31 in class I.[40]

Investigations by the Board of Education and others in the early 1930s specifically linked a high IMR to inadequate nutrition and poor health, making a similar connection between the latter and a high incidence of anaemia and toxaemia among mothers in the depressed areas. Viewed across the period 1900–40, it is, moreover, clear that the speed of the decline in infant mortality was drastically slowed during the depression years: between 1900 and 1930 the rate fell by 90 (by 20 in 1920–30 alone), whereas between 1930 and 1940 it fell by a mere 4, before tumbling again by a further 26 between 1940 and 1950.[41] The slowing in the decline of infant mortality in the early 1930s was not paralleled by any actual rise in maternal mortality in those years, but maternal mortality had remained obstinately high since the early 1920s at around 4 per thousand births, and had indeed increased by 20 per cent between 1923 and 1933. Once again, however, there was a marked regional variation: in 1936 the maternal mortality rate was 4.4 in Wales and 5.2 in the North, but 2.6 in South-east England.[42]

The picture for maternal death was more complex than that for infant mortality, however, since it involved not only social conditions, but also antenatal provision, obstetric competence and the virulence of the organisms of puerperal fever. The greater likelihood of medical intervention in the birth process among the better-to-do meant that death in childbirth was far from uncommon among the middle classes, and better nutrition was of little assistance in combating puerperal sepsis. In the well-to-do London district of Chelsea, for example, the number of maternal deaths registered in 1931 reached 5.4 per thousand births; in the socially mixed district of Hackney the rate was 3.2. Experimental programmes in Rochdale and in the Rhondda in the early 1930s, as well as evidence from poor London boroughs, suggested that the high maternal death-rate could be substantially cut by antenatal care and attention to nutrition. Nonetheless, viewed in a broad national perspective, the maternal death-rate remains suggestive: in 1928–34 it stood at 3.3 in prosperous southern towns, 4.2 in the county boroughs and 5.6 in depressed county areas. In 1936, more than thirty areas of the country experiencing severe economic difficulty had recorded an average maternal mortality rate (MMR) of more than 5 in the previous ten years.[43] In circumstances of depression and financial stringency, the allocation of resources to maternal welfare remained rare.

The health of schoolchildren, less easily measured in statistical terms, was less of a contemporary concern, since surveys by the School Medical Service appeared to suggest that real progress had been made in their social circumstances. It had been estimated before 1914, for example, that 15–20 per cent of the school population was affected by malnutrition, but by the early 1930s the problem seemed to have all but disappeared. The lack of consistency of these records with observed conditions led to an official investigation, revealing extensive errors and discrepancies in the ways in which the nutritional assessment of schoolchildren was made. One modern assessment suggests that, if the effect of low wages, periodic unemployment and large families is taken into account, between one quarter and one half of all children survived on a diet insufficient to maintain normal growth and health during the Depression.[44]

Such estimates remain to a certain extent subjective, however, since environmental factors such as poor housing and atmospheric pollution also contributed significantly to poor child health. Although interwar surveys in Durham and London indicated that more than 80 per cent of children showed signs of early rickets, this may not be unconnected with continuing sunlight deprivation, since the problem of severe atmospheric pollution by coal smoke remained almost unchanged in the great cities.

The medical response to the Depression and the social and health problems that accompanied it was mixed. There is certainly little evidence that medicine had any direct impact on ameliorating or resolving the human and local problems associated with unemployment, poverty and malnutrition in these years. The MH, in the person of the Chief Medical Officer, Sir George Newman, sought to deny that there was any serious problem of health or malnutrition, a position enforced by the political expediency of supporting the government. Local MOHs, on the other hand, varied in their willingness to criticise or endorse the optimistic pronouncements of the Ministry. Far more outspoken were various practitioners of the new medical science of nutrition, who were motivated partly by considerations of humanity and a concern for national interests, and partly by issues of scientific authority. It was a measure of the limited vision of the staff at the MH that developments in the new field of nutrition were neither followed nor integrated into any aspect of its activities in this period. By the late 1930s the nutritionists had developed a public profile and were actively involving themselves in the political promotion of their expertise.

Nutrition was one of several new scientific medical specialties to establish itself in the interwar years. The discovery of the role of vitamins and trace elements in the early decades of the century had effectively created the sub-discipline, which promoted itself in a general way as 'The Newer Knowledge of Nutrition'. Whereas nutritional adequacy had for centuries been measured in terms of a full belly, and in the nineteenth century had been redefined in terms of the absorption of adequate amounts of protein, carbohydrate and fat, the adequate diet was reconceptualised after the Great War in terms of essential vitamins. The successive leaders of the interwar Medical Research Council, Walter Morley Fletcher and Edward Mellanby, actively but unsuccessfully sought to convince the MH to implement welfare policies along the lines indicated by the new nutritional knowledge. They did, however, succeed in effecting a general shift in nutritional emphasis, among the educated classes at least, from quantity to quality, to the belief that cheap and simple changes in diet among the working classes would effect a transformation in their health and welfare, and that this change might be accomplished by nutritional education.[45]

By the 1930s MOHs and school medical officers had come to perceive micronutrient deficiency as the central problem of nutrition. Within existing financial constraints, however, policies developed on this understanding were not always as helpful in health terms as they might have been. Studies undertaken in the 1920s, for example, notably that of Corry Mann in 1925–26, appeared to show that milk had superior properties in assisting children to gain height and weight. As a result, many local authorities began to provide school milk as a cheaper alternative to school meals, in the mistaken belief that they were acting for the greater health of the children in their care.[46]

As the social crisis over the Depression and its effects on health deepened, calls began to be made for the medical specialists to describe the minimum dietary requirements for healthy living. The MH set up a Nutrition Advisory Committee in 1931, but its suggestions were quickly superseded by the BMA's publication in 1932 of its own report on the subject. The BMA defined the average daily requirement of an adult male as 3,400 calories, the needs of women, children and old people being expressed as a fraction of that figure. The monetary budget needed to achieve the upper (male) nutritional target was set at 5/11 a week, a sum that was sharply criticised as being unrealistic at a time when the family income among the poorest averaged less than 60/- a week and was often considerably less where families were dependent on insurance benefits.[47] Nonetheless, the report established the BMA as a major consultant on nutrition issues, and the document was used in many local inquiries into the extent and nature of malnutrition.[48] Nutrition was, in fact, becoming a significant international issue in this decade, and in 1935 the League of Nations published the first internationally agreed set of dietary requirements.

Britain emerged as a leading player in nutritional research during the interwar years through the establishment of several different institutions focused on this specialised area of research, including the Rowett Research Institute at Aberdeen, the Dunn Nutrition Laboratories in Cambridge, the Nutrition Department at King's College London and the Low Temperature Research Station at Reading. Among a number of prominent British nutrition scientists, John Boyd Orr, Director of the Rowett Institute between 1914 and 1945, achieved the highest public profile following the publication of his book *Food, Health and Income* in 1935.

Orr's claim that half the population of Britain could not afford to buy the minimum dietary requirements and were malnourished caused a widespread sensation but had little impact on government policy. In the first place, Orr's analysis was framed within the currently dominant micronutrient emphasis of his science, which was still viewed with suspicion within the MH, and in the second place, despite the desperate poverty and deprivation of the depressed areas, there was no evidence of any unusual prevalence of the recognised micronutrient deficiency diseases, such as rickets and scurvy. While campaigners anxious to raise the level of welfare benefit to accommodate the costs of the newly assessed nutritional requirements had hoped that Orr's pronouncements would shame government into making an additional allowance, the absence of any apparent deficiency disease served instead to reinforce government reluctance to act.[49]

The absence of the deficiency diseases serves to place some perspective on the health impact of the Depression. Although distress in the old industrial areas worst affected by the Depression was severe, and its general effect can to some extent be measured by the pattern of infant mortality, it did not return those areas to the worst conditions of the mid-nineteenth century, or even of 1900. Charles Webster has trenchantly remarked of the BMA's dietary scale that the allowance of 3d a meal for an adult 'may have been adequate to ward off an Ethiopian extreme of starvation, but it would not buy a pint of milk'.[50] A pint of milk cost 3½d, yet 3d also bought a portion of fish, and portions of chips and peas could be had for 1d. John Walton has argued that fish and chips kept the nation on its feet and eased the nutritional impact of the Depression for ordinary working people, and it has also been noted that working-class families were often adept at exploiting a range of sources of cheap food supplies.[51]

Although the welfare provisions enacted before 1930 proved incapable of cushioning working people against deprivation in adverse economic circumstances, and contemporary assessments of the condition of the people were confused, conflicting and at times misleading, it was clear that the standard set for social welfare and individual well-being had changed significantly since 1900. Where nineteenth-century public health policy had focused on disease control and the externals of a healthy life such as sanitation and clean water, the 'Newer Knowledge of Nutrition' brought a more internal, physiological conception of health to bear on questions of welfare and efficiency. It was symbolic of the tension between the two approaches that Walter Morley Fletcher thought nutrition should be the first priority for the MH, whereas the principal interwar plank of Ministry action on health remained housing.[52]

Towards a Therapeutic Watershed

It is possible to trace a contrast in purpose and perspective between the MH and the MRC in the years between 1919 and 1939, although the historical investigation of both these bodies has been limited and the career of George Newman as the first Chief Medical Officer has been largely neglected by historians.[53] The Ministry, however, appears to have been guided to a great extent by caution and tradition in its assessment of health priorities, and to have been at all times alert to the financial and political pressures on central government. The MRC, on the other hand, with a brief to support research into the causes of ill-health among the insured population, moved into a leading position as a patron of medical research and a facilitator in the introduction of new methods and treatments into British medical practice.

The financial and political pragmatism of the MH is perhaps best illustrated by its attitude towards the new immunisations against infectious disease, which began to be introduced after 1920. Diphtheria and tuberculosis were both still a major public health problem between the wars. There were on average some 50,000 cases of diphtheria a year and more than 30,000 deaths from respiratory tuberculosis. By 1920 it had become possible, through the development of the Schick test, to discover whether or not a child was naturally immune to diphtheria, and there was a reliable method of immunisation using a mix of antitoxin and antitoxoid.

Elsewhere in Europe, as well as in Canada and the United States, immunisation against diphtheria was being widely adopted. The MH consistently refused, however, to take any active part in promoting immunisation in Britain, preferring to leave such activity to the local health authorities and GPs. This reluctance was partly financial: in any national campaign, central government might be expected to bear the cost, as it did of vaccination against smallpox (and as eventually happened for diphtheria in 1940). There were also political motives, however, for there was the long history of resistance to state-imposed compulsory vaccination against smallpox, and in the 1920s the appearance of a new disease, deadly post-vaccinial encephalitis, gave further adverse publicity to the procedure. 'A Government department cannot usefully take action in advance of public opinion', a Ministry spokesman noted in 1927, and it was far from clear that public opinion would be in favour of mass immunisation against diphtheria.

It was a similar story with the anti-tuberculosis vaccine developed by Louis Calmette and Camille Guérin at the Pasteur Institute in Paris in the early 1920s. The Ministry was already acting with predictable caution when a highly publicised disaster at Lubeck in 1930, in which seventy-three infants died as a result of being given the vaccine (which had been contaminated with virulent bacilli in the laboratory), provoked a widespread reaction against the vaccine in England, France and Germany. Once again a suspicious public and administrative difficulties allowed the Ministry to remain inactive in promoting immunisation against tuberculosis.[54] Moreover, the existence in Britain of well-entrenched institutional facilities for the 'prevention' and treatment of both tuberculosis and diphtheria contributed significantly to apathy on the part of local public health services. On the one hand, the falling death-rate and reduced rate of infection appeared to substantiate the effectiveness of the isolation hospitals and sanatoria; on the other, these institutions provided many medical men with careers and salaries. The introduction of mass immunisation programmes would entail not only heavy public expenditure and probably public resistance, but also expensive and painful administrative change.

In contrast to the Ministry's reluctance to promote new immunisations, the MRC was diligent in fostering the introduction of new methods of treatment for a variety of conditions. The most medically exciting innovation of the 1920s was undoubtedly insulin treatment for diabetes. Developed in Canada by a small group of scientists working at the University of Toronto, insulin was developed commercially and marketed in America by the pharmaceutical company Eli Lilly & Co, while the University of Toronto retained the patents.[55] In 1922 the MRC were offered, and accepted, the complete British patent rights in insulin. The death-rate from diabetes had been rising steadily in Britain since the 1890s, with a brief hiatus during the war, and it has been estimated that by 1920 between 200,000 and 850,000 people were suffering from this unpleasant illness. Diabetes has two forms, both of which had increased: mature onset diabetes (usually appearing after the age of fifty-five), which is associated with an overgenerous diet; and juvenile diabetes, of which the cause is unknown. The former can be controlled by a regulated diet; the latter, untreated, is rapidly fatal, its victims being reduced within months to starving, constantly thirsty skeletons. A regular injection of insulin enabled sufferers to return to an almost normal life, and in this respect insulin was a true miracle drug, the very first of its kind.

Yet although insulin became available in Britain through the MRC early in 1923, its use only slowly diffused into medical practice, and there was little evidence that its availability contributed to an enhanced medical understanding of diabetes generally. The MRC was worried by the slow increase in consumption of the drug, and although the death-rate did fall among the under-55s, it continued to rise in the older age groups. As it was impossible to establish how many diabetic patients of each type existed, the MRC remained suspicious, well into the 1930s, that life-giving insulin treatment was not reaching many victims of the disease, and that inadequate biochemical and dietary control, resulting from its administration by unskilled hands, curtailed its therapeutic effectiveness. Although an improvement in diagnosis certainly played its part in complicating the picture, the annual number of diabetes deaths rose from 4,545 to 5,660 between 1922 and 1930, and the crude death-rate from 119 to 142 per million.[56]

The second significant therapeutic development of the 1920s potentially transformed the prospects for patients with pernicious anaemia. This condition was first distinguished from the other anaemias in the British registration data in 1920. Although relatively rare, it was a miserable and debilitating illness, and untreated was invariably fatal. In 1926 G. R. Minot and W. P. Murphy of Harvard University showed that patients with pernicious anaemia could be restored to health by a diet containing copious amounts of raw liver.[57] It was not a pleasant treatment, and techniques for administering the active principle in liver (later discovered to be vitamin B12) as an extract were quickly developed. These, in turn, were introduced into Britain and promoted there by the MRC.

Within a decade, the death-rate from pernicious anaemia among the under-65s had fallen dramatically. Death-rate in the 75-plus age group, however, was rising. As with insulin, the introduction of a miraculous new treatment did not mean that all patients automatically benefited: the availability of treatment was qualified by other factors – by the individual patient's willingness to seek treatment, as well as by the individual doctor's ability to offer or effectively administer the treatment. Such factors operated to produce a different pattern of outcome in different age groups and different parts of the country. Comparative death-rates showed that those who lived in urban areas were more likely to be offered the new treatments successfully than those who lived in the countryside.

The difference in access to new medical treatments between town and countryside was also evident for the emerging interwar specialty of radium treatment for cancer. Radium, whose medical applications had first been explored by Marie and Pierre Curie, was, like most new medical substances, used experimentally to treat a wide variety of medical conditions. Once again, the MRC was, because of the steadily rising death-rate from the disease, closely involved in the work of treating cancer with radium.[58] This rising rate partly reflected improved diagnosis, but it also reflected greater longevity and a changing pattern of behaviour. In the later 1930s the emergence of lung cancer as a major cause of death among men was beginning to cause special concern. In 1901 the total number of cancer deaths stood at 27,487; by 1920 there were more than 40,000 a year, and both the Ministry and the MRC were anxious on several counts: 'Death,' the Council noted in 1921, 'comes often in the most painful form, and from its nature and age-incidence it commonly takes the mother or the breadwinner'.[59] Although the surgical excision of cancers had been greatly extended and improved since the 1880s, it was well known not only that surgery rarely cured, generally because it was undertaken only when the cancer was already advanced, but also that many sufferers preferred not to face surgery at all. By the late

1920s many surgeons were adopting radium therapy as a substitute or an adjunct to operations. Outside London, however, the treatment was available at only twenty or so hospitals, including nine national and five regional Radium Centres.

Government concern over the rising toll of deaths from cancer found formal expression in the Cancer Act 1939. The provisions of the Act reflected the extent to which contemporary medicine viewed radium treatment as the way forward for cancer patients, as it empowered the MH to lend money to the National Radium Trust for the purchase of radium, and other radioactive substances, as well as the associated apparatus and appliances. It also required the local authorities to arrange facilities adequate to treat all cancer patients in their areas, including facilities for diagnosis and hospital treatment, and payment for the expense of travelling for treatment. Yet the interwar enthusiasm for radium therapy was largely uncritical and exposed patients, doctors and technicians to heavy doses of radiation, with results that were disastrous for many. Although both the MRC and radium specialists were concerned about this indiscriminate use of the material, it was not until the effects of the atom bomb on the inhabitants of Hiroshima and Nagasaki became known in the later 1940s that the medical uses of radium were more widely called into question.

Less controversial, and of far greater therapeutic importance, was the introduction of the sulphonamide drugs in the mid-1930s. Developed by a German scientist, Gerhard Domagk, working for the Bayer pharmaceutical company in the early 1930s, the sulphonamides proved effective against a range of bacterial infections, notably of streptococci, pneumonococci and the agents of gonorrhoea and bacterial meningitis. The MRC sponsored British trials directed by Leonard Colebrook, an expert in streptococcal infection, the drugs beginning to enter clinical practice late in 1936. Historically overshadowed by the later introduction of penicillin, the sulphonamides were the first true wonder drug, the first real fulfilment of Ehrlich's ambition of a 'magic bullet', remembered by contemporary practitioners as a more dramatic advance than penicillin.[60]

The most striking impact of the new drugs was on the death-rate from puerperal fever, the main killer of women in childbirth.

Although there had coincidentally been a marked decline in streptococcal virulence in the early 1930s, the number of deaths from puerperal fever fell to a new record low in 1937 following the introduction of the sulphonamide Prontosil, entering a steady decline thereafter. At least five proprietary brands of Prontosil were available in Britain by spring 1937, and a questionnaire distributed in December the following year showed that it was being widely used in both hospital and general practice for the prevention and cure of puerperal infections. Tellingly, the decline in death-rate from puerperal fever continued throughout the Second World War in both Britain and America, where Prontosil continued to be available. In France, Belgium and Holland, however, where supplies were restricted during the German occupation, the maternal mortality level remained steady between 1939 and 1945.[61]

In England and Wales maternal mortality fell overall, from 4.2 per thousand births in 1936 to 2.2 in 1940. Deaths from causes other than puerperal sepsis did not, however, begin to decline until 1940. In that year they were below 2 per thousand for the first time, probably as a result of war-related improvements in antenatal care. Although the interwar years also saw a significant shift in the location of childbirth from the home to the hospital – a quarter of all births taking place in the latter by 1940 – the improved survival chances of women in childbirth were clearly due to the new drug therapy rather than to increased medical attention. Hospital births were no safer than home births in the pre-sulphonamide era; what hospitals did offer was the chance to rest after the birth – greatly valued by working-class women – and a greater likelihood of receiving pain relief.[62]

The MRC's involvement in the introduction, testing and promotion of new treatments was paired with the funding and encouragement of research in other areas extending to, for example, industrial health, chemotherapy and the sex hormones, whose therapeutic potential was often long term rather than immediate. Unlike the MH, the interwar MRC acted as a dynamic contributor to the quest to improve the nation's health through medical rather than social means. Throughout the period, the officials at the Ministry took a restricted, conservative view of its role, insisting that it was for local authorities and voluntary agencies to implement new policies such as immunisation or health education. It continued to sponsor epidemiological, statistical and laboratory investigations bearing on the prevention of disease, with a view to filtering relevant information into administrative practice through these intermediaries, and to set up special committees and inquiries into particular problems. At the centre of George Newman's vision for the future of medicine was the promotion of individual health through a reorientation of general practice towards preventive medicine. Hostile forces were, however, ranged against him: medical men, more especially the powerful hospital consultants, were fiercely protective of their professional autonomy and could be counted on to resist ministerial intervention in their activities.[63] Despite the efforts of the MRC in promoting therapeutic innovation, the Ministry itself played little effective part in developing the organisation and application of new medical techniques. In this respect, its desire to reshape medical practice on a preventive model undermined its leadership potential as effectively as did its consciousness of the financial and political interests of central government.

The Social Context of Improving Health

While the contribution of the welfare services to health remains debatable, and the impact of medical innovation was essentially piecemeal, being limited to particular groups of patients in these years, a range of social and economic factors helped to generate better health, and perhaps also a greater consciousness of health. In spite of the problems in the depressed areas, the south of England and the Midlands experienced a degree of relative prosperity, and there was a new emphasis on consumption and leisure, which, together with new political power, gave ordinary people a greater sense of choice and control in their lives. The advent of radio, paid holidays, cheap motor transport and hire purchase, together with the increasing influence of the popular press, raised expectations as well as standards of living. Certain beneficial patterns of consumption and expenditure engendered during the Great War endured after it. The MRC, for example, was impressed by the nation's new sobriety: in 1933 it noted that the postwar conversion from a culture of drunkenness was one of the main factors contributing to improved health.[64] Quite apart from the specific benefits noted by the Council – cirrhosis of the liver had become rare, the overlaying of babies was greatly reduced and there was comparative peace in urban casualty departments on a Saturday night – a reduced expenditure on alcohol meant more in the family budget to spend on food and other items.

A continuously falling birth-rate was also important in raising the family's living standards. Whereas the average family was composed of 4.6 persons in 1901, by 1951 this was only 3.2.[65] As families became smaller, they were better fed, and children were more easily cared for. Although birth control remained a contentious issue in this period, the falling birth-rate indicates that family limitation was being successfully practised by a significant number of couples. Fewer children per marriage also had health benefits for mothers, in terms of less physical wear and tear, less exhaustion and a reduced risk, not only of death in childbirth, but also of such debilitating medical conditions as prolapsed womb and varicose veins. Questions of sexual intercourse and child-bearing created tension in many households, however, as was later evident in many requests from married women for the contraceptive pill. The continuing frequency of abortion as a desperate preventive resort, and of numerous deaths from septic abortion, made contraception and abortion issues of concern not only for organisations involved with women's health and welfare, but also for those anxious about the manpower consequences of the continually falling birth-rate. In 1920 the birth-rate stood at around 20 per 1000 population; by the 1930s it was down to 15.

While families with many young children were too often held down in poverty, as Rowntree's investigations in York demonstrated, smaller families were, conversely, better able to take advantage of the opportunities that postwar society offered them. Notable among these was increased leisure time. The working week had been reduced to forty-eight hours in 1919, and with the arrival of the motor bus as a cheap and flexible form of transport, outings and excursions became a regular feature of working people's lives. By the 1930s many employers were offering paid holiday, and in 1938 this innovation was regularised by the Holidays with Pay Act.[66] In other respects, too, leisure opportunities expanded, as the cinema, dance halls, cricket, football, and horse and greyhound racing became popular interests. While the direct health impact of increased leisure time and an increasing variety of ways of using it cannot be measured, there can be little doubt that a clearer demarcation of work and leisure added interest and enjoyment to many lives. Physical fitness also became more highly prized and an objective for an increasing number of people.

After the First World War, efforts were made to spread the traditional English public school emphasis on team games and fresh air more widely, and additionally to develop more rigorous forms of physical training. Dancing, hiking and cycling became popular pastimes, and clubs and societies devoted to physical exercise flourished in urban areas. Voluntary organisations such as the National Playing Fields Association (1925) and the Women's League of Health and Beauty (1929) were joined, as the threat of war drew perceptibly closer in the 1930s, by public bodies like the Council for Physical Recreation and Training. In 1935 medical awareness of these issues was signalled by the BMA's establishment of a physical education committee.[67] The spirit of international competition certainly lent an edge to these endeavours. Britain's poor showing at the Olympic Games in 1936 (four gold medals compared to Germany's thirty-three) spurred the government into action, and in 1937 the MH and the Board of Education launched joint publicity campaigns to raise the national consciousness of physical fitness.[68]

The new popular media such as the BBC, as well as mass-market daily papers and weekly magazines, provided effective methods of communicating both commercial and non-commercial interests. Public interest in matters medical meant columns in the press, while there was a great expansion in advertising, and a levelling – whether up or down – began of standards and practices nationally. Cigarettes and soft drinks, proprietary foods and medicines, clothing and household goods, and beauty and cleaning products all received nationwide exposure. Nancy Tomes has pointed to the importance of advertising in establishing the norms of domestic hygiene in the United States, and although no similar survey exists for Britain, there can be little doubt that advertising between the wars contributed significantly to educating the British people in domestic cleanliness and sanitary practices, just as it did in educating them in the importance of vitamins for health.[69] Channels for popular education multiplied between the wars, among the most important being the radio. By 1935 two-thirds of the nation owned a radio set, and the BBC had become an important educational medium. Even the MH had come to see the advantages of media exposure by the 1930s, although George Newman's weekly addresses to the nation on subjects related to health were redolent of the department's desire to encourage individuals towards self-improvement, rather than seriously to inform them on matters of health and medicine.[70]

Conclusion

The paradox of interwar Britain lies precisely in the steady modernisation and expansion of standards of living and expectations of life and health for many on the one hand, and the miseries of the Depression in the old industrial areas on the other. For the British people in general, life and health appeared to be improving, if judged by the traditional measures of deathrate and life expectancy, and by memories of life in the Victorian and Edwardian past. Developments in medical science contributed to transforming the life prospects of certain specific groups of people such as mothers and diabetics, but medical specialists also began to move towards a more prescriptive type of medicine, which, as with the 'Newer Knowledge of Nutrition', held out the prospect of achieving a new standard of health through individual self-improvement or adjustments to the quality of individual diets.

4

MEDICINE AND THE MAKING OF WAR, 1939–45

Introduction

The outbreak of the Second World War in September 1939 found Britain only half-prepared. Although it had been recognised since the early 1930s that another war was possible, the country's political elite was anxious not to create public alarm. Much of the necessary preparation for war, both military and civilian, had therefore to be made in secret, and the arrangements suffered accordingly. When the war began, Neville Chamberlain's government was unenthusiastic at the prospect, and as Germany was at this time preoccupied with the situation elsewhere in Europe, it was not until Winston Churchill took over as Prime Minister in May 1940 that the 'phoney' war ended, and the real war got underway. The nine months before this happened were crucial to Britain's later war effort, for they allowed construction of the defensive and support systems that carried her through the last four years of conflict.

In sharp contrast to the war of 1914–18, the critical theatre of this war lay at home and not abroad. The development of the aeroplane as a means of transport and a weapon of war had effected a radical change in the nature of warfare, which became almost as much a process of attrition against civilians as a contest between armed forces. Civilian casualties in the First World War were negligible (a thousand people being killed in the Zeppelin raids on London); in the Second World War they amounted to nearly a quarter of the forces' dead, and three-quarters of the forces' wounded, with a total of 60,595 civilians killed and some 218,000 injured.[1] In this war, the importance of the home front as the supporting base of operations was well recognised from the beginning, this sharply differentiating it from previous conflicts. The presence of a large standing army within the country, of conscripts in training or waiting to be deployed abroad, resulted in an unprecedented mix of problems of civilian and service welfare. Air raids, the population movements caused by planned and voluntary civilian evacuation from cities, the management of civilian and service patients within the same hospital system; and the urgency of returning both civilian and military casualties to fitness as efficiently as possible were new social and medical features characteristic of this war.

For the first time, the medical establishment at home was as fully involved in the war effort as the doctors who served with the armed forces. Between the fall of France in June 1940 and America's entry into the war following the Japanese attack on Pearl Harbour in December 1941, Britain was to a great extent isolated in defiance of Germany in north-western Europe, and from 1942 it acted in addition as a front-line base for the American contribution to the fighting. In the maintenance of manpower, and in the planning, construction and administration of national defensive systems for the support of public health and national fitness, medicine played a key part. During this war, for perhaps the first time in history, medicine found itself centre stage in the nation's engagement with health.

A War at Home

The national mythology of the Second World War, influentially expounded by Richard Titmuss in his classic account of Britain's wartime experience, emphasises Britain's national unity, the disappearance of class divisions and the solidarity of communal defiance of the enemy.[2] It is a picture that frays on closer historical inspection, in both its political and social dimensions.[3] Inequalities in health experience and health care certainly remained a feature of British people's lives in wartime, as they had done in peace. Geographical and social divisions did not disappear for the duration and, as in the Great War, minority groups such as unmarried mothers, the elderly and chronic sick, and refugees suffered neglect or the effects of prejudice.[4]

In general terms, however, Britain's overall health experience during the war was favourable. The first two years were the worst, partly because of the physical trauma of mobilisation, evacuation and new patterns of work, but also because of:

- the psychological impact of a return to global war;
- the strain imposed by the country's isolated stand against the Axis Powers in 1940–41;
- the enemy bombing campaign of those years.

The demographic measures available for the first two full years of war are significant, and perhaps give some indication of the importance to national morale of America's entry into the war. The death-rate for the old – those over sixty-five, who had been through the Great War – soared in 1940 and remained above normal until the end of the war (Table 4.1). The death-rate from all forms of tuberculosis rose by around 11 per cent in 1940 and 1941, returning to its prewar level in 1942; in 1944 the downward trend in tuberculosis mortality resumed (Table 4.2). The IMR rose sharply in 1940 and 1941 but returned to its prewar trend in 1942 (Table 4.3). On these indications, civilian health was most affected in the first two years of war (1940 and 1941), when the dislocation caused by evacuation and bombing was most severe, and doubt as to the eventual outcome of the fighting most draining.

As in the Great War, the pattern of civilian health does not appear to have been directly shaped by the availability or reduced accessibility of professional medical treatment. In April 1940, the Ministry of Labour announced the conscription of doctors aged under 41; a year later the limit was raised to 46, and women doctors under 31 were included. By the end of 1945 a total of 15,701 medical personnel had been recruited, roughly a third of the country's medical manpower. Already in 1943, many of the general practitioners remaining in civil life were aged over 50, some 8 per cent of them being over 70, and a great many more were women. By this time the ratio of patients to practitioners for

Table 4.1   Deaths among persons aged
over 65, England and Wales, 1938–44

Year	Men	Women	Total
1938	118,302	128,530	246,832
1939	127,907	141,669	269,576
1940	142,362	158,479	301,111
1941	129,947	142,536	272,483
1942	122,875	131,999	254,874
1943	129,825	143,799	273,624
1944	129,365	139,150	268,515

Source: Chief Medical Officer's Report for 1939–45, p. 260.

more than half the population of England and Wales was 3,000:1, reaching, by the end of the war, 4,500:1 in some districts.[5]

The remaining doctors were hard-pressed, more so than in 1914–18. As well as covering for colleagues who had been called up, they variously took charge of first aid posts, worked part-time in the emergency hospitals, attended bombing 'incidents', served on recruiting boards, acted as medical officers to the Home Guard and as works doctors in munitions factories, and in between times trained nursing and auxiliary staff for the voluntary services. If the shortage of civilian doctors seems generally to have had little adverse effect on civilian health, and organised medicine clearly did not prevent the rise in the number of deaths

Table 4.2   Deaths from respiratory
tuberculosis, England and Wales, 1938–44

Year	E & W	Year	E & W
1938	21,282	1942	20,989
1939	21,542	1943	21,382
1940	23,660	1944	20,104
1941	23,633		

Source: Chief Medical Officer's Report for 1939–45, p. 16.

Table 4.3   Infant mortality in England
and Wales, 1900–44

Deaths under one year per 1,000 live births			
1901–10	128	1939	51
1911–20	100	1940	57
1921–30	72	1941	60
1931–35	62	1942	51
1936	59	1943	49
1937	58	1944	45
1938	53		

Source: Chief Medical Officer's Report for 1939–45, p. 15.

in the first two years of war, the effectiveness of civilian medical arrangements can be seen in the failure of the death-rate from tetanus to increase despite the 200,000 plus bomb-related injuries. The preventive immunisation of all civilians having been considered impractical, the rescue services had been instructed 'rigorously' to administer prophylactic injections to all civilian wounded.[6]

Concern for the medical consequences of war to civilians centred around four main issues: population movement, infectious diseases, air raids and food. In September 1939 the immediate problem was evacuation and the resulting mass egress of young children from the cities into the countryside. It had long been anticipated that Germany would launch an immediate heavy bombing offensive on London and the great cities on the outbreak of war, but when war did come the evacuation arrangements had to be put hastily into place. Although more than a million children and young mothers with babies were successfully evacuated in the first three days of September 1939, some parts of the operation were shambolic, with bewildered children enduring, unfed, long train journeys to strange destinations.[7]

The translation of these inner-city working-class children into country areas proved to be an essentially divisive social experiment, confirming middle-class prejudices and official beliefs about the inadequacy of the poorest classes, as well as subjecting many individual children – and other evacuees – to traumatic experiences of separation and isolation.[8] Many host families, usually middle-class families whose homes would most comfortably accommodate additional bodies, and local MOHs were shocked by episodes of bed-wetting and by the revelation of a relatively high incidence of head lice, while children reft from their own caring communities responded to their new situation by failing to thrive. It had been expected that the health of inner-city children would be improved by their translation to the country; not only was no such improvement recorded, but also many children continued to demonstrate a degree of disturbance for many years afterwards. When the expected autumn bombing campaign failed to materialise, evacuees began to drift back to the cities, and by early in 1940 nearly 80 per cent had returned to the urban danger areas. As an exercise in safeguarding the health of city children, the evacuation of 1939 must be counted as a failure, but later waves of evacuation during the blitz in the late summer of 1940, and with the V1 and V2 rocket attacks of 1944, were better thought out and organised, proving less problematic.[9]

The perceived poor condition of many child evacuees had social and political repercussions well beyond the immediate shock of the middle-class rural host communities. Richard Titmuss first suggested that the 1939 evacuation was critical in shaping a growing wartime reforming consensus that led to the implementation of the Welfare State in the later 1940s, while John MacNicol argues that it also reinforced among civil servants and social workers a 'conservative, behaviouristic analysis of poverty' that traced the children's problems to 'family failure, poor parenting and general social inadequacy', so developing the concept of the 'problem family', which was to be widely influential among social workers into the 1960s.[10]

As well as influencing social policy, the evacuation debacle also influenced medical thinking more specifically in the direction of child welfare. The effectiveness of the School Medical Service was now questioned, in the light of revelations about dirt, scabies, head lice and incontinence that had surely been its business to deal with, and reacted with the traditional defence that its role was essentially educational so it could bear no responsibility for conditions caused by children's home lives.[11] If, in this respect, the School Medical Service betrayed the limitations of its operation, the experience of evacuation galvanised other medical professionals into a deeper involvement with issues of children's welfare. Paediatrics, which had been a small and unimportant specialty before the war, developed an increasingly crusading political profile, as younger members of the British Paediatric Association – an organisation that previously had existed largely as a social club – responded to the problems of evacuation. In the field of mental health, similarly, the new sub-specialty of child psychiatry expanded on foundations established in the 1920s by the pioneering Tavistock Clinic and child guidance clinics, essentially as a response to the problems thrown up by the experience of evacuation.[12]

Public health anxiety about head lice among evacuee children was lent an edge by the knowledge that the human head louse is a possible vector for typhus, even though the disease had long ceased to be indigenous in Great Britain. Fears of infectious disease sweeping rampant through a population dislocated by severe bombing, and surviving among shattered housing stock and sanitary facilities, had been highly influential among epidemiologists and public health personnel before the war. William Whiteman Carlton Topley, who had experienced the Serbian typhus epidemic of 1915, later elucidating the concept of herd immunity, and now the highly distinguished professor of bacteriology at the London School of Hygiene and Tropical Medicine, was indeed so possessed by the likelihood of such an eventuality that he swept aside military fears of bacteriological warfare, to insist instead on the implementation of plans for emergency sanitation. In particular, the safeguarding of water supplies was deemed vitally important, and, for the first time, the MH required all water providers permanently to chlorinate their water supplies to prevent dangerous contamination as a result of either bomb damage or acts of sabotage.[13]

The problems with vermin were not, however, limited to schoolchildren, and the military experience of both head lice and scabies in the early months of the war went a long way towards confirming the idea of these afflictions being family-related problems. The experience in recruiting into the womens' services was particularly influential. Investigations by Keith Mellanby on behalf of the Board of Education had revealed infestation running as high as 50 per cent among girls aged 2–12, but in some industrial areas as many as 65 per cent of women enrolling were found to infested – a phenomenon blamed on the fashion for permanent waves, whereby hair went unwashed for weeks at a time. After various trials among schoolchildren, lethane hair oil was found to be a quick and effective louse-killer, subsequently being widely used in the forces.

Scabies, or itch, proved equally prevalent among children and recruits, although this was less surprising since the incidence of scabies had been known to be rising sharply even before the outbreak of war. Military expediency led to the identification of benzyl benzoate as a solution to the problem, but it was the needs of children that led to the development of an emulsion formula that did not irritate sensitive skin. Although scabies had been recognised as a public health problem since the Great War, it was only in the Second World War that army medical officers made the observations that produced a strategy for control: that the mite lived in bedding; that it was highly susceptible to temperature; that 'silent' carriers existed; and that family habits, especially that of all sleeping in one bed, were a critical factor in its transmission. In the case of domestic entomology, at least, the experience of war precipitated the elucidation and solution of long-standing problems of hygiene in the home.

Despite the problems of mass evacuation, one expected hazard did fail to materialise: there was no serious outbreak of infectious disease as a result of mixing the urban and rural child populations. Indeed, one of the demographic features that contemporaries found remarkable about the years 1940–45 was the continuing low mortality from infectious disease among children. This was only in part the result of preventive action. Immediately before the war, alarm at the possible consequences of urban evacuation had spurred public health authorities, the MH and the BMA into launching a campaign to maximise the level of immunisation against diphtheria, with a considerable degree of success. There were serious worries about the prospects for measles and whooping cough, both of which were known killers and for which preventive immunisation was not yet available. Measles did indeed become seriously epidemic in 1941 and 1942 but caused few fatalities, one indication that social factors and the level of nutrition were not too adversely affected by wartime conditions. Neither, when they did come, did the air raids result in epidemics of typhoid and dysentery through disrupted or contaminated water supplies. The most striking epidemic outbreak on the home front during the Second World War was of meningitis. It came as something of a surprise, even though it was a possibility that had been suggested by the experience of the Great War.

Beginning in the winter of 1940, the outbreak carried over into 1941 and was undoubtedly the result of the mixing of populations of young adults some of whom had not had the opportunity to build up resistance against current viral or bacterial strains of the disease. A total of 23,848 cases were recorded, four times as many as in the previous worst outbreak in 1915. Treatment with the new sulphonamide drugs, however, reduced the number of deaths to some 10 per cent, the lowest recorded fatality rate, although the death-rate among forces personnel was less than half that among civilians. A knowledge of the new treatments, drug supplies and expertise in their administration were more readily available within the service than the civilian hospitals sector.[14]

The circumstances that generated the 1940 meningitis outbreak were not dissimilar from those that provoke outbreaks in British universities today. Military enrolment and training brought the mixing of civilians and forces personnel from many different areas. It was a cold winter, and economies in fuel, as well as the black-out, which had been in force since 1 September, meant that many buildings were poorly ventilated. Such conditions are ideal for the transmission of meningococcal meningitis. The factors contributing to the epidemic spread of the disease were already well recognised in 1940, and it had been thought that control over the disease might be obtained through the detection and treatment of carriers. The circumstances of war defeated this hope: so many carriers were found both among the contacts of meningitis cases and among non-contacts that isolation and treatment proved impracticable, while it proved technically impossible to determine the virulence of meningococci in specimen swabs. Following a recommendation from the MH, the army abandoned its search for meningitis carriers in October 1940.

This early and unfortunate experience with meningitis enhanced fears about the probable results of aerial bombardment when a large number of people in urban areas began to use bomb shelters as night-time dormitories later that autumn. At the beginning of the war, it had been assumed that bombing raids would be conducted in daylight, and in the early stages of the Battle of Britain, when Germany was targeting ports and airfields in southern England, daylight raiding was the usual practice. As a result, a large number of surface air raid shelters had been built on the assumption that they would be used for a relatively brief period of time while a raid was in progress.

In September 1940, however, the German air force changed tactics and began bombing civilian targets by night. As a result, a large number of people who sought both safety and an escape from the noise of the raids began to spend their night in London's underground railway stations, and in natural or man-made tunnel networks, such as the Chislehurst Caves in Kent, the old London and South-eastern railway tunnel between Broadstairs and Ramsgate, and the Ouseburn Culvert at Newcastle-on-Tyne. This unexpected development resulted in major sanitary headaches. In the London region, on the night of 5 January 1941, for example, more than a million people slept in the underground shelters, while some 10,000 regularly used the Chislehurst Caves. Between September 1940 and May 1945, more than 53 million attendances were recorded at London's tube shelters alone. By every possible epidemiological criterion, it was a usage that represented a potentially explosive health hazard.

The sanitary upgrading of the underground shelters to meet the requirements of hundreds of thousands of nightly users was one of the major civilian achievements of the Second World War. Initially, arrangements were chaotic and conditions appalling.[15] Overcrowding was a serious problem, there were no beds and no washing facilities, many were below the level of the sewers, making pail closets essential, and many were damp. Local authorities and shelter managers strove to provide sanitary facilities, with a fair degree of success, and, less successfully, to improve ventilation. The night-time atmosphere was generally thick with the smell of massed humanity. Although inspecting medical officers were at times overcome by nausea in the small hours of the morning, it was noted that the shelterers came to no apparent harm.[16] Water closets or latrines, piped water supplies, lighting, ventilating fans and hot-air disinfectors (for personal belongings) were installed, and bed-bugs were combated by chemical means.

The Central Council for Education and the BBC were enlisted to publicise measures for preventing droplet infection and respiratory disease, especially the importance of immunisation against diphtheria. An unexpected small rise in pulmonary embolism among shelter users in the early months ended when chairs and deck-chairs were replaced by bunks. In February 1941 the MH set up an Epidemiological Committee to investigate the spread of infection in shelters and methods for controlling it, but the anticipated epidemic outbreaks never materialised. Their absence can be attributed in part to the heroic efforts made to provide basic sanitation, but social factors were undoubtedly important as well. Most shelterers were middle aged, they were mostly women, and they usually came from the same local area and social group. In these circumstances, the likelihood that individual shelterers would be exposed to new pathogens was greatly reduced, and the chance of epidemic outbreaks was correspondingly diminished.[17]

The problem of the shelters was a novel one, but at least it appears to have been resolved with minimal damage to civilian health. More worrying was an old problem that inevitably resurfaced with every fresh war: that of STD. The interwar policy of tackling STD by establishing treatment centres had apparently achieved a measure of success: in 1939 the number of new cases of syphilis coming forward reached an all-time low, and while the incidence of gonorrhoea remained difficult to assess, two of the new sulpha drugs available since 1937 gave a 90 per cent cure rate for the disease after a short course of treatment.

With the outbreak of war, the number of cases quickly spiralled. Not only had relations between the sexes become much freer in all social classes since 1914, but the great wartime population mobility, the disruption to family life brought about by evacuation and conscription, and the country's role as a service training ground and a base for the fighting forces of other combatants (notably the American forces after Christmas 1941), taken together, meant, as the Chief Medical Officer memorably put it, that 'sexual promiscuity must have been practised on a scale never previously attained in this country'.[18] By 1942 the MH was seriously alarmed and intensifying its campaign of public education, Defence Regulation 33B being implemented to facilitate the examination and treatment of known carriers. Following these measures, the incidence among men began to fall, among both civilians and forces personnel. Among women, however, the rate continued to rise until the end of the war, a phenomenon popularly blamed on the resident Allied Forces, especially the Americans.

Anxieties over the not unexpected resurgence of STDs in wartime had to some extent been reduced by the development of drug therapies in the years immediately before the war. At that time, the relevant drugs, sulphathiazole and sulphadiazine, were classified as poisons and were subject to medical monopoly and control: they could only be taken under the supervision of a qualified orthodox practitioner. The pressure of war brought with it a relaxation of control, these drugs being made widely available in an attempt to limit the spread of disease among women.[19] The measure, in opening the door to self-medication and the uncontrolled use of the drugs, patients too often not finishing courses of treatment after the worst symptoms had faded, backfired; in an ominously short space of time, drug-resistant strains of gonorrhoea began to appear. By 1945 the success rate against gonorrhoea with the sulpha drugs was falling fast, to the consternation of both military and civilian authorities.

The arrival of penicillin, which proved outstandingly successful against both syphilis and gonorrhoea, restored medical control over these diseases, initially among the military, but after 1945 also among civilians. The emergence of sulpha-drug-resistant strains of gonorrhoea was, however, a portent that the health authorities failed to heed. The use of penicillin in treatment was initially circumscribed by the fact that it had to be administered in hospital so that the absorption rate of the drug could be carefully monitored. As long as its administration was closely supervised, penicillin continued to be effective in the treatment of both syphilis and gonorrhoea. In the 1950s, however, it became possible to administer the drug by mouth, and while this meant that it became much more widely prescribed, it also followed that the drug became much more carelessly used. Although the organism of syphilis is notoriously fragile and remains responsive to penicillin, penicillin-resistant strains of gonococci had emerged by the mid-1960s.

While neither the emergence of drug-resistant gonorrhoea nor the problem of the night shelters could probably have been foreseen, the MH's general response to the potential medical and public health problems of war was not as efficient as it might have been. Despite the serious fears about bombing, the first evacuation of city children was substantially underplanned; the programme of immunisation against diphtheria became effective only after the Ministry finally accepted the cost of providing vaccine free late in 1940; and the campaign against the STDs was only developed with any degree of seriousness in October 1942, when recollections of the Great War must surely have indicated that vigilance should be exercised from the start of mobilisation.

Similarly, provision was not made for the consequences of setting aside hospital beds for potential air raid casualties. The focusing of hospital facilities on acute injury resulted in a crisis for the long-term sick and frail elderly, 140,000 of whom were discharged from hospital within two days of the declaration of war.[20] By 1940 urban air-raid shelters had come to harbour a large population of such people who had nowhere else to go. As a result government was for the first time obliged to take direct financial responsibility for the care of civilians, which it did by establishing hostels for the aged and infirm in requisitioned country houses. It was a care innovation that set a significant precedent for the postwar development of private nursing homes for the elderly.[21] These examples suggest that there was little cohesive, comprehensive or far-sighted strategic planning to meet known or anticipated problems of health in wartime before the outbreak of hostilities.

As with these issues of welfare and disease, so it was with that other significant health concern of war – food and nutrition. Despite the fact that it had long been recognised that the outcome of this war, as of the last, would depend critically on Britain's ability to maintain its food supply, and although plans had been under consideration since the mid-1930s, a reserve of essential foodstuffs had not been built up, and the Ministry of Food was set up only with the outbreak of war, on 8 September 1939.[22] A public opinion poll was then necessary to establish whether the nation would accept rationing, which was finally introduced in January 1940. By then imports of food and supplies had already been seriously reduced as the merchant fleet came under fire from German warships and submarines. Between October 1939 and June 1940, imports ran at a yearly average of 45.4 million tons, as against 55 million before 1939. In the first year of the war, the Ministry of Food operated on a bare margin of safety, the period of the 'phoney war' being essential for it to complete its organisation and to build reserves. In the opinion of one authority, starvation might have ended Britain's war effort before the first Christmas of the war had the Germans at the outset attacked the country on the scale that had been anticipated.[23]

Although introduced with belated formality, the rationing system was in fact based on the model of that adopted in the Great War.[24] Although nutrition experts such as Sir Jack Drummond quickly tried to claim a rational scientific basis for the system, and exalted their own contribution to this aspect of the war effort, it was not until the war was into its second year that science came to dominate policy within the Ministry of Food.[25] The system of rationing was in fact only partial, in that it applied to the protein foods (meat, bacon, cheese and fats), which were regarded as essential to health, and to the minor luxuries that enhanced the British way of life (tea, sugar and preserves). The allowances, which included a weekly pound of meat at the close of the war, were intended to provide no more than a third of total calorie intake: the remainder was to come from unrationed foods.

Experience in the early years of the war showed, however, that on this basis there developed a pattern of inexplicable local shortages and surpluses, so that towards the end of 1941 a points system was introduced to try to regulate the demand for a wide range of foods, tinned, dried and processed, such as sausages and breakfast cereals. Among the essential staple foods, bread and potatoes were never restricted, but milk and fresh eggs were. With the now inevitable eye to the future, nursing mothers, infants and schoolchildren were granted a special allowance of such nutritive items as milk and fruit juice. The uptake of these privileges was disappointing, but there is little evidence that the health of these groups suffered as a result.[26] Efforts were also made to improve the nutritional value of one or two basic foodstuffs according to the latest scientific criteria. Margarine, for example, was fortified with vitamins A and D in order to raise its nutritional value closer to that of butter.

Britain's wartime rationing programme was generally accepted by the public, whose grumbles seem to have fallen largely within the traditional British spectrum of acceptance. The national loaf, for example, was eaten even though its grey colour came in for adverse comment. In its aim of feeding the nation without compromising health, wartime food control has generally been adjudged successful, although whether the policy in fact contributed to making the nation healthier than ever before or since, as is now often claimed, is doubtful. The number of deaths from cancer, leukaemia, hepatitis, gastroenteritis, and coronary and arterial disease increased during the war, although that from cancer (excluding lung cancer) remained in line with what might be expected given the increasing number of people surviving to a susceptible age.[27] Jack Drummond, as specialist adviser to the Ministry of Food, was indeed determined to improve the nation's health through the food control programme, but while the equality of protein distribution brought by rationing probably did help to raise nutritional standards for the poorest classes, other factors were also at work, and by the close of war many people, especially women, were suffering from a continuing fatigue, which the more severe postwar rationing did not alleviate.[28]

An assessment of the success of rationing *per se* is further qualified by the development of catering networks that operated outside the rationing system. Communal feeding centres were initially established to supply the needs of those bombed out of their homes. Aiming to provide substantial meals at the lowest possible price and renamed, at Churchill's insistence, British Restaurants, they rapidly became an institution. By September 1943, 2,160 British Restaurants were serving some 630,000 meals daily.[29] Extra ration meals were also available to industrial and other workers through employer canteens, which became widespread in these years. A further complication in evaluating the rationing system lies in the government's efforts to stabilise wages by means of food subsidies. This strategy helped to hold the cost of living steady, and contributed to peaceful industrial relations and stable production in munitions and other important industries.[30] On balance, however, wartime food policies were successful but not outstandingly so, except in so far as real starvation was avoided and the country literally kept on its feet. The Chief

Medical Officer's assessment of the success of the rationing programme was certainly very modest: 'the nutritional state of the nation is, at least, not worse than it was at the beginning of the war'. Children, he admitted, seemed to have fared better.[31]

Changes in the origin, storage and preparation of foodstuffs as a result of wartime exigencies had some negative effects on health. In the effort to ensure that essential workers received an adequate diet, the Ministry of Food encouraged the establishment of works canteens and British Restaurants in cities and places where many small manufacturers were concentrated. The introduction of mass catering, together with the need to conserve food stocks and fuel, brought important changes to the technical aspects of the British diet. In these catering establishments, quantities of foods were, for example, prepared in advance and reheated, while even in the home, left-over foodstuffs began to be reused in further meals, practices that had been virtually unknown, at least in better-to-do households, before the war. The precooking and reheating of foods, and the increasing shortages of soap, clean towels and hot water, resulted in an increase in the number of episodes of dysentery and food poisoning, with reported cases rising markedly through the war years. The importing of new foods from abroad also had its dangers: imported dried egg from the United States, for example, was discovered to have introduced new and exotic strains of salmonella, and old people and small children had to be advised against eating reconstituted dried egg.

The MH did not remain unaware or inactive in the face of these new food hazards. As with other areas of public health concern, it stepped up its efforts at public health education. Compared with countries like America, British public education in health and hygiene had not developed very far in the years before the war.[32] It was only during the war that the MH began to deploy modern techniques of health education: 'the full orchestra of propaganda, press editorial and advertisements, radio, films, posters, leaflets and exhibitions... attuned to the older instruments of direct, personal education'.[33] As the Chief Medical Officer noted somewhat wryly, in wartime the admonition 'Keep yourself fit' had meaning; in peacetime the response too often was, 'Fit for what?' An important contribution to this intensified educational effort was made by Charles Hill, the 'Radio Doctor', whose fatherly broadcasts on medical issues of current concern won him a vast and regular following throughout the country. The Ministry also recognised the propaganda importance of the national media and made an effort to diffuse adverse health publicity. Well aware of the damaging power of the press when it came to health scares, the Chief Medical Officer began to court the media, arranging regular briefing sessions in an effort to curtail any alarmist rumours over outbreaks of infectious disease.

The MH's manipulation of the media on wartime health issues, and the widespread national awareness of the uses of propaganda that characterised the war effort, makes the balanced assessment of Britain's wartime health record a question of some delicacy. Most of the available historical documentation on the health experiences of the war comes from official sources, contemporary accounts or oral history sources, which, while they have their merits, also have their limitations; regional and local inequalities in health survived and persisted throughout the war, as Helen Jones has noted.[34] In the balance, however, Britain's people survived the war, and survived it relatively well. Once again, the underlying mortality trends remained undisturbed.

The Medical Services in Wartime

A radical reorganisation of the formal medical services was the inevitable companion to the extended intervention in social organisation that characterised the Second World War. Preparations for this reorganisation were advanced further in the years before the war by the need to provide for the armed services' requirements, and by the anticipation, based on the model of the Spanish Civil War, of an immediate major bombing campaign and subsequent disruption of personnel and facilities. Already in June 1938 an Emergency Medical Service (EMS) was established under the auspices of the MH, this being supplemented by an Air Raid Precautions Scheme following the Munich Crisis that September. The latter was intended to meet the needs of those injured and dispossessed by the bombing; the EMS itself had a much broader brief. It was to provide hospital beds for civilians and service personnel, casualty clearing facilities in areas vulnerable to attack and base hospitals outside them, and fully equipped specialist hospitals. In addition it was responsible for appointing consultant advisers to the Ministry itself, to the regional administration and to the hospitals, with a view to ensuring the effective delivery of services. The necessity of coping with both civilian air raid casualties and wounded service personnel at home meant that most hospitals were brought under the management of the regional civil defence administration.

At a basic level this reorganisation exposed the inadequacies of the country's fragmented, traditionalist hospital system and initiated a laborious process of modernisation to meet the medical needs of war. The development of specialist treatment facilities, inhibited by the generalist ethos of the interwar medical establishment, formed a part of this response; so too did the provision of a regional blood transfusion service and of a national Public Health Laboratory Service (PHLS). In these respects the potential ability of medicine to contribute to individual and community health was greatly extended by the war. Although the wartime priority was for acute and casualty services at the expense of the system as a whole, and despite initial difficulties in renovating and updating neglected hospital facilities, the Emergency Hospital Scheme (EHS), and the EMS in general, marked a breakthrough in both organisation and experience that was to be critical in accelerating plans for a national health service.[35]

Within this vast and complex system, front-line civilian defence was provided by the civil defence casualty service organised on a local basis. Manned First Aid Posts were established in areas thought vulnerable to air attack, while unmanned first aid points containing essential equipment were provided in rural and semi-rural areas. Those medical practitioners who remained unconscripted played a central part in the staffing and organisation of these services since they trained the volunteer staff essential to the successful running of the scheme, as well as providing medical cover at the First Aid Posts. Mobile paramedic units, rescue parties for air raid casualties, and ambulance services completed the local arrangements. The main responsibility of the First Aiders was to cope with the immediate aftermath of bombing: to deal with minor injuries and shock, and to provide shelter, comfort, warmth and nourishment to the victims of enemy bombardment. The rescue of those trapped in bombed buildings, the treatment of shock and the proper handling of the wounded were important contributions to civilian welfare, in the successful management of which medically trained staff, whether doctors or auxiliaries, were essential.

The two new medical bodies created under the EMS at the outbreak of war, the PHLS and the Blood Transfusion Service, were important supplementary components of civilian casualty care. The conviction of leading bacteriologists, such as W. W. C. Topley, that major problems of epidemic disease would result from bombardment and evacuation led to the establishment of a network of emergency laboratories, principally in the south of England, to provide diagnostic services, vaccines and immune sera to non-combatants.[36] (Blood serum contains gammaglobulin, which carries inherited and acquired immunity to infectious diseases. It can therefore be used therapeutically. Diphtheria antitoxin, for example, is carried in the serum.) Although disruption to the sewage systems and water supplies by bombing did not produce any serious outbreaks of disease during the war, the PHLS was reconstituted on a permanent basis after the war and has continued to play an important part in research into, and the monitoring of, human health in respect of micro-organisms.

Despite its relatively subdued wartime role, the creation of the PHLS was significant. Here, as in other aspects of the development of the wartime health service, medical men took an active advantage of the perceived needs of war to extend their specialist interests. Medical officers and microbiologists had for many years been anxious to achieve a more comprehensive provision of laboratory services for public health purposes, and the prospect of devastating bomb damage to urban areas provided the means of convincing government of the need for such an establishment.

The Blood Transfusion Service, in contrast, did prove an immediately important innovation in the context of war. Although blood transfusion had become the resuscitation method of choice for military surgeons during the Great War, the difficulty of organising and storing large quantities of blood had prevented the technique passing into regular hospital practice after 1918. With the outbreak of the Second World War, however, the MRC initiated the organisation of a proper service in London and sponsored research into improved handling and storage techniques. A network of regional transfusion centres was established in 1940 under the aegis of the EMS, and a formidably efficient service was rapidly put in place. Intended as an adjunct to the hospitals at home, the service also assisted the hard-pressed Army Blood Transfusion Service in times of emergency as, for example, on D-Day.

Before the war, blood transfusion had been virtually unknown outside London and some of the large provincial cities; by 1945 it had become an indispensable part of medical practice and was recognised as being of profound potential in many medical procedures. The critical technical and organisational innovation in this development was the institution of the blood bank, where supplies could be typed and stored until needed. Yet, as with the sulphonamides and the antibiotics, there were early indications that this new procedure was not risk-free, and that there were serious potential complications for patients, as well as wider consequences for society as a whole. It was not until late in the war that it was realised that the rising toll of hepatitis deaths was linked to transmission through infected blood and blood products: one of the bitter lessons of this wartime experience was that 'blood and blood products are highly dangerous materials', which ought only to be used under constant supervision by highly trained personnel.[37] The emphasis on highly trained, skilled personnel was characteristic of the many different medical facilities that found themselves raised to positions of national importance through the necessities of war, and it was to result in a new professionalism in many medical sectors in the years after 1945.

Under the EHS, some 3,000 hospital beds were provided for civilian casualties and for such personnel as the services could not accommodate. From a miscellaneous national collection of medical institutions, the EHS reorganised a selected thousand or so into front-line treatment centres having priority in the allocation of skilled staff and modern equipment. The policy of reserving beds in existing hospitals for EMS patients involved the displacement of long-stay, chronically sick patients, especially in the great cities where hospitals had already come to function as resident care units for the elderly and infirm whose families were no longer able or willing to cope with them. Through the efforts of the local authorities, many of these patients were transferred in the first months of the war to large hospitals in rural areas.[38]

The EMS bed allocation had been calculated on an estimate of 200,000 casualties a week, a total that was never even remotely approached at any stage in the war, and many of the reserved beds remained under-utilised. Although a large number of hospitals suffered more or less extensive bomb damage, few were destroyed outright, and bed shortage never became critical. In London 175 hospitals were damaged on 438 occasions – St Thomas' receiving no fewer than six direct hits – but in the city as a whole enough beds were always available.[39] This sufficiency was not accidental: the inner-city hospitals in areas thought vulnerable to bomb damage had been designated as casualty clearing stations, whose patients were transferred to the safer base hospitals and specialist units as soon as circumstances permitted.

The outstanding feature of the EHS lay in the emphasis placed on specialist services, which maximised the efficiency with which patients received appropriate treatment. There were 120 specialist centres in all; the needs of war had broken up the generalist consensus of interwar medicine, and the specialists came into their own. In the years after 1945, with escalating innovations in the technical and therapeutic capacity of medicine, specialisms developed and multiplied. The wartime centres were, in fact, indicative of the strength of specialisms to come. With their emphasis on the solution of particular problems in very specific areas of medicine, specialties were to grow in importance as changes in postwar society brought hitherto relatively rare problems into new prominence. Such postwar social changes as the overseas holiday in hot climates and the massive increase in car ownership increased the significance of specialties such as dermatology in the detection of skin cancers, and accident and emergency facilities.

The most important wartime centres in numerical terms were those for orthopaedic surgery and skin diseases (20 each), followed by those for neuroses (14), children's diseases (13), faciomaxillary injuries (12), head injuries (11), chest injuries (10), amputations (7), spinal injuries (4), peripheral nerve injuries (3), burns (3), rheumatism (2) and effort syndrome (1).[40] These centres apart, specialist consultants in medicine and surgery regularly visited the EMS hospitals with a view to spreading information on new techniques and encouraging research. The active promotion of modernising medicine was very much a part of the medical war effort as managed and directed by the consultants influential at the MH. Specialists were also called in to review existing conditions in the various institutions and to recommend improvements. Serious shortcomings were revealed in many, notably pathology, radiography and anaesthesia, and attempts were made to institute a general updating in both facilities and technology in hospitals under EMS control, for the benefit of both civilian and forces patients.

Many of the visiting specialists were shocked by the old-fashioned nature of the hospital facilities they came to inspect. Poverty, tradition and distance from the great teaching and research hospitals had left many provincial institutions with facilities that had changed little since they were founded in the Victorian period. In particular they often lacked pathology laboratories, even though pathology had become increasingly important to clinical practice in the twentieth century. Victorian pathology had concentrated on the study of abnormal changes in the body through post-mortem studies; since 1900 new techniques, such as the X-ray, had extended these studies into living tissue. By the 1940s tissue studies had become, in the modernised hospitals at least, an integral part of the assessment of a patient's disease process. Surveys undertaken early in the war revealed a dearth of pathology services countrywide, a comprehensive reorganisation being undertaken with a view to ensuring an adequate provision in all regions. The relocation of London consultants to provincial hospitals as a part of the emergency response also helped to spread new practices into the provinces. By 1945 clinical pathology had begun to establish itself in hospital practice across the country.[41]

Wartime surveys similarly showed up serious widespread deficiencies in the arrangements and equipment of the radiography and anaesthetic services, even though these were well-established components of hospital work by 1939. Shortcomings here were especially evident in the tuberculosis sanatoria and mental asylums that had been taken into the EHS, whose specialised nature had enabled them to develop apart from mainstream medicine. The upgrading of these institutions to meet the requirements of wartime medicine, and the general extension of such facilities in the EMS hospitals, resulted in a severe shortage of qualified personnel, and training courses were hastily instituted. Both radiography and anaesthetics expanded professionally as a direct result of these measures, becoming recognised specialties in their own right. Anaesthetic services, for example, had hitherto largely been provided part time by GPs, but they now rapidly evolved into a full-time specialist occupation. As one observer noted:

> It was officially recognised at long last that the administration of anaesthetics was a highly skilled occupation, that anaesthetists were indeed specialists, and that the skill and experience of the anaesthetist was in many instances far more important than the actual anaesthetic agent employed.[42]

The Second World War was in many ways more instrumental in establishing the relevance of the medical specialist than was its predecessor. Because so much of the treatment of war-wounded took place within the context of the 'civilian' hospital, the innovations and reorganisations resulting from wartime needs could be related much more directly to normal conditions. As the doctors who had experienced the medical organisation of war on the Western Front in 1914–18 brought back knowledge of new and more advanced techniques and technologies to their own surgeries, so in 1939–40 the consultants and specialists spread the standards and expectations of modern metropolitan medicine into provincial hospital culture. In so doing they prepared a basis for the expansion of modernising medicine through the hospital sector in the years after the war, notwithstanding the persistence of regional inequality and the continued dilapidation and under-equipment of much of the national hospital stock.

The Mending of Men

The social and cultural impact of the Second World War was far outstripped by that of its predecessor. In 1914–18 more than 700,000 men were killed on active service, in 1939–45, 264,000. Although roughly the same number of men served in both wars, the risk of death for fighting men in the Second World War was about a third to a half of that seen in the Great War, and the risk of injury was very much less: whereas 30 per cent of all servicemen were wounded at least once in the Great War, only 6 per cent suffered thus in the Second World War. In all, civilians included, the losses of the Second World War were about half those of the First.[43]

The conditions of this war showed that the science that can mend will always be outstripped by the science that can mar. Where tanks and aircraft had played a small part in the conflict of 1914–18, they played a central role in 1939–40. The shells and grenades that characterised the fighting on the Western Front were replaced by aerial bombs of infinitely greater capacity, while on the ground vehicles and long-range guns permitted new forms of extensive damage, and in the seas the submarine and torpedo made naval warfare greatly more hazardous than of old. The Royal Navy and the Air Force played a much greater part in the Second World War than in the Great War, and for the first time their casualties outnumbered those of the army.[44] Yet the servicemen who were blinded, maimed and disabled during the Second World War have not lingered in history as have the gassed and the disabled from the Great War. The virtual disappearance of the distinction between the home and fighting fronts spread the fortunes of war across whole societies, while the mechanisation of war, preceded by the rise in motor transport in civil society and followed by greatly increased mechanisation after 1945, helped to blur the distinction between the injuries of war and those of peace.

War, on the other hand, did concentrate the demand for medical skills as yet under-utilised in peace. The very different conditions and practices of 1939–45 favoured different specialties from those in demand during the Great War. The orthopaedic surgeons, for example, who had anticipated the resurgence of their specialty and another starring role as wartime medical heroes, did indeed contribute significantly to the rehabilitation of both service and civilian wounded, but found themselves quite displaced in popular esteem by the plastic surgeons.[45] The bulk of orthopaedic work in this war lay in the unexciting business of industrial sprains and fractures, and the popular heroes of the moment were the crews who fought the war in the air, and whose injuries too often consisted of the burns inevitably associated with petrol-driven means of transport. During this war the prospects for burns patients were transformed through the development of new methods of treatment.[46]

Plastic surgery was one of a number of specialties that had been quietly developing its expertise during the interwar years while working to maintain a specialist identity.[47] Cardiologists, thoracic surgeons and burns specialists all similarly found new calls on their expertise. Occupational therapy and physical medicine, which had barely retained their independent identities since 1918, re-emerged with new prominence in the context of the wartime emphasis on rehabilitation. The multiple and lacerated wounds complicated by foreign bodies, so characteristic of the weaponry of explosive shells, bombs, mortars, grenades and landmines, were inevitably present, but the simpler wounds caused by swords and hand guns had all but disappeared.

The advent of motorised transport brought a new range of emergencies. Tanks and aeroplanes, falling masonry, motor crashes and overturning vehicles resulted in an unprecedented number of casualties suffering crushes and crush wounds to tax the skill of the thoracic surgeons. The careless use of petrol in cooking and cleaning resulted in a great many more burns cases than even the vehicles of war provided.[48] Mechanisation also improved the efficiency with which the wounded were removed for treatment and increased their chances of survival. Accordingly, the various specialists were able to develop long-term restorative techniques to supplement emergency practice. But the chances of survival still hinged to a great extent on conditions in the immediate theatre of war: in conditions of great hardship, as in the fighting in Sicily in July and August 1943, the death and sickness rates among wounded significantly increased.[49]

From the beginning of the Second World War, too, psychiatry took its place as a key specialty in both the training of fighting men and the management of civilians. Because of the total nature of this war, fear and acute anxiety beset both soldiers and civilians.[50] Although the recruitment boards paid special attention to mental fitness, psychiatric disorders constituted by far the largest cause of discharge among military personnel: some 118,000 men and women were discharged from the services on psychiatric grounds between September 1939 and June 1944. In 1943 psychiatric disorders accounted for more than a third, and in 1945 for more than two-fifths, of army discharges on grounds of disease.[51] The picture for civilians is even less clear, despite the likelihood of psychiatric damage through experiences of evacuation, of constant bombing and of personal damage and loss in that bombing. Moreover, while the specialists working in hospitals within the EHS system were detailed to return forces personnel to active service as soon as possible, and generally offered forceful but supportive short-term treatment, civilian patients about whom there was no urgency were often subjected to experimental and potentially damaging therapies.[52] For such patients, and for the many service patients who were discharged for their conditions, the stresses of war had serious long-term consequences.

While both surgery and psychiatry had demonstrated their relevance to modern warfare in 1914–18, it was in the field of chemical pathology that medicine made its outstanding contribution to winning the Second World War. The discovery of the drug penicillin was perhaps the most important medical innovation of the war, whose significance far outstripped developments in surgery, rehabilitation and management. Although the relevant mould spore had been discovered by Alexander Fleming in 1927, the drug was only developed for clinical application by Howard Florey's research team at Oxford during the early months of the war. Penicillin's power of destroying wound infections, curing STD and relieving a range of life-threatening infections earned it the reputation of being a 'miracle drug', the ultimate magic bullet, overshadowing in the popular imagination the sulphonamide drugs that had preceded it. Penicillin was of enormous importance to the war effort partly because of its curative powers, especially in respect of war wounds and gonorrhoea, but also as a morale booster.[53] It was the first true antibiotic (a substance produced by one organism that destroys others) to be discovered, and has usually been seen as opening a new era in modern medicine in which the power of the doctor to cure reached previously undreamed of heights. As it filtered into civilian practice after 1945, penicillin helped to raise popular expectations of medicine's ability to cure dangerously high.

Although the research work demonstrating the curative potential of penicillin took place in wartime Oxford, the production of the new drug on a scale adequate to the needs of war was only achieved through the development of mass-production techniques in America.[54] American and Canadian medical aid was crucial in the maintenance and development of Britain's wartime medical effort, the production of penicillin being an extreme example of the problems of development and supply experienced by the country's medical services for the duration of the war. Items as diverse as ambulances, operating tables, modern steam sterilisers, aspirin tablets and syringes were channelled from North America through the Red Cross Societies and the Order of St John. America's Lend Lease Act of spring 1942, designed to ease acute shortages that threatened the efficient running of Britain's war effort, enabled British hospitals to acquire high-quality, modern equipment, which played a significant part in the endeavour to bring them up to date.[55]

Self-sufficiency was, however, also encouraged: throughout the country women's volunteer groups toiled in making nightgowns, bandages and other homely essentials for the hospitals, as well as in the knitting of socks, stockings, gloves, scarves and hats for the fighting forces. The distribution of medical supplies of all kinds was supervised by the MH, which decided between regional needs and organised the supply of such miscellaneous essentials as paraffin, insulin, liver extract and benzyl benzoate. Considerable ingenuity was often exercised in the effort to secure supplies. The country's attempt to produce enough liver extract and insulin, for example, resulted in the virtual disappearance of offal as a food resource because of its diversion for medical purposes. An important part in the overall procuring and organisation of essential supplies for the EMS and the fighting services was played by the Medical Supplies Branch of the London County Council, which had extensive prewar experience in supplying the city's municipal hospital network. Several remarkable innovations were achieved by the London County Council team, their resourcefulness being well illustrated by the production of artery forceps from the drop stampings supplied by a firm of London cutlers.[56] Over the whole period of the war, some 80 per cent of the MH's medical and surgical supplies were obtained through the London County Council.

Wartime medical enterprise was equally manifest in the national Reserve of Drugs and Vegetable Drugs Committee, which organised the production of agar-agar (the vegetable gelatin essential to several bacteriological and pharmacological processes), until then entirely supplied from Japan, from indigenous seaweeds. Members of the Women's Institutes, the Boy Scouts, the Girl Guides and the volunteer services were mobilised into collecting wild plants useful in drug production, such as foxglove leaves (for digitalis for heart conditions), belladonna (for atropine and hyoscyamine used with anaesthetics and for the relief of colic) and rose hips (for vitamin C). In the maintenance of the supply of essential drugs and medical equipment, ingenuity and a co-operative spirit can be seen to have featured in some aspects at least of Britain's civilian war effort.

Conclusion

The immense effort of organisation and endurance that Britain's people underwent during the years 1939–45 appears by the conventional measurement of mortality experience to have left them relatively unscathed. Despite the adverse experiences of the first two years of the war, medical observers were deeply impressed by the extent to which the general level of health and fitness had been sustained. Yet while the general level of health may have risen, especially among the poor, in part through the more equal distribution of crucial foodstuffs under the rationing system, it is not true to say, as is often said, that the nation's physical health was better under rationing than before or since. Britain survived the war, but it was a weary country in 1945, and the stricter rationing that followed in the first decade of peace, not finally lifted until 1954, only served to deepen that weariness.

Medicine contributed in many ways to Britain's war effort and to her survival of the war, from the organisation of emergency medical care, through the development of food strategy in the later years of the war, to the elaboration of new treatments for burns and crush injuries. The war saw the implementation of new medical technologies, such as the Blood Transfusion Service, and the application of recently discovered drugs on an extensive scale, but it also revealed the dangers and drawbacks associated with the introduction of new medical techniques and treatments – dangers that were to become of increasing concern with the explosion of new therapeutic drugs and practices that followed the return of peace. The Second World War was, in many respects, a specialists' war, in terms of both actual warfare and civil defence. The medical specialists played a significant part in maintaining the nation's health and fitness between 1939 and 1945, but they also took every opportunity to use that experience for political ends in furthering the interests of their own disciplines.

5

A Golden Age? 1945–2000

Introduction

The immediate postwar years saw a transformation in both the organisation of medical services and the competence of medicine to alleviate suffering and cure disease. At the heart of this 'therapeutic revolution' lay medicine's growing ability to relieve most patients of the minor ills that constitute a considerable part of the perception of 'health' and well-being. This was not just a British phenomenon. The immediate postwar years saw an acceleration of medical innovation in the developed world, especially in the United States, and the emergence of a culture in which new ideas and practices were swiftly diffused through medical and scientific communities. The success of the new NHS must be seen in the context of this therapeutic revolution, the continuing long-term decline of the old infectious diseases and the great social changes that followed on the war.

By 1960 the infectious diseases had virtually disappeared as a cause of death and of serious disablement. The plans for national regeneration formulated by Sir William Beveridge during the war years, which enshrined his conviction that 'the purpose of victory is to live in a better world than the old world', were being enacted even before the conflict was over. The 1944 Education Act delivered education free to all children between the ages of five and fifteen. The year 1945 saw the introduction of family allowances, and in that year government for the first time accepted the principle that every family should be able to live in a separate dwelling. Three million houses were built over the next decade, although, in the event, social change once again ensured that

139

demand continued to outstrip supply.[1] Once rationing was finally abandoned, in 1954, a much greater range and variety of food-stuffs and other consumer goods became available.

Social change, postwar prosperity and technological develop-ment transformed the daily routine of domestic life. By the late 1960s more than half of all British households owned a washing machine and a refrigerator, very nearly half owned a car, and nearly a quarter had central heating. By the early 1970s nearly every household owned a television; by 2000 a great many, not just among the wealthy, owned two or more. In the 1990s the house-hold computer and the arrival of the Internet were promising further transformations. These and other social changes brought rising expectations and a rising standard of living, as well as estab-lishing a much higher level of apparent health. They also led to a change in the way in which health care was delivered and in the public attitude towards orthodox medicine and its practitioners. For medicine the years 1945–80 were a period of innovation, excitement and the expectation of progress; in the last decades of the century, the rate of innovation slowed while public expecta-tions, and financial pressure, generated a more critical approach to the delivery and practice of medicine, which qualified much of the earlier optimism of the profession.

A National Health Service

The establishment of the NHS in 1948 in theory made medical care available to the whole population of Britain, free at the point of delivery. The intention behind the NHS was from the begin-ning to provide an adequate health service for all, but from the beginning it failed to meet this objective. Despite a very great contribution to the welfare of individual patients, local and regional disparities and inequalities, as well as more general prob-lems in the delivery of particular specialist services, remained. From the earliest days there was apparent a continuing tension between provision and financing that threatened to overwhelm the original ideals behind the service. Nor did the government's assumption of responsibility for the financing and organisation of basic medical services imply any significant capital investment in the reorganisation, updating and equalisation of services. The old voluntary, municipal and specialist hospitals were taken over as they stood; the GPs, employed on new contracts of capitation, remained in their old surgeries with their existing equipment. The concept of an adequate, integrated system that had animated the plans for the NHS was in practice implemented on a take-over basis negotiated to accommodate various existing interests, notably those of the hospital consultants. From the moment it began operation, on 5 July 1948, the NHS was entangled in the difficulty of matching reality to the ideals of politicians, medical practitioners and patients.[2]

The new service was divided into three distinct component parts: the hospitals, managed by regional hospital boards (except for the teaching hospitals, which retained their local independence); primary care, as provided by GPs and dentists, who retained considerable independence in the management of their practices; and the auxiliary services, such as ambulances, maternal and infant welfare, and home helps, which were left in the hands of the local authorities. Besides being inimical to the concept of an integrated service, the division made for problems of communication between the three different sectors, as well as for local disparity in the nature and quality of services offered.

The principal innovation of the new system was the state-owned and state-funded hospital sector.[3] As the wartime surveys had revealed, a great many of the provincial hospitals in particular were woefully dilapidated and old fashioned, both in their equipment and facilities, and in the range and type of services they offered. The distribution of the very hospitals themselves was uneven, still on the pattern established by eighteenth- and nineteenth-century philanthropic and municipal initiatives, reinforced by the financial realities of the country's regional economies. London, for example, was notoriously well provided with hospitals. The south of England and the Midlands were moderately well endowed, but in the north, east and west, especially in East Anglia and Wales, hospitals were mostly to be found in the cities, and the smaller towns and country areas were poorly served.

It was also often the case that institutions established many decades previously with no thought for meeting general demand had not attempted to accommodate increased local populations, while hospital building, as a philanthropic and municipal activity, had vanished with changing economic and cultural conditions. Nor were the financial circumstances of postwar governments favourable to major capital investment in hospital-building. It was not until the 1960s that government began to implement plans to modernise the hospitals, or to take steps to achieve a greater equality of provision between regions.[4] The 1962 Hospital Plan envisaged a national network of District General Hospitals, which was to involve the building of ninety new hospitals, and the rebuilding of 134 more, over the next ten years. It was an over-ambitious programme in view of the financial problems encountered by local authorities involved in the undertaking, but some headway had been made before the oil crisis of 1973 again placed a large question mark over major demands for government capital investment and, more insidiously, over the energy costs incurred in the running of modern, open-plan hospitals.

In the primary care sector, too, the NHS inherited an uneven distribution of GPs nationwide, with a wide range of competencies and facilities among them. In the early 1950s it was estimated that 34 per cent of GPs were working from inadequate premises, and that about a quarter of all GPs were themselves unsatisfactory.[5] For many practitioners, who had often had little opportunity to keep up with such developments as there had been in general medicine since they left medical school, practice consisted largely of handing out sickness certificates and prescriptions for unspecific medicines. The new availability of free care meant a rising demand for attention from a number of patients, putting family doctors under pressure. Surgery waiting times lengthened, and consultations were often reduced to a couple of minutes. Like the hospital sector, the GP service was in need of systematisation and modernisation. In 1952, however, the establishment of the Royal College of General Practitioners fulfilled a long-held practitioner ambition and heralded changes in medical education and in the organisation of practices, which conferred a new professional confidence and standing.[6]

The therapeutic revolution, meanwhile, contributed significantly to the doctors' confidence by giving them unprecedented means to alleviate and to cure, and a rising real income, especially after the negotiation of a new deal on GP pay in 1956, enhanced their sense of standing within the wider community. The concept of the family doctor, entrenched in the GPs' image of themselves and in the popular imagination, for a century, perhaps reached its apogee in these years, even while waiting and consultation times remained problematic. Many patients received a sub-standard service, and confidence at times turned to arrogance. Patients had been trained to possess a low expectation of their practitioners, but as general educational standards rose, and as the popular expectation of the capabilities of medicine itself changed under the impact of the therapeutic revolution, so standards of general practice became increasingly criticised. Charles Webster has noted this as the paradox of modern general practice, that on the one hand it is lauded as 'economical, humane and versatile', but that on the other it offers 'an inferior quality of service, delivered by practitioners of limited competence, whose deficiencies are disguised by the availability of hospital referral'.[7]

It was, nonetheless, through GP surgeries, and through the dentists and opticians associated with family doctors in the primary care sector, that the real benefits of the NHS and the therapeutic revolution reached ordinary people and improved the quality of their lives. For women in particular, for so many of whom conditions such as varicose veins and prolapsed wombs, untreated through poverty, had made life a misery, the service proved a special boon; among children minor ailments, such as ear infections, began to be treated before they did lasting damage; and for the elderly problems of eyesight and hearing became remediable, while new drug treatments offered relief from rheumatism and arthritis.

In the early years of the NHS, there was an enormous demand for false teeth and spectacles: in 1949–51, 7.5 million pairs of spectacles were supplied in England and Wales alone, and in 1950–51, 65.6 million artificial teeth.[8] The alarming cost of these services led to the introduction of charges to help to cover the material costs of frames and dentures in 1951. Patient demand, together with the new availability of effective drugs, had, meanwhile, sent the cost of GP-prescribed drugs soaring: between 1949 and 1953 the cost of pharmaceutical services rose from £35 to £53 million.[9] As a result the 1/- prescription charge was levied from 1952, although with exemption for a significant range of social groups, including children, pregnant women and old age pensioners. There is little evidence that the new charge deterred demand from either patients or doctors, and the cost of supplying drugs under the NHS continued to rise exponentially.[10]

The structure of medical provision under the NHS was organised to meet the general needs of the ordinary population rather than special needs of those for whom general provision was not sufficient. Shortcomings in health provision under the NHS can be argued for almost all social groups, but after 1950 they became increasingly evident in respect of particular minority groups, notably the elderly and the mentally ill, and the ethnic minorities, who entered Britain in increasing number from the 1960s.[11] Even before the advent of the NHS, the elderly were becoming a problem population for local government health services. Increasingly, small modern families with no more than two or three children, with a rising standard of living and rising expectations of quality of life, were reluctant to undertake the care of elderly relatives in their homes. Medical services for the elderly were generally depressing, and frequently inadequate, and between 1929 and 1948 an increasing number of frail elderly people spent the latter end of their lives in municipal hospitals. In the immediate aftermath of the war, this problem became increasingly acute as a result of the housing shortage. By 1948 local MOHs were worried about the prospects for these patients under the NHS, when hospital admissions policies would no longer be controlled by local interests and seemed likely to become more exclusively medical.[12]

Worries about the care of frail elderly people were compounded by demographic factors: the number of people aged over 65 had been rising steadily in Britain since 1900. At the turn of the century, 5 per cent of the population were aged over 65, by 1951 11 per cent. In 1991 the proportion reached 16 per cent, of whom more than a quarter were aged over 80. Yet the new health service failed to engage with this growing problem, and the prospect for action was disproportionately affected by the general financial stringency that engulfed the NHS.[13]

Two developments in social and medical thinking meanwhile offered a new possibility for resolving some of the problems surrounding the care of the elderly. The first was the concept of community care, which had evolved between the wars as a desirable way of looking after vulnerable social groups, through the provision of residential homes, short-stay accommodation and domiciliary after-care and support systems. The second was the new medical specialty of geriatrics, which emerged in the 1950s.[14] Both offered the means of improving health and health care for many elderly persons, since it soon became apparent that specialist attention was often the key to resolving individual problems. More than sixty specialist geriatric units were established during the 1950s, but the rising population of elderly people, combined with the special needs of many of them meant that the cost of making such services in any degree widely available remained prohibitive. In the 1980s, however, the introduction of social security vouchers for residential care of the elderly led to a rapid expansion in the number of private residential homes, where elderly people could receive state-supported special care.[15]

Similar problems over funding and integration within the formal structure of provision arose over the care of the mentally ill. The Victorians had regularised the care of the mentally ill on an institutional basis, with the asylum and the specialist 'mad doctor', and institutionalisation had become the accepted method of dealing with this particular social problem. By 1948 there were some 200,000 patients in private and public mental institutions, with a further 150,000 thought to be receiving care of some kind within the community.[16] At this period, when there seemed little hope of discovering effective treatment for mental illness, these special hospitals, like their general counterparts, were old-fashioned, over-stretched and under-funded, often suffering a serious shortage of nursing staff. In 1948 they were designated the responsibility of the Regional Hospital Boards, thus in theory being brought into a closer relationship with the general health services.

Integration into the NHS did not, however, bring improved conditions to the mental hospitals, which remained spartan, inhospitable and subject to periodic scandal and investigation. The health and welfare of patients maintained under their regime was constantly open to question, yet social and financial pressure ensured that the institutions survived, and without significant remedial action. The concept of community care began to be extended to the mentally ill following the recommendations of the Royal Commission on Mental Illness of 1957, initially being envisaged to be provided by local community services under local authority supervision.[17] As with the care of the elderly, many of whom had found their way into mental institutions before 1948, the implementation of such a programme was gradually subverted by financial considerations: by the 1980s community care had essentially been redefined to mean care provided by family and neighbours, supported by the health services.[18] It was a redefinition facilitated by the availability of increasingly effective drug therapy, but by the 1990s it had become clear, following several tragic murders committed by mental patients released into the community, that clinical judgement continued to be an indispensible adjunct to the successful implementation of community care for the mentally ill.

In the effort to keep the overall cost of the health services within bounds, central government generally sought to delegate 'peripheral' health concerns – those which lay beyond conventional hospital medicine and which could not be adequately catered for by GPs – to local authorities, whose spending did not impinge on general taxation. 'Special needs' cases, for example, whether of individuals or social groups, fell into this category. Local authorities, however, also had budgets, and became increasingly subjected to central control in the effort to keep down the overall level of taxation: at local level there has been little spare money to develop specialised health care services.

When in the 1960s immigrants from Britain's former colonial possessions began to arrive in large numbers from the Caribbean, former African dependencies and the Indian sub-continent, it fell to the local authorities to cater for their medical problems. Often beginning their new lives in poor material conditions and frequently, especially for women, with little or no spoken English, these minority groups manifested patterns of health and illness different from those of the indigenous population and often from each other. They presented special problems of health provision and education as they adjusted to their new environments. Rickets, for example, re-emerged as a problem among Asian children in the northern counties in the 1970s, while the IMR of the immigrant communities remained twice as high as that of the rest of the population into the 1990s.[19] By 1991 minority groups constituted some 6 per cent of the population, but their special health needs were far from receiving consistent professional attention.

The implementation of the NHS therefore by no means resolved the problem of delivering adequate health care to Britain's people, although it did offer a considerable improvement over the combination of private and insurance medicine that had preceded it. How far the NHS in fact contributed to improving the country's health by accelerating the downward trend of mortality and reducing morbidity is a large question. The medical services offered under the 1948 Act were pre-eminently providers of treatment for existing illness rather than agents for preventing its development.

Between 1936–40 and 1976–80, the classic years of the implementation of the health service and of the therapeutic revolution, the average death-rate per thousand population fell from 12.5 to just under 12, a decline achieved through a slight fall in male mortality, the death-rate for women remaining steady at around 11.6 per thousand.[20] By the 1990s comparative international mortality statistics showed Britain to be lagging behind other developed countries in key health indicators such as infant mortality and heart disease, while comparative local death-rates revealed that the outcome of medical treatment offered for, for example, breast cancer varied significantly depending on the local presence of specialist facilities. The provision of free medical services was not, apparently, a critical factor in achieving a measurable improvement in the nation's health, nor did it encompass equality of provision between regions and social groups.

Beyond the NHS: Government Health Policies and Preventive Medicine

The concerns, techniques and organisation of public health and preventive medicine changed significantly in the twentieth century. As the major infectious diseases retreated, and as, in the interwar period, local authorities became involved in the delivery of hospital and welfare services, so the emphasis on disease prevention decreased.[21] In the 1950s, however, a new type of preventive ethos emerged with the development of the new medical specialty of statistical epidemiology in both England and America.[22] By studying long-term trends in mortality statistics using new methodologies such as the prospective study of mortality rates for particular medical conditions within a selected population, epidemiologists were able to reach startling and novel conclusions about the causative factors involved in various diseases. (Such techniques are currently used to excess, often in population samples too small to offer a sound conclusion.)

The first such study to make an impact on public health thinking was published in 1950, coincidently at much the same time as an American study reaching a similar conclusion. The English study had been commissioned by the MRC, who had become concerned by the rising level of lung cancer among British men. Various causative factors, including atmospheric pollution, had been proposed, but the investigations of Sir Austin Bradford Hill and Richard (later Sir Richard) Doll demonstrated conclusively that the rising mortality from this particular cancer was linked to cigarette smoking.[23]

This was the beginning of a curious relationship between the science of epidemiology, government health policies and informal methods of health education, epidemiology providing information on which policies for the improvement of national health could be based, and government generally failing to take effective action. Successive governments proved reluctant to intervene directly where medicine demonstrated the risks or benefits of particular types of environmental action or social behaviour. In various disputed areas, where centrally directed action for prevention was a possibility – cigarette smoking, clean air, alcohol consumption, the fluoridation of water supplies and the national diet – financial and political considerations, vested interests and vocal pressure groups, and issues of personal freedom and administrative practicality proved more influential than considerations of health and mortality. In these postwar years health education, most often through reports in the popular press and admonitions to the individual to take responsibility for his or her own health, replaced intervention as the standard political strategies for the promotion of preventive medicine. The proliferation of health-related pressure groups was one indication of a deepening public interest in issues of health and medicine.

The power of economic interests to influence health policy was demonstrated by one exception to the general inertia during the 1950s. Air pollution had been a significant environmental problem in Britain since at least Victorian times, being almost as obtrusive in the 1940s and 50s as it had been when Charles Dickens described the London particular in graphic detail.[24] By the 1870s heavy fogs were known to cause a sharp rise in the death-rate from respiratory disease, but Victorian attempts to curb air pollution resulted, in the words of Anthony Wohl, in little more than turning Britain's skies from gritty black to dull grey.

The 'massive discomfort' from smarting eyes, foul smells and closed windows, which Wohl assessed as possibly the greatest health consequence of air pollution, lingered well into the twentieth century.[25] In the 1920s it was calculated that 2.5 million tons of soot escaped into the atmosphere every year from domestic fires alone, and the yearly deposit of soot in urban areas could be as high as 650 tons per square mile.[26] Disastrous fogs continued to occur in London and elsewhere during the earlier twentieth century. In December 1952 London again fell victim to a five-day fog 'of catastrophic proportions', as a direct result of which some 4,000 people died. Persistent agitation by the National Smoke Abatement Society, public health men and the media followed, the Clean Air Act, which introduced smokeless zones and the control of domestic smoke emission, eventually being passed in 1956. Public pressure was, however, significantly underpinned by economic incentive: the productivity of the British coal industry had begun to decline in 1952, and political concern to conserve the national coal supply and the jobs of coal miners undoubtedly eased the path towards legislation.[27]

If the effect of public pressure for cleaner air was perhaps not quite as influential as it might have appeared, the negative power of the pressure group was, in contrast, clearly demonstrated by the history of attempts to introduce the fluoridation of the water supply between the mid-1950s and the early 1980s. The effectiveness of fluoride in the water supply as a preventive factor in tooth decay had first been noted in the United States in the 1930s.[28] Although scientific studies confirmed the benefit of the procedure as an inexpensive measure that promised a major saving on dental treatment (the cost of which was running at about £40 million a year in 1955), legal ambiguities and vociferous opposition by local pressure groups, notably in Conservative constituencies, deterred most health authorities from implementing the measure until government eventually regularised the legal situation with the Water (Fluoridisation) Act 1985.[29]

Perhaps the clearest illustration of the negative influence of vested financial and political interests on government action on health issues lies in the case of smoking and tobacco. Hill and Doll, and the American researchers E. L. Wynder and E. A. Graham, published their first sets of independent results linking cigarette smoking and lung cancer in 1950. The epidemiological evidence of the link was widely accepted within the medical community, but, despite rising pressure from the profession, entrenched economic interests and political anxieties surrounding intervention with regard to an established popular habit served both to delay and to minimise government action. Cigarette smoking had become ubiquitous since the Great War, being vigorously promoted by advertisers as a liberated and sophisticated activity. The many and various interests involved in the consumption of tobacco inhibited government action. Cigarette advertising on television was not banned until February 1965, health warnings were added to advertising and cigarette packets only in 1971, and health education on the perils of smoking was delegated to the local authorities.

Meanwhile, the death-rate from lung cancer among men continued to rise inexorably until 1973, reaching at its peak a total of 26,000 deaths a year, and the death-rate among women also began to rise.[30] This was by any account a major epidemic of a chronic disease causing distressing and expensive illness and premature death: cigarette-related deaths, which also include many arising from coronary heart disease, were estimated to be costing the NHS £165 million a year in the mid-1980s. Behind the government's dilatory performance on public information and prevention, however, lay an annual revenue from tobacco tax of

£4 billion, thousands of jobs in associated industries, a healthy balance of payments, and important economic investment and political goodwill in developing countries where tobacco was grown.[31] Substantive efforts at education were finally initiated in the 1970s following the formation in 1971 of the pressure group Action on Smoking and Health, these becoming by the 1980s increasingly, if partially, effective. Publicity for the effects of passive smoking added weight to the argument, and during the 1980s smoking in public places, offices, educational establishments, public transport and so on gradually became unacceptable to non-smokers. The death-rate from smoking-related diseases began to decline among men, although it continued to rise among women into the 1990s.[32] At the turn of the century, however, government was still delaying the implementation of a full advertising ban on tobacco products.

Similar economic and political interests underpinned government inertia on other issues in which the health benefit was less clear cut, but in which health activists thought action desirable, such as alcohol consumption, the airborne lead level, food additives, pesticides and the encouragement of healthy eating. In all these areas, powerful economic interests, including commercial and government revenues, were in operation, as were such voter-sensitive issues as employment, the cost of living and personal liberty. Action proved easier to achieve where health issues could be related to the welfare of the wider environment, and where the area in question did not directly touch on individual choice. The regulation of pesticide composition, the introduction of lead-free petrol and the labelling of foodstuffs to indicate their content and additives had all been achieved by 1990. The question of inducing 'desired behaviour' with regard to the individual choice of food and drink proved more difficult, especially where government was reluctant to interfere with powerful and lucrative vested interests. Attempts originating with the medical profession from the later 1960s onwards to alert people to the danger of excess alcohol consumption, and to change the rising national trend of increased consumption, made little headway in a context in which government was not prepared to act.[33]

Popular taste in food also proved somewhat intransigent in the face of medically endorsed efforts to improve public health by improving the national diet. By the mid-1970s epidemiologists studying the causation of heart disease had concluded that the Western diet, with its heavy emphasis on saturated fat and sugar, together with smoking habit and a lack of exercise, was responsible for the continuing high level of heart disease. In 1976 the Department of Health and Social Security published the report *Prevention and Health: Everybody's Business,* which marked renewed government interest in the national diet and publicised the new medical thinking on heart disease.

Government, however, remained committed to the indirect route of health education as the means of achieving the desired end. This was to some extent effective: the 1980s saw an explosion of media interest in 'healthy eating', people began to eat less sugar, and there was a decline in the consumption of saturated fats such as butter and lard (although the overall level of fat consumption did not change). In general, however, food preferences were slow to change. Despite strenuous promotion by government and health professionals in the 1990s, health education initiatives designed to encourage the eating of less fat and more fruit and vegetables faltered over the obstacle of decided consumer preference. Although women, for example, showed themselves susceptible to dietary advice, they gave priority to family preferences in the food they bought and the meals they prepared.[34]

The Therapeutic Revolution

The second half of the twentieth century was, for Britain as for other developed countries, a period in which medicine appeared to have achieved an astonishing victory over the ancient scourges of infection, and to be making equally astonishing strides towards the alleviation of a great many other pathological conditions. The virtual disappearance in the 1960s of death from the common infectious diseases such as measles, diphtheria and whooping cough produced a general confidence that lethal infections were a thing of the past. This confidence survived the 1970s, to be rudely shaken, for a time at least, by the emergence of the human immunodeficiency (HIV) viruses and acquired immune deficiency syndrome (AIDS) in the early 1980s. The failure of HIV to spread as rapidly in the West as had initially been feared restored a measure of that previous confidence, however groundlessly, to the general public, although medical scientists and health organisations throughout the world continued to worry about HIV and also the possible global spread of other emerging infections such as the Marburg and Ebola viruses.[35] The period 1945–2000 effectively divides in 1980, with the realisation that new problems will always occur in medicine, and with a recognition that, despite years of research, there had been little real advance in prospects for patients with many serious diseases, most notably cancer, but also other conditions less frequently seen, such as muscular dystrophy, multiple sclerosis, Parkinson's disease and Alzheimer's disease.

Between 1945 and 1980, however, modern scientific biomedicine appeared to have come into its own. The horizons of therapy were greatly extended for general medicine and psychiatry by new drug treatment, and for surgery by developments in antibiotics, anaesthesia, immunology and technology. Medical research made possible revolutionary breakthroughs in the regulation of fertility and the management of the biological consequences of femininity, with far-reaching implications for individual women. The apparent miracle of two particular therapeutic innovations, the antibiotic and steroid drugs, which in Britain were delivered to the general population through the agency of the NHS, and which helped to alleviate a great range of acute and chronic conditions, contributed substantially to the perception of dramatic medical progress and a notable improvement in health in these years.

Yet the impact of the therapeutic revolution on health was variable, and medical observers in the 1990s were reticent about the extent of the improvement in general health since 1945.[36] Modern morbidity surveys repeatedly demonstrate a significant presence of 'ill-health', mortality statistics suggesting essentially the same story.[37] The substantial improvements in death-rate and life expectancy achieved in the first half of the twentieth century were not sustained at the same rate after 1945. The standardised death-rate fell from 16 to 12.5 per thousand between 1900 and 1936–40, but only fractionally after that.[38] Against this statistical pattern stands that of a radical alteration in the nature of life-threatening disease: death from infectious disease constituted 25 per cent of all deaths in 1900 but less than 1 per cent by 1990.

The apparent stagnation in the health level recorded in the statistics and the surveys suggests both the inevitability of occurrence of much minor illness and the inevitability of the diseases of ageing, and the importance, as well as the mutability, of individual perceptions of health. As with the provision of medical services under the NHS, the enormous extension in the competence of modern medicine to alleviate and cure has laid bare only the continuing nature of ill-health, both real and perceived. This does not mean that the new competence of medicine has not altered the experience and nature of ill-health, or that it has not achieved some notable successes over some of the health-related causes of human misery. The so-called therapeutic revolution was a very real one, beginning with the discovery of penicillin and continuing through a range of distinctive innovations that greatly extended the range of both medicine and surgery.

The discovery of penicillin, which was released for civilian use in Britain in 1945, marked the beginning of a new era of pharmaceutical research in which international drug companies competed in an extensive search among natural and chemical compounds for new drugs of use against disease. Penicillin was quickly followed by other antibiotics, such as streptomycin, the first drug effective against tuberculosis, and rapidly came to include whole new groups of drugs, such as the broad-spectrum antibiotics and cephalosporins.[39] The chemical structure of penicillin itself was established by Dorothy Hodgkin in 1945, and this led to the development of synthetic penicillins, many elaborated with a view to specific medical problems. While these drugs had an important impact on a number of serious infectious diseases, such as puerperal fever and bacterial meningitis, and led to the disappearance of such minor infectious inconveniences as impetigo, they were also important in the achievement of such major surgical innovations such as organ transplantation and heart surgery, and in the treatment of burns.[40]

As with the sulphonamides, however, it was not long before drug resistance became a problem. The first penicillin-resistant strain of *staphylococcus aureus* (the most common cause of wound infections) was identified in 1942, and the first signs of resistance to streptomycin were noted in 1946. By 1948 nearly 60 per cent of the staphylococci isolated at Hammersmith Hospital in London were penicillin resistant. After about 1950 the drug companies were engaged in a continuous struggle to maintain the crucial centrality of antibiotics in modern medical practice against the rapid evolution of drug-resistant bacteria. The problems of resistance were compounded by the tendency first of doctors to prescribe, and later of patients to demand, the prescription of antibiotics for a whole range of conditions against which they are useless (the common cold being the most notorious example), and by the extensive use of these drugs to support intensive modern industrial farming of animals for food. By the 1990s many scientists were predicting imminent defeat for the pharmaceutical effort to stay ahead of drug resistance.[41]

In the 1940s, however, the arrival of the antibiotics laid the foundations of confidence in the powers of modern medicine. Nonetheless, it was by no means clear in late 1940s and early 1950s that any kind of watershed in the history of the infectious diseases had been reached. Poliomyelitis is a disease that has almost been forgotten in Britain except by its survivors, but in the immediate postwar years it appeared as the most significant epidemic threat seen since the beginning of the century.[42] Although the disease had caused repeated epidemics in America and Scandinavia since around 1900, the first serious outbreak occurred in Britain in the autumn of 1947. Further outbreaks followed in 1950, 1952 and 1957.

In the early 1950s polio looked like the new infectious scourge of the later twentieth century. The Americans had been working fruitlessly at the problem since 1910, but it was only in 1953 that Jonas Salk finally developed the first vaccine against the disease. Countered finally in the midst of the upsurge in new treatments and vaccines that followed the Second War, the experience of polio did little to dent the developing confidence of the new medicine. The polio vaccine joined those against diphtheria, tetanus, whooping cough, and the later additions of rubella, measles, mumps and eventually chicken pox, in what became a comprehensive protective package against the major childhood infections. In the 1960s the cycle of infection experienced by generations of children in the past, and with it the attendant miseries of fever and the possibility of damaging complications, was broken by mass immunisation programmes. While new generations of parents subsequently proved susceptible to scares about the effects of these different vaccines, the overall contribution of childhood immunisation to safeguard the short- and longer-term health of children and the adults they became should not be underestimated.

The second great pharmacological discovery of the 1940s, the almost accidental realisation of the therapeutic powers of the naturally occurring hormone cortisone (a steroid), came about as a result of the interwar interest in hormonal deficiency. Elucidated by Philip Hench and Edward Kendall at the Mayo Clinic in New York State, cortisone was initially heralded as a miracle cure for rheumatoid arthritis. It quickly became apparent that the drug provoked such severe side effects that it was almost unusable in the treatment of arthritis, although it had its uses in stimulating pharmaceutical interest in developing more satisfactory treatments for that widespread, painful and demoralising condition.[43] There was, however, an unexpected corollary. Medical researchers and practitioners in the immediate postwar years continued to experiment widely with new drugs, and were willing to try out pharmaceutical innovations against a wide range of different conditions in the hope of extending their application.

At almost the same time as the rheumatologists reluctantly abandoned the use of cortisone, experimental applications revealed its usefulness against a wide range of other conditions from allergy (used externally and in small doses) to meningitis and multiple sclerosis. Within a short time the steroid group of drugs, to which cortisone belonged, had acquired a central role in modern therapeutics, and transformed the prospects for treatment of a whole range of conditions within the medical specialties of rheumatology, opthalmology, gastroenterology, dermatology and renal and respiratory medicine. By the 1990s more than eighty separate disorders were known to be responsive to steroid therapy.[44] Far less hyped than the discovery of the antibiotics, the steroids were at least as important in extending the competence of modern medicine and enabling patients with a range of chronic conditions to live a more comfortable life.

The great transformation in the power of modern medicine with respect to physical illness was also extended into the underworld of mental illness by this postwar surge in pharmacological research. Once again the initial breakthrough occurred in an almost accidental fashion, to be picked up and developed by the international drug companies on a commercial basis.

Progress in the treatment of mental illness had been slow in the years since the Great War. The adoption of techniques of Freudian psychoanalysis after 1918, although useful for patients depressed and unsettled by events in their own lives, offered little prospect of cure to those suffering extreme psychiatric illness. For the latter the outlook remained dreary: psychoanalysis for the well-to-do (in an era of private medicine, such treatment being expensive) and confinement for the poor. As the number confined in mental hospitals continued to swell in the 1920s and 30s, asylum doctors experimented with a number of dramatic and unpleasant treatments in the search for a measure of therapeutic success. Such treatments included the use of insulin to obtain a deep coma, barbiturate-induced deep sleep, electro-convulsive therapy, and psychosurgical techniques such as lobotomy and leucotomy.[45] These treatments did not always secure patients any significant improvement in their condition, and the nature of many were such as to induce further acute mental and physical misery. They remain controversial to this day.

In the early 1920s research into the chemistry of the brain resulted in the isolation of the first neurotransmitter, the chemical acetylcholine, which mediates the transmission of nerve impulses. This discovery turned the attention of psychiatrists to the potential of pharmaceutical intervention, and widespread experimentation with drug treatment for mental illness followed, with little initial success. In fact the breakthrough to reach drugs that influenced the chemistry of the brain occurred only after the Second World War, and was as fortuitous as the other major breakthroughs for innovative drug therapies had been.

A French naval surgeon, Henri Laborit, had been studying the treatment of shock using the antihistamine promethiazine. He noted that the administration of the drug produced a 'euphoric quietude' in his patients, and persuaded psychiatric colleagues at the Val-de-Grâce military hospital that it might be worth trying in the management of restless psychiatric cases. Over a period of weeks, the drug worked a spectacular improvement in the condition of a manic patient. Follow-up research under the auspices of the drug company Rhône-Poulenc resulted in the discovery of chlorpromazine, a drug with a dramatic effect on hitherto incurable schizophrenic patients.[46] It was a discovery that opened the way for the mass screening of chemical compounds characteristic of drug companies anxious to improve their profit, and led to the production of a range of drugs suitable for use across the whole spectrum of psychiatric illness. It was a development that significantly underpinned the British movement towards implementing community care schemes for the mentally ill after 1970.

The appearance of drugs for use in psychiatric medicine had an effect that reached far beyond the walls of the mental hospitals. In particular, the introduction of tranquillisers in the 1950s opened up a whole new dimension of popular, patient-driven illness as the threshold of tolerance towards stress and sadness plummeted with the prospect of instant relief in a tablet.[47] Valium, first marketed in 1963, became the single most successful drug in pharmaceutical history until it was in the 1990s supplanted by Prozac, thought to be effective for mood disorders in general and depression in particular. While the new psychopharmacology undoubtedly offered real relief to many thousands of people who suffered from many problems of sadness and desperation, there is little doubt that it also vastly increased the number of people more or less dependent on medication who considered themselves to be, in one sense or another, unwell or at least not attaining a 'normal' degree of mental well-being.

The major innovations in medical treatment represented by the antibiotics, steroids and psychiatric drugs was complemented by a great extension in the number and effectiveness of other drug treatments in the years after 1950. Hypertension, asthma, peptic ulcers and Parkinson's disease were among the many conditions for which new and more effective treatments were found.[48] The growth in therapeutic competence initiated by the drug revolution in medicine was paralleled by a similar expansion in the surgeon's ability to correct, reconstruct and repair the body. In 1939 it had been thought that surgery had reached the limits of the possible, but the introduction of the antibiotics, of new anaesthetics and of the immunosuppressive drugs, together with technical innovations such as renal dialysis and the heart–lung machine, allowed surgeons to develop expertise in types of operation that had previously existed in the realms of fantasy.

Classic examples of such new operations include organ transplantation and open heart surgery. By the 1990s these had become commonplace, but the path by which these operations achieved the routine was far from smooth. For both patients and their families, as well as for the surgeons, there were many tragedies in the early stages of their elaboration. Open heart procedures were initially developed by paediatric surgeons, who were faced with the immediate family tragedy of babies born with congenital heart defects. Because the life expectation of so many of these infants was very limited, and because their hearts were so small, it was both ethically and technically easier to practise experimental surgery on them than on adult heart patients. The critical breakthrough to routine success came with the development of an effective heart–lung machine, which supported the patient's breathing and blood flow during the operation. By the 1960s surgeons were able to repair all operable heart defects in children. In the 1970s they moved on to explore the possibilities of replacing diseased heart valves in adults. The medical challenge that this development presented should not be underestimated – James Le Fanu has called these operations 'staggeringly difficult' – but by the 1990s the heart bypass operation had become a routine slot in the surgeon's diary.[49]

Medical concern at the pitiful wastage of young lives was also central to the development of organ transplantation. As with blood transfusion, organ transplant had been attempted in animals without success by a number of experimentalists since the seventeenth century. The fundamental problem with transplantation was that of rejection: the patient's immune system recognises and repels tissue originating in other bodies.[50] Yet for some conditions, replacement seemed the only ultimate solution. This was especially true of patients with defective kidneys, often young people in their teens and early twenties who were condemned to a painful, lingering death with their lives still before them.

Although renal dialysis had been possible since 1943, it was rarely used, it then being considered unethical to prolong the lives of patients with chronic disease, for whom it could only delay inevitable death.[51] It was, in any case, a trying procedure and an especially wearisome prospect for otherwise healthy young patients whose only problem was their defective kidney function. Technically, the replacement operation was possible in the 1950s, the first successful transplant being carried out between identical twins in 1953. Subsequent operations between siblings, and even between twins, nonetheless continued to show a high failure rate, and it was only with the discovery of the right combination of immunosuppressive drugs that the kidney transplant became a surgical reality.[52] It was not until 1963 that the use of the drug azathioprine in combination with steroids was shown to be the key to preventing rejection. The subsequent introduction of cyclosporin in the late 1970s reduced the need for steroids and placed the whole science of immunosuppression on a firmer basis. By this time dialysis had been accepted in the treatment of kidney patients, and the two treatments together offered a considerably better prospect for those afflicted with renal disease.[53]

Once the problem of rejection in kidney transplantation had been successfully resolved, surgeons quickly moved on to attempt other types of transplant. Within four years of the mastering of the technique of immunosuppression, the South African surgeon Christian Barnaard performed the first heart transplant, to the accompaniment of worldwide publicity. It was an operation that had a disastrous early history. Barnaard's first patient died within days, but the incentive had been given to surgeons the world over to try the operation on selected patients. Within a year fatalities among transplant patients had reached such a level that the operation was abandoned for a time; yet surgeons are persistent, and by the 1980s they had achieved a survival rate in the region of 80 per cent. Although heart transplant operations remain a technique of last resort, there were by the 1990s many hundreds of patients whose lives had been prolonged for many years in a condition of much greater comfort and fitness than they could have hoped to achieve before 1970.

Less emotive in its appeal than organ transplantation, but at least as important to a great many older patients, was the development of techniques to replace osteoarthritic or worn-out joints such as hips, fingers and knees. Hip replacements were pioneered by the Manchester surgeon John Charnley in the early 1960s, initiating a series of procedures that transformed the lives of many elderly patients, restoring them to an active and pain-free life. Physical activity and enjoyment of life by the elderly could also be seriously curtailed by impaired vision, and the introduction of techniques of corneal replacement using a plastic lens as a substitute for the natural cornea obscured by cataracts was another liberating medical contribution to the welfare of the elderly.[54]

By the 1970s the ability of medicine to alter and to repair the body, together with rising standards of living and expectations of life among ordinary people, and growing media interest in medicine and personal health, was beginning to foster a new approach to medical treatment. This is the so-called 'lifestyle medicine', in which medical intervention is required less for the resolution of the causes of ill-health than to confer a perceived improvement on the quality of patients' everyday lives. Such medicine is essentially social in its intentions, often accommodating patients' own perceptions of the improvements needed in their lives. Many such interventions were originally designed to meet specific medical needs within a social context, but they have had their application extended by popular demand for the enhancement of life. Recent examples include Prozac and the anti-impotence drug Viagra (1998).

The original lifestyle drug was perhaps the oral contraceptive pill, developed in the 1950s by the American endocrinologist Gregory Pincus, with the support of leading American birth control reformer Margaret Sanger. Although it did not, as has sometimes been suggested, inaugurate the modern revolution in sexual behaviour, the pill did initiate a change in the doctor–patient relationship that subsequently extended across the spectrum of medical practice. Whereas in the past patients had waited for the doctor's diagnosis and prescription, the advent of the pill encouraged women to identify their own medical problem (fertility) and to ask their medical practitioner to prescribe a specific treatment.[55] While the pill undoubtedly contributed to the health of those women whose health had been, or was imminently about to be, undermined by too-frequent pregnancies, it also freed many more women to enjoy sexual activity outside the bounds of marriage.

Despite periodic scares about health problems associated with using the pill, oral contraception quickly became the most popular method of birth control in Britain. By the mid-1970s, when free family planning services were made available, it was used by 58 per cent of married couples in England and Wales, and by an estimated 2.25 million women, both married and unmarried.[56] Despite the scares, the health risk associated with the pill appeared to be very small indeed, while its health benefit for many women lay not only in the avoidance of unwanted and debilitating pregnancies, but also in a monthly reduction of the physical discomforts of menstruation.

The introduction of the oral contraceptive did not, however, put an end to abortion, that ancient and controversial method of avoiding an unwanted pregnancy. In the nineteenth century, the medical profession had acted to tighten the legal control on abortion, but in the twentieth century doctors began gradually to extend the application of the law as they recognised that there were mental and well as physical justifications for the operation. In the years after 1950, as the social pressure for abortion in certain circumstances began to be recognised, reform of the restrictive abortion laws began to be considered. The issue became increasingly contentious, as the women's rights movement adopted the cause of reform, and anti-abortion pressure groups took action to resist it. The medical profession, however, was anxious to retain control over the performance of the operation and proved influential in effecting both the passage and the scope of the revised law. The Abortion Act 1967 legalised therapeutic abortion and extended possible justifications to include social considerations such as existing family circumstances and the possibility that the child might be seriously handicapped.[57]

While the medical prescription of oral contraception and the medical supervision of abortion both had implications for women's health as regards childbirth, which been a medical concern since at least the eighteenth century, it was only in the 1960s that medicine began to enter the related field of infertility. Here again the identification of infertility as a medical problem, and role of infertile couples in their own diagnosis and their requirements of the doctor, formed part of the shift towards lifestyle medicine so clearly demonstrated by the demand for the oral contraceptive pill. Fertility drugs to stimulate ovulation were introduced in the 1960s, but they proved a mixed blessing in their tendency to induce multiple pregnancies. In the wake of the women's rights movement and of changing popular expectations of medicine, infertility became a major social issue in that decade.[58]

The identification of infertility as a medical condition and as a health and lifestyle issue encouraged researchers to investigate the various types of infertility and to explore methods of overcoming them. By 1977 Patrick Steptoe and Bob Edwards had developed a technique enabling them to fertilise human eggs in vitro before returning a fertilised single egg to the mother's womb. In July 1978 the first baby conceived as a result of this process, Louise Brown, was born. Steptoe and Edwards' technique proved applicable to several other types of infertility, and by the 1990s, although the problem of infertility was by no means totally resolved, many thousands of couples had been relieved of the sadness of childlessness through specific medical interventions.[59]

Medicine also produced an improvement in quality of life for women at the end of their reproductive lives. For a great number of women the menopause is a time of both physical and mental suffering, and the introduction of long-term hormone replacement therapy in the 1980s was greeted by many with relief. Besides modifying the symptoms of menopause, hormone replacement therapy was reported by many users to restore libido, and was considered to have medical benefits in reducing the risk of osteoporosis and heart disease – benefits that were thought to outweigh an increased incidence of breast cancer and thrombosis. By the early 1990s around a tenth of women in the relevant age group were using the therapy, and among women doctors the proportion was closer to half.[60]

Despite the great improvements, even transformations, that medicine wrought in the lives of patients with many different conditions and diseases, the diseases of ageing remained a generally problematic area, continuing to elude the best efforts at their resolution. Mental frailty, osteoporosis, arthritis, heart disease, cancer and others remained largely resistant to successful long-term treatment. With the growing number of elderly people, cancer became an increasingly high-profile disease, generating its own specialist consultants, specialist epidemiologists, charities and support networks. The number of cancer deaths continued to increase, even among children, reaching a total of over 100,000 a year for the first time in 1962.

Technological advance in the years immediately after the war resulted in the replacement of radium therapy by more sophisticated mechanical interventions, radiotherapy becoming integrated into treatment regimes throughout the hospital system. Chemotherapy became available with the development of new drugs, while screening programmes were put in place for two of the most preventable female cancers, those of the breast and cervix, in 1963 and 1965 respectively.[61] Yet while successful treatments were discovered for certain cancers, such as Hodgkin's disease and acute lymphoblastic leukaemia, these were generally among the rarer forms of the disease.[62] Advances in the treatment of childhood leukaemia were heartening, but for the most common adult cancers, those of lung, bowel, breast and cervix, the prospect remained at best moderate, early detection offering the best hope of cure. Into the 1990s treatment for disseminated cancer continued to be a question of management and control. At the end of the century, the annual death toll from all cancer had reached 150,000, and 200,000 new cases were yearly coming forward for treatment.[63]

The rising toll of deaths from cancer continued a trend apparent since the late nineteenth century but was a constant feature in a changing picture. As patients began to develop a more demanding approach to medical treatment, and as the pace of medical innovation increased and the standard of living rose, so the kinds of illness being brought before medical practitioners changed. A recent comparison by Irvine Loudon and Mark Drury of the disorders that have become more and less common in general practice between 1950 and the mid-1990s reveals how the balance has changed from a past in which physical ailments dominated the spectrum of health concerns to a present in which socially generated disorders and conditions previously rarely recognised contribute a more considerable share than specifically 'new' diseases such as AIDS and Legionnaire's disease. For the 1990s Loudon and Drury's list of the more common conditions includes, as well as various cancers, child abuse, autism, dyslexia and drug abuse; bulimia and anorexia nervosa; obesity; suicide in young males; infertility in women; and teenage pregnancy. In contrast the diseases that have become less common have a large infectious, congenital or environmental component: tuberculosis and the common infections of childhood; minor infections such as impetigo, ringworm and scabies; spina bifida and hydrocephalus; stillbirth; chronic bronchitis, bronchiectasis and childhood anaemia. The list of diseases less common because of such medical interventions as immunisation, the screening of target populations, therapy and improved clinical care is considerable and impressive.[64]

Despite the very real achievement of modern medicine in improving health by removing many of the older afflictions, the range of disorders for which medical assistance was sought increased. With the decline in the acute infectious diseases and growing public attention to matters of health, the failures and shortcomings of medicine became more apparent, acting as a source of tension between patients and the profession.[65] Following reports that linked the combined measles, mumps and rubella vaccine with autism in a very small number of cases, for example, parents began in the late 1990s to demand single-shot, or measles/mumps vaccine only for their children, to the consternation of the British medical profession.

In this decade also, new developments in medical science promised the genetic modification of individuals as a remedy for many diseases, but the initial application of similar methods to improve the quality and yield of food crops was met with suspicion and hostility by consumer groups. Public sensitivity towards foodstuffs had undoubtedly been heightened by the long-running crisis over the epidemic of bovine spongiform encephalopathy in Britain's cattle herds, but the outcry over genetically modified foodstuffs was characteristic of the newly critical public attitude towards medical and scientific innovation.[66] By the 1990s popular perceptions of risk and responsibility had shifted significantly away from unquestioning trust in the doctor's prescription and from an uncritical acceptance of scientific innovation.

Reaction

The rapid intensification of the search for new therapies in the years after 1945 created problems as well as bringing benefits, although societies across the world were slow to accept that this could be the case. Before the Second World War, Western medicine was subjected to very little in the way of control over its research activities and therapeutic practices. In Britain the Cruelty to Animals Act of 1876 imposed certain limitations on the use of animals in medical research, and the General Medical Council had existed since 1858 to supervise the social and ethical behaviour of registered medical practitioners, but the development, testing and introduction of new treatments and drug therapies remained essentially in the hands of the researchers and practitioners themselves.[67] The situation began to change in the 1940s, when Austin Bradford Hill, professor of medical statistics and epidemiology at the London School of Hygiene and Tropical Medicine, pioneered the randomised controlled clinical trial, after which the statistical evaluation of the risks and benefits of treatment began to permeate clinical as well as epidemiological practice.[68]

The need for probity and rigour in the testing of new treatments especially in the field of pharmaceuticals, became urgent with the rapid expansion of the chemical exploration of new drugs by the pharmaceutical industry after 1945. The inadequacy of most national medical systems was tragically demonstrated in the years around 1960. Between 1956, when the drug thalidomide was released in Germany, and 1961, when it was withdrawn, thousands of babies were born with more or less severe physical malformations of the hands, limbs and oesophagus. Sold over the counter in Germany (on prescription in Britain) as a general tranquilliser and morning sickness preventive, the drug had not been subjected to sufficiently rigorous trials, the omission of its effects in pregnant animals being a key failing.[69] As a result, most Western nations introduced controls over the introduction of new drugs.

In Britain the process followed the characteristic pattern of adoptive legislation, with subsequent more stringent controls stemming from the old political reluctance to interfere with private enterprise and the free market. A supervisory body, the Committee on the Safety of Drugs, chaired by Sir Derrick Dunlop, was set up in 1962, but the drug companies' submissions were to be made voluntarily. The Dunlop Committee implemented a three-stage assessment through laboratory toxicity trials, clinical trials and surveillance. The latter was supplemented by the yellow card system, under which doctors were supplied with forms for reporting adverse drug reactions, but practitioner feedback proved unreliable. As was almost inevitable, the arrangement for voluntary drug submission proved unsatisfactory as the pressures of commerce and competition remained, especially for the smaller companies.

In 1968 the Medicines Act extended external control over the industry, but in practice close co-operation between the drug companies and regulators, the frequent interchange of personnel between regulator and industry, and government reluctance to damage the industry's profitability allowed considerable leeway within the regulatory system. Drug-testing through full-scale clinical trials proved an expensive procedure and was not always effective in predicting side effects that became apparent with long-term clinical use. In 1981 the Conservative government introduced a scheme under which companies could be exempted from the full programme of controlled clinical trials required by law, which effectively reduced the extent of safety regulation within the industry.[70] The intention was to establish an early warning system that would enable government to issue warnings or to withdraw drugs from the market if necessary, thus maintaining the principle that even if drugs do not positively contribute to health, they should at least not harm the patient.[71]

The thalidomide tragedy was one among a number of factors that helped to shape a more critical public attitude towards medicine and medical practitioners during the 1960s. Postwar social change, with the great expansion in the number of the middle classes and the relatively well educated, the emergence of environmental awareness, and mass means of communication (especially, perhaps, television) all contributed to the development of a society increasingly able and willing to question and criticise established institutions and long-accepted standards. Thalidomide, and the long struggle for compensation on the part of the affected British families, which was not resolved until 1973, seemed to demonstrate that the good faith of governments and commercial companies could not be depended on.[72] The proliferation of popular pressure groups and self-help groups from the 1960s onwards helped to raise public awareness of single, separate medical issues, and reinforced a growing impression of the inadequacy of organised medicine to meet all medical needs. At the same time, new voices began to criticise the achievements and attitudes of modern medicine.

In 1961 Thomas Szasz put forward the idea that mental illness was 'manufactured' by psychiatrists and (sometimes) the state, and by the 1970s Archie Cochrane had questioned the effectiveness of most therapeutic interventions, with Thomas McKeown arguing that an improving standard of living rather than medical innovation had initiated the great decline in the death-rate since 1870.[73] There was increasing criticism of the medical profession for its assumption of authority over patients: in 1971 an American organisation, the Boston Women's Health Collective, published *Our Bodies Our Selves*, which emphasised the importance to women of an informed response on issues concerning their own personal well-being. In 1976 Ivan Illich argued more broadly that modern medicine made people ill, and in 1981 Ian Kennedy's Reith Lectures condemned modern medicine for its exclusive focus on the disease process rather than the needs of the patient. Indeed, Kennedy went so far as to recommend that patients take greater responsibility for their own health, to the extent of questioning the power exercised by doctors.[74]

Such criticism helped to change the public attitude towards the modern practice of medicine, as it was filtered through to the general population by television and the popular press. Already in 1972, for example, a BBC documentary on the history of Charing Cross Hospital, London, ended by contrasting the humanity of the interwar hospital, where little could be done to cure the disease but the consolation and comfort of the patient was a priority, with the isolating experience of treatment in the modern high-technology hospital.[75] A sharp reminder of the power of television to shape public opinion came in October 1980, when *Panorama* broadcast a programme on brain death, highlighting the cases of four individuals declared brain dead by

American physicians, who later recovered. The removal, with donors' or relatives' consent, of organs from those deemed brain dead for transplant purposes had by this time become a not unusual procedure, and public consternation at the *Panorama* programme was reflected in a two-year stagnation in transplantation number.[76]

The effect of social and intellectual developments on the public attitude towards modern medicine and the medical profession itself was complex. On the one hand, people generally became much more sensitive towards their own health and more demanding of the health services: in 1987 it was calculated that public expectations of the NHS were rising at 5 per cent a year, because of, among other things, an awareness of what could be provided, advances in medical treatment and a reduced tolerance of discomfort.[77] On the other hand, the public also began to take more independent action in preserving its own health. Membership of the Vegetarian Society soared from the later 1970s, and in the 1980s attendance at swimming pools and gymnasia significantly increased. Non-smoking became an issue in restaurants and public places. The later 1980s and the 1990s were beset by continuing crises over the epidemic of bovine spongiform encephalopathy among British cattle, and public anxiety about the possible transmission of the disease to consumers. In the 1990s supermarkets began stocking organic produce, and the year 1999 was distinguished by a public outcry against the introduction of genetically modified foods. In the meantime, non-orthodox medicine became increasingly popular. By 1981 GPs had been outnumbered by alternative therapists in Britain, and in the 1990s several of the more prominent alternative therapies, such as homeopathy and chiropractic, were brought within the provisions of the NHS.[78]

By the end of the twentieth century, public confidence in the altruism of doctors and the competence of modern medicine was beginning to fragment. While government attempts to control spending on health were generally blamed for deteriorating facilities and services within the NHS, the periodic uncovering of scientific shortcomings in services, for example, repeated local breakdowns in the cervical cancer screening programme, helped to undermine general confidence in the judgement of doctors and medical scientists. In 1998 publicity surrounding the high failure rate of heart operations at the Bristol Children's Hospital led to the suspension of three surgeons and the call for tougher control over medical practice. In the following year similar accusations (subsequently unproven) of medical negligence against child heart patients were levelled at the country's premier centre for cardiac surgery, the Brompton Hospital. In that year also, legal sanction was sought for parents to over-rule doctors' decisions on the treatment of severely handicapped and terminally ill children.

It was increasingly apparent that, especially where children were involved, the professional authority of medicine no longer went unquestioned by families concerned in the treatment of one of their number. It was a development that raised the level of stress and anxiety within the medical profession itself. Although the situation had by no means reached the extreme then current in the United States, where the likelihood of a successful outcome of a medical procedure had become almost a determining factor in whether it was undertaken, British medical practice in the 1990s was increasingly aware of the threat of litigation for clinical negligence.

The growing public unease over real or perceived shortcomings in medical treatment, organisation and preventive services within the NHS occurred alongside a rising concern among health professionals from the later 1970s over continuing inequality in health between different regions of the country and different social classes. Comparative international health statistics showed that, in key indicators such as infant death and heart disease, British mortality rates had not improved as fast as those of other wealthy Western societies. In 1977 the Secretary of State for Social Services appointed a Research Working Group under Sir Douglas Black to investigate inequalities in health across the country.

Published amid heated political controversy in 1980, the Black Report demonstrated the existence of a significant class-related disparity in health, the poorest (social class V) suffering a death-rate twice as high as the wealthiest (social class I). It was a pattern that held good for a wide range of medical conditions, from obesity through arthritis to accidents. The group could only explain these differences as being the result of poverty and material deprivation. They called for a comprehensive strategy to eliminate poverty, a radical redistribution of resources to include measures aimed at reforming the lifestyle and living conditions of the poor, as well as the provision of medical services, and for these measures to be targeted particularly at children.[79] The government, however, balked at the perceived expense of implementing such a programme, despite reinforcement of the Black Report findings on health and social class by a second investigation, Margaret Whitehead's *The Health Divide*, published in 1987. The emphasis of general government policy on health continued to be on individual responsibility and on a change in lifestyle to fit the emergent model of healthy living: the consumption of plenty of fresh fruit and vegetables, no smoking, little or no alcohol and regular exercise.

The achievement of a common level of health for all became an issue not only in Britain, but also in the world community in the late 1970s. In 1978 the World Health Organization declared its aim of *Health For All by the Year 2000*, a programme based on the social relations of health rather than on medical intervention, on housing, education and health promotion rather than on the provision of medical services. In the years that followed, several countries, including the United States, began to publish health strategies of their own, based on the World Health Organization blueprint. It was not until 1992, however, that Britain's Conservative government (in power since 1979) produced its own such document, the White Paper *The Health of the Nation*. It adopted an individual approach, framing strategy in terms of specific problems rather than in terms of broad social improvement. Key areas for action were identified as coronary heart disease and stroke, cancer, HIV/AIDS and sexual health, mental illness and accidents. The desired results were set in line with existing trends, a decision that blurred any obvious impact of subsequent government action.[80] Interested researchers, meanwhile, were beginning to develop more radical and democratic solutions, for example that better health is directly related to the degree of equality and social cohesion present within a given society.[81]

When the Labour Party came to power in 1997, the issue of inequality in health assumed a more prominent place in government pronouncements on future health policy, in line with the party's long-standing commitment to social equality and an improvement in living standards for working people and the poor. In July 1999 the then Health Secretary, Frank Dobson, announced a £96 million plan for reducing the number of deaths from heart disease, cancer, suicide and accidents, with a view to saving 300,000 lives over ten years. Following the example of the Black Report and *The Health Divide*, Dobson's White Paper, *Saving Lives*, again stressed that the poorest social groups had a life expectancy five years less than that of the well-to-do, and that they were more likely to die from heart disease and cancer. Twenty-six Health Action Zones were to be established in the country's poorest areas, offering such socially based strategies as first aid training for 11–16-year-olds, and 'Expert Patients' programmes to help people to manage their own illnesses. A few weeks later, the BMA published a report of its own, which argued that the children of Britain's poor were among the unhealthiest in the developed world and were destined to become illness-prone adults.[82]

Conclusion

At the turn of the twentieth century, British medical and social observers were agreed that, despite the achievements of modern medicine, and despite fifty years of largely free medical provision, the health of the nation's poorest classes remained unsatisfactory. One survey published in 1998 emphasised the continuing relevance of the old mortality and morbidity division along the north/south divide and the urban/rural axis. Twenty-seven British communities were identified as having a 'high and rising' mortality ratio, of which twenty were urban, including Oldham, Salford, Manchester, Liverpool and Edinburgh. Five London boroughs, with Hackney in the lead, and the rural counties of Stirling, Durham (a former mining county) and Perth, also featured in the list. The authors noted an increasing polarisation of death-rate by area in Britain, an inequality of mortality so striking that 'if the Registrar General of 1851 were to repeat the study of mortality carried out then, he would no doubt be shocked by the extent, persistence and widening of the basic divided British society'.[83] Despite the 1978 World Health Organization declaration, Britain had not achieved health for all by the year 2000. Yet in general health and life expectancy had improved significantly since 1945, partly as a result of social change and partly as a result of the contributions of biomedicine. Definitions of both health and poverty had themselves changed since the Second World War with the general rise in expectations and in the standard of living. While these changing cultural standards and expectations altered the concept of health itself over time, the statistical accounts provided a continuing reminder of the very real ways in which health and life expectancy had improved since 1860.

CONCLUSION

Between 1860 and 1960 there was, in the words of Jay Winter, 'an astonishing change' in the expectation of life at birth. From 40.5 years for men and 43 years for women in 1861, life expectancy had risen to over 70 years by the 1960s.[1] In the 1860s most people in Britain, especially those who lived in the cities, suffered from under-nutrition, a polluted water supply, adulterated food, heavy atmospheric pollution, overcrowded living conditions and the ravages of infectious disease. Even the well-to-do were not immune from the effects of these adverse environmental conditions, as the health concerns of mid-Victorian intellectuals from Darwin to Charles Dickens too clearly show. The transformation that occurred in the conditions of life and health in the century that followed was slow, uneven and unequally distributed between the different social classes, yet a century later not only were actual standards of health and well-being much greater, but also the expectations of ordinary people in terms of their own physical and mental well-being had been transformed.

By the turn of the twentieth century, the transformation in expectation had become established, so much taken for granted that demands for an ever-healthier life have often come to focus on the minute details of the individual daily regime. Many factors played a part in this process of dramatic social reformation, and their relative importance has been variously and often polemically assessed by historians in recent times, but throughout this history there runs the theme of medical intervention, not least because medicine has historically been a principal resource for those seeking not only to cure illness and ill-health, but also to maintain health and well-being.

Since at least the 1860s, health and medicine in Britain have been linked not simply through the doctor–patient relationship but also through the wider social and political activities of medical men concerned about human welfare and the state

174

of the nation. The radical medical journal the *Lancet* was an early pioneer of outspoken social criticism on a medical basis, by the 1860s performing a notable function in drawing the attention of the educated classes to urgent social and health issues. The formation of the BMA in 1855 gave British medicine a corporate identity through which a powerful political influence emerged in the twentieth century. The creation of the London MOHs in 1855–56, and of the central Medical Department (transformed into the MH in 1919) in 1858, established a cadre of medical men professionally concerned with issues of sickness, health and disease, which was to exert significant pressure on the ways in which government health strategies developed. Through these specialist and general medical organisations, as well as the development of socially aware and politically conscious medical journalism, nineteenth-century medicine acquired the mission and the methods for active intervention in wider issues of public health.

Although medicine, as a curative art, remained to a large extent powerless directly to cure disease during the Victorian period, the growing scientific authority of the profession probably enhanced its influence over patients, partly through increased effectiveness in the management of illness, but also through patients' increasing respect for and confidence in the doctors' knowledge and powers. As medicine and medical men acquired a greater scientific and professional status because of medical research and the reform of medical education, so the placebo effect of their treatments was also enhanced. Beginning in the 1890s with antitoxin treatment for diphtheria, and continuing with anti-tetanus serum, immunisation against typhoid, cholera and diphtheria, and the anti-syphilis drug Salvarsan, the new science-based medicine had begun to deliver visibly potent new measures against disease by the outbreak of the Great War.

These developments in medical competence were relatively small, however, being overshadowed by the widespread concern about national degeneration and physical fitness that was aroused by the recruiting experiences of the Boer War, when nearly 35 per cent of volunteers were rejected as being unfit for military service. It was the evidence of medical men, however, that convinced the Interdepartmental Committee on Physical Deterioration of 1904 that heredity degeneration was a myth, and led to the introduction of legislative measures designed to alleviate the impact of poverty and under-nutrition on the health of babies and schoolchildren. The National Insurance Act 1911, with its emphasis on sickness provision for those social classes just above the poverty line, on the provision of medical treatment for victims of tuberculosis, and on research into the causes of ill-health among insured persons, marked a further extension of medical involvement in the health of the nation.

The contribution of the new medical science to the successful conduct of Britain's war effort in 1914–18 has not been fully explored. Yet medical science and military medical management combined to give the soldiers of the Great War a better prospect of survival than those of any previous war, notwithstanding the appalling loss of life and the terrible conditions in the trenches. Indications of the ways in which new medical skills and understanding of disease processes made themselves felt lie in the absence of severe epidemic disease undermining strength on the Western Front, the improved survival rate of the injured through new techniques of wound management, and some of the medical endeavours to resolve the mental agony of men traumatised by war.

The medical profession's contribution to civilian health during the Great War was less impressive, in part because the medical services were overstretched by the absence of half the country's doctors on war service, and partly because of the continuing limitations of civilian medicine. The depletion of civilian medical resources appeared to have little adverse impact, however, except perhaps for certain exceptional groups, such as patients in asylums and sanatoria. The established pattern of a generally declining death-rate was little interrupted by the war, although increased mortality among the elderly and among young women from tuberculosis may relate in part to a reduced medical management of illness, as well as to the immense emotional strain imposed on these particular groups by the intensity and duration of the conflict. The overall health of the civilian population remained relatively good by contemporary standards, despite anxiety over industrial poisoning and levels of nutrition. The terrible impact of the influenza epidemic of 1918 cannot be ascribed either to war-related malnutrition or to the inadequacy of the medical response to the epidemic: in terms of mortality and morbidity, Britain's experience of the epidemic was no worse than that of non-combatant countries or of the United States.

The concerns over the physical condition of the working classes, which had been so aggravated by the recruitment experience of the Boer War, were not allayed by the experiences of medical boards assessing the physique of recruits after the introduction of conscription in 1916. Despite the falling death-rate, even among infants, both recruitment experience and records of child development suggested that there had been little real improvement in the general health of the country's poorer classes since 1900. In this respect, however, the Great War seems to have constituted a watershed. Although the interwar period was characterised by more or less severe economic depression, and by a high level of unemployment, the death-rate continued to fall, and schoolchildren began to gain markedly in height and weight. Tuberculosis and the common infectious diseases of childhood continued to decline as causes of death.

The impact of medicine on these developments is debatable. During these years government continued to add to the welfare provisions begun in the early 1900s, with further legislation relating to, for example, mothers and babies. As insurance medicine became increasingly popular, GP surgeries often became the means by which preventive health advice was disseminated, while a growing number of specialised, independent health organisations took advantage of the new popular press to publicise their views and activities. Even the MH made use, in a somewhat limited fashion, of the new medium of radio to suggest ways in which people might improve their health and enjoyment of life.

It was in the interwar period that scientific medicine began to yield effective treatment for a number of previously highly fatal and incurable diseases, such as diabetes, pernicious anaemia and puerperal fever. The introduction of the sulphonamide drugs in the mid-1930s stands out as an innovation of particular significance, although it was subsequently overshadowed by the politics of penicillin. During these years the MRC was active in the introduction and promotion of new medical treatments, while the MH focused on housing reform rather than the implementation of more specifically medical policies for the promotion of public health. The local impact of the Great Depression brought to a head debates over the relationship between nutrition and health that had been simmering for some time. The new medical sub-discipline of nutrition, which had evolved largely as a result of the discovery of vitamins, developed an increasingly prominent political profile in these years, notably as a result of the activities of John Boyd Orr. An edge was added to these debates by the recognition, growing since the rearmament of Germany in the early 1930s, that another major European war was possible. Medical men played their part as specialist consultants in some of the early preparations for war, and when war came the profession was thoroughly engaged in the war effort, not least on the home front.

With the return of peace in 1945, medicine came to engage with health more directly than at any previous period since 1860. The development of penicillin for medical use during the war gave the profession the most potent remedy yet against a whole spectrum of bacterial infections, and within a decade the antibiotics had been joined by the steroids as crucial keys in the effort to alleviate suffering. The establishment of the NHS in 1948 greatly extended the reach of organised medicine, encouraging to come forward for consultation and treatment those who had previously been too poor or too reticent to call for medical attention.

At the same time, new environmental measures and a rising standard of living raised the threshold of health and began to change the pattern of disease seen in GP surgeries. The common infectious diseases virtually disappeared as a cause of death, and increasingly of illness, as new immunisations were developed and offered through baby clinics and surgeries. Old-established problems of poverty and poor housing, such as bronchitis and rheumatism, began to decline as a cause of ill-health, to be replaced by a different range of conditions. Contrary to some expectations, the growing power of modern scientific medicine to alleviate suffering and cure disease did not result in a fall in the demand for medical services; instead, the demand continued to grow. As the disease profile of an increasingly well-to-do population changed, in terms not just of the diseases that killed, but also those which caused minor discomfort, so people sought help for a wider range of problems. And as the levels of general health and expectation of medical competence rose, so to did the thresholds of intolerance towards physical and mental discomfort.

The period since 1860 had been characterised by a growing (albeit often reluctant) involvement by government and medical men in providing for improved health first through environmental improvement and the control of infectious disease, then by the provision of welfare services, and finally by making medical treatment universally available. Faced with an apparently intractable problem of demand for medical services, with growing concern over the toll of cancer and heart disease and with an increase in such socially related problems as obesity, medical men and policy-makers began in the 1980s to return to an ideal of personal responsibility for health. In parallel with this new emphasis, which an increasingly health-conscious public seemed enthusiastically to adopt, came the recognition that, despite the very real gain in living standard made by even the poorest in society during the twentieth century, a significant inequality in health and well-being continued to exist between the higher and lower social classes.

APPENDIX

Table 1   Birth-rates (B/R), crude death-rates (D/R) and infant mortality rates (IMR), England and Wales, 1851–1991

Years	B/R	D/R	IMR
	per 1000 living		*per 100 births*
1851–60	35.5	21.3	148 (1860)
1861–70	35.8	21.5	160 (1870)
1871–80	35.4	21.4	149
1881–90	32.4	19.1	142
1891–1900	29.9	18.2	153
1901–10	27.2	15.4	128
1911–20	21.8	14.4	100
1921–30	18.3	12.1	72
1931–40	14.9	12.3	61
1941–50	17.0	12.3	43
1951–60	15.9	11.7	25
1961–70	17.5	11.8	20
1971–80	13.7	11.9	15
1981–90	13.2	11.5	9
1992	13.6	10.9	7

Sources: Supplement to the Registrar-General's 65th Annual Report, Part 1, p. 13; *Medical Officer's Report for the Years 1939–45*, Ministry of Health, p. 15; Klim MacPherson and David Coleman, 'Health', in A. H. Halsey (ed.), *British Social Trends Since 1900*, pp. 400–1; Office of Population, Surveys and Statistics, *Mortality Statistics 1841–1990*, 1992.

Table 2 Life expectancy at birth, England and Wales, 1838–1995

1838–54	40.9
1871–80	43.0
1881–90	45.4
1891–1900	46.0
1901–10	50.5
1920–22	57.6
1930–32	60.8
1950–52	69.0
1960–62	71.0
1970–72	72.0
1980–82	74.0
1992	74.4
1997	75.5

Sources: Supplement to the Registrar-General's 65th Report, p. 50; Klim MacPherson and David Coleman, 'Health', in A. H. Halsey (ed.), *British Social Trends Since 1900*, pp. 404–5; Department of Health, *On the State of the Public Health*, 1992, 1997.

Table 3 Expectation of life at birth, and infant mortality rate, Britain and other European countries, *c.* 1995–96

Country	Year	Life expectancy	IMR
UK	1995	76.8	6.2
France	1994	78.6	5.9
Germany	1995	76.7	5.3
Sweden	1995	79.0	4.0
Italy	1993	77.9	7.1
Spain	1995	78.1	5.5
Netherlands	1995	77.7	5.5
Ireland	1993	75.4	6.1
Finland	1995	76.7	4.0
Greece	1996	78.1	7.3
EU average	1995–96	77.4	6.0

Source: Department of Health, *On the State of the Public Health*, 1996, Table A.11, p. 280.

NOTES

Place of publication is London unless otherwise stated.

Introduction

1. See John Pickstone, 'Dearth, Dirt and Fever Epidemics: Rewriting the History of British "Public Health", 1780–1850', in Terence Ranger and Paul Slack (eds), *Epidemics and Ideas: Essays on the Historical Perception of Pestilence* (Cambridge, 1992); Ann de la Berge, *Mission and Method. The Early Nineteenth Century French Public Health Movement* (Cambridge, 1992); Christopher Hamlin, *Public Health and Social Justice in the Age of Chadwick, 1800–1850* (Cambridge, 1998).
2. For the history, development and influence of the GRO, see John M. Eyler, *Victorian Social Medicine: The Ideas and Methods of William Farr* (Baltimore, 1979); *Social History of Medicine*, Special Issue, 4.3 (1991); Anne Hardy, '"Death Is the Cure of All Diseases": using the General Register Office's Cause of Death Statistics', *Social History of Medicine*, 7 (1994), 472–92; Simon Szreter, *Fertility, Class and Gender in Britain, 1860–1940* (Cambridge, 1996).
3. See, for example, Thomas McKeown, *The Rise of Modern Population* (1976); Robert Woods and John Woodward, *Urban Disease and Mortality* (1984); Anne Hardy, *The Epidemic Streets: Infectious Disease and the Rise of Preventive Medicine 1856–1900* (Oxford, 1993); Klim McPherson and David Coleman, 'Health', in A. H. Halsey (ed.), *British Social Trends Since 1900* (Basingstoke, 1988).
4. For Scotland see M. W. Flinn, *Scottish Population History from the 17th Century to the 1930s* (Cambridge, 1977); David Hamilton, *The Healers: A History of Medicine in Scotland* (1981); Olive Checkland and Margaret Lamb, *Health Care as Social History: The Glasgow Case* (Aberdeen, 1982).
5. See, for example, Joseph Melling and Bill Forsyth (eds), *Insanity, Institutions and Society, 1800–1914* (1999); Peter Bartlett and David Wright (eds), *Outside the Walls of the Asylum. The History of Care in the Community, 1750–2000* (1999).
6. See especially Elizabeth Malcolm and Greta Jones (eds), *Medicine, Disease and the State in Ireland, 1650–1940* (Cork, 1999); Greta Jones, *Tuberculosis in Ireland* (Amsterdam, 2000); Ruth Barrington, *Health, Medicine and Politics in Ireland 1900–1970* (Dublin, 1987).
7. Robert Woods and Nicola Shelton, *An Atlas of Victorian Mortality* (Liverpool, 1997).
8. Paul Huck, 'Infant Mortality in Nine Industrial Parishes in Northern England, 1813–36', *Population Studies*, **48** (1994), 515–26; Naomi Williams and Graham Mooney, 'Infant Mortality in an "Age of Great Cities": London and the English Provincial Cities Compared, c. 1840–1910', *Continuity and Change*, **9** (1994), 185–212.

Notes

9. Flinn, *Scottish Population History*, p. 416; for general patterns of death in this period, see Anne Hardy and Simon Szreter, 'Patterns of Mortality and Fertility 1849–1950', in Martin Daunton (ed.), *The Cambridge Urban History*, vol III (Cambridge, 2000); for patterns of morbidity, James Riley, *Sick Not Dead: Sickness among British Workingmen in the Later Nineteenth Century* (Baltimore, 1997), especially Chapter 8.
10. A valuable example of how such data may be used can be found in Riley, *Sick Not Dead.*
11. Arthur K. and Elaine Shapiro, *The Powerful Placebo: From Ancient Priest to Modern Physician* (Maryland, 1997). On the effectiveness of old folk remedies, see Robert and Michele Root-Bernstein, *Honey, Mud and Maggots. The Science Behind Folk Remedies and Old Wives Tales* (New York, 1997).
12. For these developments see Michel Foucault, *The Birth of the Clinic. An Archaeology of Medical Perception*, translated by A. M. Sheridan (1976); Erwin Ackerknecht, *Medicine at the Paris Hospital, 1794–1848* (Baltimore, 1967).
13. Herbert Spencer, *Education. Intellectual, Moral and Physical* (1949 edn), p. 177. For the Larmarckian position see Ludmilla Jordanova, *Lamarck* (Oxford, 1984).
14. The effect of this influence is explored in Geoffrey Searle, *Eugenics and Politics in Britain, 1900–1914* (Leyden, 1976); Daniel Kevles, *In the Name of Eugenics: Genetics and the Uses of Human Heredity* (New York, 1985); Richard Soloway, *Demography and Degeneration: Eugenics and the Declining Birth-rate in Twentieth-century Britain* (Chapel Hill and London, 1990).
15. Simon Szreter and Graham Mooney, 'Urbanisation, Mortality, and the Standard of Living Debate: New Estimates of the Expectation of Life at Birth in Nineteenth-century British Cities', *Economic History Review*, **51** (1998), 84–112, p. 110. See also Simon Szreter, 'Economic Growth, Disruption, Deprivation, Disease and Death: On the Importance of the Politics of Public Health for Development', *Population and Development Review*, **23** (1997), 693–727.
16. For the incidence of infectious disease in the 1860s, see Hardy, *The Epidemic Streets*; on the issue of venereal disease, see Judith Walkowitz, *Prostitution and Victorian Society* (Cambridge, 1980). See also Bruno Latour, *The Pasteurisation of France*, translated by Alan Sheridan and John Law (Cambridge, MA and London, 1988); Christopher Lawrence and Richard Dixey, 'Practising on Principle: Joseph Lister and the Germ Theory of Disease', in Christopher Lawrence (ed.), *Medical Theory, Surgical Practice. Studies in the History of Surgery* (1992).
17. Bruce Haley, *The Healthy Body and Victorian Culture* (Cambridge, MA, and London, 1978), pp. 12–13. A detailed study of such Victorian health consciousness may be found in Ralph Colp Jr, *To Be An Invalid. The Illness of Charles Darwin* (Chicago and London, 1977).
18. E. Dawson and S. R. Royal (eds), *An Oxfordshire Market Gardener. The Diary of Joseph Turrill of Garsington 1841–1925* (Gloucester, 1993).
19. Haley, *The Healthy Body*, pp. 19–20; The World Health Organization, *The First Ten Years of the World Health Organization* (Geneva, 1958), p. 459. Recent discussions of medical and lay understandings of health include Mildred Blaxter and E. Patterson, *Mothers and Daughters: A Three Generations Study of Health Attitudes and Behaviour* (1982); Michael Calnan, *Health and Illness. The Lay Perspective* (1987); Mildred Blaxter, *Health and Lifestyles* (1990); Sarah Curtis and Ann Taket, *Health and Societies. Changing Perspectives* (1996), Chapter 2.

Notes

20. Riley, *Sick Not Dead*, pp. 199–202.
21. Stanley Reiser, 'Technology and the Use of the Senses in Twentieth Century Medicine', in W. F. Bynum and Roy Porter (eds), *Medicine and the Five Senses* (Cambridge, 1993), pp. 265–70.
22. Mabel C. Buer, *Health, Wealth and Population in the Early Days of the Industrial Revolution* (1926).
23. Thomas McKeown, and R. G. Record, 'Reasons for the Decline in Mortality in England and Wales during the Nineteenth Century', *Population Studies*, **16** (1962), 94–122; T. McKeown, R. G. Record and R. D. Turner, 'An Interpretation of the Decline in Mortality in England and Wales During the Twentieth Century', ibid., **29** (1975), 391–422.
24. For critiques of McKeown see Woods and Woodward (eds), *Urban Disease and Mortality in Nineteenth Century England*; Simon Szreter, 'The Importance of Social Intervention in Britain's Mortality Decline c.1850–1914: A Reinterpretation of Public Health', *Social History of Medicine*, **1** (1988), 1–18; Bill Luckin, 'Perspectives on the Mortality Decline in London, 1860–1920', *London Journal*, **22** (1997), 129–30.
25. Szreter, 'The Importance of Social Intervention'. See also Szreter and Mooney, 'Urbanisation, Mortality and the Standard of Living Debate'; Szreter, 'Economic Growth'.
26. Blaxter, *Health and Lifestyles*, p. 6.
27. Examples of this type of analysis may be found in Derek Oddy, 'The People's Health', in Theo Barker and Michael Drake (eds), *Population and Society* (1982); Roderick Floud, Kenneth Wachter, and Annabel Gregory, *Height, Health and History. Nutritional Status in the United Kingdom, 1750–1980* (Cambridge, 1990); Bernard Harris, 'The Demographic Impact of the First World War: An Anthropometric Perspective', *Social History of Medicine*, **6** (1993), 343–66.

Chapter 1

1. Supplement to the Registrar-General's Twenty-fifth Annual Report, British Parliamentary Papers 1865, xiii, pp. 33–4.
2. Supplement to the Registrar-General's Fifty-fifth Annual Report, B.P.P. 1875 xxiii, part I, p. xxxvi.
3. Ibid., p. xlviii: table 5.
4. On the creation of the family practitioner, see Irvine Loudon, *Medical Care and the General Practitioner, 1750–1850* (Oxford, 1986); on the consultant–general practitioner divide, Rosemary Stevens, *Medical Practice in Modern England: The Impact of Specialisation and State Medicine* (New Haven, 1966).
5. Keir Waddington, 'Unsuitable Cases: The Debate Over Outpatient Admissions, the Medical Profession and Late-Victorian London Hospitals', *Medical History*, **42** (1998), 26–46.
6. Anne Digby, *Making a Medical Living: Doctors and Patients in the English Market for Medicine, 1720–1911* (Cambridge, 1994), p. 170.
7. See Christopher Lawrence, *Medicine in the Making of Modern Britain* (1994), pp. 64–7.
8. Irvine Loudon, 'The Historical Importance of Outpatients', *British Medical Journal*, i (1978), 975: In contrast, the attendance rate at NHS hospital

184

outpatients and casualty departments in 1949 was 240 for England and Wales, and that in England in 1974, 346.

 9. The emergence, function and significance of the specialist hospital has been well covered in various publications by Lindsay Granshaw: see 'Stepping to Fame and Fortune by Means of Bricks and Mortar', in Lindsay Granshaw and Roy Porter (eds), *The Hospital in History* (1989); *idem*, 'The Rise of the Modern Hospital in Britain', in Andrew Wear (ed.), *Medicine in Society* (Cambridge, 1992); and *St Mark's Hospital, London: A Social History of a Specialist Hospital* (1985).
10. Steven Cherry, 'Change and Continuity in the Cottage Hospitals c. 1859–1948: The Experience of East Anglia', *Medical History*, **36** (1992), 271–89; see also M. Emrys Roberts, *The Cottage Hospitals 1859–1990* (1991).
11. For London see Gwendolen Ayers, *England's First State Hospitals* (1965); for the provinces, John Pickstone, *Medicine and Industrial Society* (Manchester, 1985), Chapter 8.
12. Digby, *Medical Living*, pp. 15–20.
13. D. G. Green, *Working Class Patients and the Medical Establishment* (Aldershot, 1985).
14. James Riley, *Sick Not Dead: Sickness among British Workingmen in the Later Nineteenth Century* (Baltimore, 1997), pp. 49–50.
15. Ibid., p. 202.
16. Jeanne L. Brand, *Doctors and the State: The British Medical Profession and Government Action in Public Health, 1870–1914* (Baltimore, 1965), p. 99.
17. R. P. Hastings, 'A Nineteenth Century Dispensary at Work', *Local History*, **10** (1973), 5; I. S. L. Loudon, 'The Origins and Growth of the Dispensary Movement in England', *Bulletin of the History of Medicine*, **55** (1981), 322–42.
18. For Poor Law medicine under the Poor Law Board, see Ruth Hodgkinson, *The Origins of the National Health Service. The Medical Services of the New Poor Law, 1834–1871* (1967); for the later period, Brand, *Doctors and the State*, Chapter 5.
19. Brand, *Doctors and the State*, p. 97.
20. Anne Digby, *The Evolution of British General Practice 1850–1948* (Oxford, 1999), pp. 250–1.
21. Ernest P. Hennock, *British Social Reform and German Precedents: The Case of Social Insurance, 1880–1914* (Oxford, 1987).
22. S. W. F. Holloway, 'The Regulation of the Supply of Drugs in Britain before 1868', in Roy Porter and Mikuláš Teich (eds), *Drugs and Narcotics in History* (Cambridge, 1995); Stanley Chapman, *Jesse Boot of Boots the Chemist* (1974), Chapter 1; Geoffrey Tweedale, *At the Sign of the Plough. Allen and Hanbury and the British Pharmaceutical Industry 1715–1990* (1990).
23. *Lancet*, ii (1894), 1151, 1515. For the wider culture of drug-taking in nineteenth-century Britain, see Virginia Berridge and G. Edwards, *Opium and the People. Opiate use in Nineteenth Century England* (1981).
24. N. D. Jewson, 'The Disappearance of the Sick-man from Medical Cosmology, 1770–1870', *Sociology*, **10** (1976), 225–44.
25. The GPs' struggle for reform is well recounted in Loudon, *Medical Care and the General Practitioner*.
26. On the functioning of the Council in this period, see Margaret Stacey, *Regulating British Medicine* (Chichester, 1992); P. S. Brown, 'Medically Qualified Naturopaths and the GMC', *Medical History*, **35** (1991), 50–77; R. G. Smith, 'The Development of Ethical Guidance for GPs by the GMC', *Medical History*, **37** (1993), 56–67.

27. Jeanne L. Petersen, *The Medical Profession in Mid-Victorian London* (Berkeley and London, 1978); Thomas Bonner, *Becoming a Physician: Medical Education in Great Britain, France, Germany and the United States, 1750–1945* (Oxford, 1995); Christopher Lawrence, 'Incommunicable Knowledge: Science, Technology and the Clinical Art in Britain, 1850–1914', *Journal of Contemporary History,* **20** (1985), 503–20.

28. For the use of these technologies in hospital practice, see Charles Newman, 'Physical Signs in London Hospitals', *Medical History,* **2** (1958), 195–201; for their slow diffusion, A. J. Youngson, *The Scientific Revolution in Victorian Medicine* (London, 1979), pp. 18–21; Digby, *The Evolution of British General Practice,* pp. 187–8; Malcolm Nicolson, 'The Introduction of Percussion and Stethoscopy to Early Nineteenth-century Edinburgh', in W. F. Bynum and Roy Porter (eds), *Medicine and the Five Senses* (Cambridge, 1993).

29. Anne Hardy, '"Death is the Cure of All Diseases": Using the General Register Office's Cause of Death Statistics, 1837–1921', *Social History of Medicine,* **7** (1994), 472–92.

30. Anne Digby, *Making a Medical Living: Doctors and Patients in the English Market for Medicine, 1720–1911* (Cambridge, 1994), p. 102.

31. Frederick Cartwright, *The Development of Modern Surgery* (1967), pp. 212–13.

32. Charles Singer and E. A. Underwood, *A Short History of Medicine* (Oxford, 2nd edn, 1962), pp. 390–1.

33. W. F. Bynum, *The Science and Practice of Medicine in the Nineteenth Century* (Cambridge, 1994), pp. 140–1.

34. Miles Weatherall, *In Search of a Cure. A History of Pharmaceutical Discovery* (Oxford, 1990), pp. 36–7.

35. Deaths from hydrophobia averaged 32 a year in England and Wales in the 1880s. Two national centres of rabies infection had been identified by the mid-1880s, in London and Lancashire, and the number of human deaths diminished dramatically after the introduction of the 1890 Muzzling Order in these districts.

36. Peter Baldwin, *Contagion and the State in Europe 1830–1930* (Cambridge, 1999).

37. The history of smallpox is one of the best documented of nineteenth century infections. For the implementation of preventive strategies against it, see R. J. Lambert, 'A Victorian National Health Service: State Vaccination 1855–71', *Historical Journal,* **5** (1962), 1–18; Anne Hardy, *The Epidemic Streets: Infectious Disease and the Rise of Preventive Medicine 1855–1900* (Oxford, 1993), Chapter 5. For the anti-vaccinationist position see R. M. MacLeod, 'Law, Medicine and Public Opinion: The Resistance to Compulsory Health Legislation 1870–1907', *Public Law* (Summer 1967), 107–28; (Autumn 1967), 189–211; Dorothy Porter and Roy Porter, 'The Politics of Prevention: Anti-vaccinationism and Public Health in Nineteenth-century England', *Medical History,* **32** (1988), 231–52.

38. See Frank Fenner, *Smallpox and its Eradication,* (Geneva, 1988); Jack W. Hopkins, *The Eradication of Smallpox. Organizational Learning and Innovation in International Health* (San Franscisco and London, 1989).

39. Riley, *Sick not Dead,* pp. 174, 197.

40. Cartwright, *The Development of Modern Surgery,* pp. 36, 101.

41. Anne Hardy, 'Rickets and the Rest: Childcare, Diet and the Infectious Children's Diseases', *Social History of Medicine,* **5** (1992), 389–412.

42. Riley, *Sick Not Dead,* pp. 120–3.

43. See Simon Szreter, *Fertility, Class and Gender in Britain, 1860–1940* (Cambridge, 1996), pp. 190–237.
44. See Royston Lambert, *Sir John Simon, 1816–1904: and English Social Administration* (Bristol, 1963).
45. Elizabeth Fee and Dorothy Porter, 'Public Health, Preventive Medicine and Professionalisation: England and America in the Nineteenth Century', in Andrew Wear (ed.), *Medicine in Society* (Cambridge, 1992.)
46. John M. Eyler, 'Mortality Statistics and Victorian Health Policy: Program and Criticism', *Bulletin of the History of Medicine*, **50** (1976) pp. 335–55; Robert Millward and Sally Sheard, 'The Urban Fiscal Problem 1870–1914: Government Expenditure and Finance in England and Wales', *Economic History Review*, **48** (1995), 501–35; Robert Millward and Frances Bell, 'Economic Factors in the Decline of Mortality in Late Nineteenth Century Britain', *European Review of Economic History*, **2** (1998), 263–88.
47. For the debates that raged over water quality and water analysis, see Christopher Hamlin, *A Science of Impurity. Water Analysis in Nineteenth-century England* (Bristol, 1990).
48. A. S. Wohl, *Endangered Lives. Public Health in Victorian Britain* (1983), p. 111.
49. Ibid., pp. 62–3.
50. The problems and practices of non-water carriage towns are well described in Martin Daunton, *House and Home in the Victorian City: Working Class Housing 1850–1914* (1983).
51. Ian Buchanan, 'Infant Feeding, Sanitation and Diarrhoea in British Coal Mining Communities, 1880–1911' in D. J. Oddy and D. S.Miller (eds), *Diet and Health in Modern Britain* (1985).
52. Wohl, *Endangered Lives*, Chapter 8.
53. Leonard Hill and Argyll Campbell, *Health and Environment* (1925), pp. 1–4.
54. Enid Gauldie, *Cruel Habitations. A History of Working-class Housing* (1974), p. 168. For a concise discussion of nineteenth-century working-class housing, see John Burnett, *A Social History of Housing* (2nd edn, 1986), Chapter 6.
55. Barbara Harrison, *Not Only the Dangerous Trades: Women's Work and Health in Britain, 1880–1914* (1996); Marguerite Dupree, *Family Structure in the Staffordshire Potteries, 1840–1880* (Oxford, 1995).
56. Wohl, *Endangered Lives*, p. 281. On gout see Roy Porter and G. S. Rousseau, *Gout. The Patrician Malady* (New Haven and London, 1998).
57. Jim Phillips and Michael French, 'Adulteration and Food Law, 1899–1939', *Twentieth Century British History*, **9** (1998), 350–69. See also John Burnett, *Plenty and Want: A Social History of Food in England from 1815 to the Present Day* (3rd edn, 1989), Chapter 10.
58. Burnett, *Plenty and Want*, pp. 108–11.
59. Derek Oddy, 'Food, Drink and Nutrition', in F. M. L. Thompson (ed.), *The Cambridge Social History of Britain* (Cambridge, 1990), vol. 2, pp. 272–5. See also Anna Davin, 'Loaves and Fishes: Food in Poor Households in Late Nineteenth-century London', *History Workshop Journal*, **41** (1996), 167–92; Burnett, *Plenty and Want*, Chapters 7 and 8; Jack Drummond and Anne Wilbraham, *The Englishman's Food: Five Centuries of English Diet* (revised edn, 1957), p. 403.
60. For the *fin-de-siècle* crisis, see Mike Jay and Michael Neve (eds), *1900* (1999).
61. For Galton, his ideas and influence, see Daniel J. Kevles, *In the Name of Eugenics. Genetics and the Uses of Human Heredity* (Harmondsworth, 1985). See also Richard Soloway, *Demography and Degeneration: Eugenics and the*

Declining Birth Rate in Twentieth-century Britain (Chapel Hill and London, 1990); Mathew Thomson, *The Problem of Mental Deficiency. Eugenics, Democracy, and Social Policy in Britain c. 1870–1939* (Oxford, 1998).

62. Geoffrey Searle, *The Quest for National Efficiency: A Study in British Politics and Political Thought, 1899–1914* (Oxford, 1971).

63. Dorothy Porter, '"Enemies of the Race": Biologism, Environmentalism, and Public Health in Edwardian England', *Victorian Studies*, **34** (1991), 160–77.

64. Searle, *The Quest for National Efficiency*; Anna Davin, 'Imperialism and Motherhood', *History Workshop Journal*, **5** (1978), 9–66; Jane Lewis, *The Politics of Motherhood. Child and Maternal Welfare in England 1900–1939* (1980).

65. For the reasons behind the dominance of this attitude, see Christopher Hamlin, *Public Health and Social Justice in the Age of Chadwick* (Cambridge, 1998).

66. Gareth Stedman Jones, *Outcast London* (Oxford, 1975).

67. Charles Booth, *Life and Labour of the People in London*, 10 vols (1892–97).

68. B. Seebohm Rowntree, *Poverty: A Study of Town Life* (1901).

69. Kenneth W. Carpenter, *Protein and Energy: A Study of Changing Ideas in Nutrition* (Cambridge, 1994).

70. Deborah Dwork, *War is Good for Babies and Other Young Children. A History of the Child and Infant Welfare Movement in England 1898–1918* (1987); John Welshman, 'Image of Youth: The Issue of Juvenile Smoking, 1880–1914', *Addiction*, **91** (1996), 1379–86.

71. For the School Medical Service, see Bernard Harris, *The Health of the Schoolchild. A History of the School Medical Service in England and Wales* (Buckingham, 1995).

72. For contemporary debates about the family and its position in society, see George K. Behlmer, *Friends of the Family. The English Home and its Guardians, 1850–1940* (Stanford, CA, 1998).

73. For the potential impact of such measures see Lewis, *The Politics of Motherhood*, pp. 101–2; Pat Thane, 'Visions of Gender in the Making of the British Welfare State: The Case of Women in the British Labour Party and Social Policy, 1906–1945', in Gisela Bock and Pat Thane (eds), *Maternity and Gender Politics. Women and the Rise of the European Welfare States 1880s–1950s* (1991), pp. 102–3.

74. Frank Prochaska, *Women and Philanthropy in Nineteenth-century England* (Oxford, 1980).

75. Wohl, *Endangered Lives*, pp. 36–8, 67–70; Frank Prochaska, 'Body and Soul: Bible Nurses and the Poor in Victorian London', **60** *Historical Research*, (1987), 336–48; *idem*, 'A Mother's Country: Mothers' Meetings and Family Welfare in Britain, 1850–1950', **74** *History*, (1989), 379–99.

76. For the respiratory tuberculosis pattern, see Gillian Cronjé, 'Tuberculosis and Mortality Decline in England and Wales', in Woods and Woodward (eds), *Urban Disease and Mortality*, pp. 79, 83–5; for typhoid, Hardy, *The Epidemic Streets*, p. 155. See also Robert Woods and Nicola Shelton, *An Atlas of Victorian Mortality* (Liverpool, 1998).

77. For increased middle-class health consciousness, see Patricia Branca, *Silent Sisterhood: Middle Class Women in the Victorian Home* (1975), Chapter 4. The impact of Florence Nightingale's *Notes on Nursing* in America is discussed in Suellen Hoy, *Chasing Dirt. The American Pursuit of Cleanliness* (New York and Oxford, 1995), pp. 30–2. See also Alison Bashford, *Purity and Pollution. Gender, Embodiment and Victorian Medicine* (Basingstoke and London, 1998).

Chapter 2

1. J. Drummond and A. Wilbraham, *The Englishman's Food*, p. 529, cited in J. M. Winter, *The Great War and the British People* (Basingstoke and London, 1985), p. 104; Sir Clifford Allbutt, cited in Roger Cooter, 'War and Modern Medicine', in W. F. Bynum and Roy Porter (eds), *The Companion Encyclopaedia of the History of Medicine* (1993), vol. 2, p. 1546. See also Roger Cooter, 'Medicine and the Goodness of War', *Canadian Journal of Medical History*, **7** (1990), 147–59.
2. Winter, *Great War*; See also Roger Cooter, Mark Harrison and Steve Sturdy (eds), *War, Medicine and Modernity* (Gloucester, 1999).
3. Tim Jeal, *Baden-Powell* (1989), p. 358 *et seq.*
4. Daniel Pick, *The War Machine. The Rationalisation of Slaughter in the Modern Age* (New Haven and London, 1993); John Gooch, 'Attitudes to War in Late Victorian and Edwardian England', in Brian Bond and Ian Roy (eds), *War and Society* (1975); Mark Girouard, *The Return to Camelot: Chivalry and the English Gentleman* (London and New Haven, 1981); J. A. Mangan and James Walvin (eds), *Manliness and Morality. Middle-class Masculinity in Britain and America 1800–1940* (Manchester, 1987); Anne Summers, *Angels and Citizens. British Women as Military Nurses, 1854–1914* (1988).
5. Samuel Hynes, *A War Imagined. The First World War and English Culture* (1992).
6. Richard Wall, 'English and German Families and the First World War, 1914–1918', in Richard Wall and Jay Winter (eds), *The Upheaval of War. Family, Work and Welfare in Europe, 1914–1918* (Cambridge, 1988), pp. 45–6.
7. Winter, *Great War*, Chapter 3.
8. David Cannadine, 'War and Death, Grief and Mourning in Modern Britain', in Joachim Whaley (ed.), *Mirrors of Mortality* (1981), pp. 193–217.
9. James Munson (ed.), *Echoes of the Great War. The Diary of the Reverend Andrew Clark 1914–1919* (Oxford, 1985), p. 177.
10. For the wartime controls and their context, see John Burnett, *Liquid Pleasures. A Social History of Drinks in Modern Britain* (1999), Chapters 6, 8. See also R. B. Weir, 'Obsessed with Moderation: the Drink Trade and the Drink Question (1870–1930)', *British Journal of Addiction*, **79** (1984), 93–107; John Turner, 'State Purchase and the Liquor Trade in the First World War', *Historical Journal*, **23** (1980), 589–615. For the economic and technological factors behind the rising popularity of the cigarette, see Matthew Hilton, *Smoking in British Popular Culture* (Manchester, 2000), Part II.
11. The drug nicotine, the active ingredient in tobacco addiction, is a slow carcinogen, whose effects on the body take decades to become apparent.
12. The comparative civilian health experiences of Britain and Germany, and their relationship to food supplies, are analysed in Avner Offer, *The First World War: An Agrarian Interpretation* (Oxford, 1989), Chapter 3.
13. For the detail of Britain's wartime food management, see L. Margaret Barnett, *British Food Policy During the First World War* (Boston and London, 1985); see also Drummond and Wilbraham, *The Englishman's Food*, pp. 431–42.
14. Registrar-General's Annual Report for 1915, pp. xxxix–xl. Civilian mortality in the South stood at 80 per million persons; in the Midlands, 35; in Wales, 25; and in the North, 12.
15. Linda Bryder, 'The First World War: Healthy or Hungry?', *History Workshop Journal*, **24** (1987), 141–57; J. M. Winter, 'Public Health and the Political

Economy of War', ibid., **25** (1988), 163–73; *idem*, 'Surviving the War: Life Expectation, Illness and Mortality Rates in Paris, London and Berlin, 1914–1919' in Jay Winter and Jean-Louis Robert (eds), *Capital Cities at War: Paris, London, Berlin 1914–1919* (Cambridge, 1997), pp. 520–2.

16. The migration factor is stressed in Catherine Rollet, 'The 'Other War' II: Setbacks in Public Health', in Winter and Robert, *Capital Cities*, pp. 471–2; Winter, 'Surviving the War', ibid., pp. 520–1.

17. Linda Bryder, *Below the Magic Mountain. A Social History of Tuberculosis in Twentieth-century Britain* (Oxford, 1988), pp. 3–4.

18. See Vera Brittain, *The Testament of Youth* (1978), pp. 462–3.

19. Rollet, 'The "Other War" II', pp. 467–8.

20. Lara V. Marks, *Metropolitan Maternity: Maternal and Infant Welfare Services in the Early Twentieth Century* (Amsterdam, 1996), Chapter 5.

21. Winter, *Great War*, pp. 184–7.

22. Gail Braybon, *Women Workers in the First World War* (1981), Chapter 2.

23. Anne Digby, *The Evolution of British General Practice 1850–1948* (Oxford, 1999), pp. 158–9; James Stuart Garner, 'The Great Experiment: The Admission of Women Students to St Mary's Hospital Medical School, 1916–1925', *Medical History*, **42** (1998), 68–88.

24. Antonia Ineson and Deborah Thom, 'T.N.T. Poisoning and the Employment of Women Workers in the First World War', in Paul Weindling (ed.), *The Social History of Occupational Health* (1985), pp. 89–107.

25. Winter, 'Public Health', p. 166; Offer, *The First World War*, Chapter 3; Winter and Robert, *Capital Cities*.

26. Mark Harrison, 'Medicine and the Management of Modern Warfare', *History of Science*, **34** (1996), 379–410.

27. Cooter, 'War and Modern Medicine', p. 1541.

28. Anne Hardy, '"Straight back to Barbarism": Typhoid Inoculation and the Great War, 1914', *Bulletin of the History of Medicine*, **74** (2000), 265–90.

29. David K. Patterson, 'Typhus and Its Control in Russia, 1870–1940', *Medical History*, **37** (1993), 361–81.

30. Fielding H. Garrison, *A History of Medicine* (Philadelphia, 1929), p. 2.

31. Cooter, 'War and Modern Medicine', pp. 1536–54.

32. Frederick W. Cartwright, *The Development of Modern Surgery* (1967), Chapter 6, pp. 106–13.

33. J. C. Bennett, 'Medical Advances Consequent to the Great War 1914–1918', *Journal of the Royal Society of Medicine*, **83** (1990), 738.

34. John Boyd, 'Tetanus in Two World Wars', *Proceedings of the Royal Society of Medicine*, **52** (1958), 109–10.

35. Roger Cooter, *Surgery and Society in Peace and War. Orthopaedics and the Organisation of Modern Medicine, 1880–1948* (Basingstoke, 1993).

36. Saul Benison, A., Clifford Barker and Elin L. Wolfe, 'Walter B. Cannon and the Mystery of Shock: A Study of Anglo-American Co-operation in World War I,' *Medical History*, **35** (1991), 217–49.

37. Joel Howell, '"Soldier's Heart": The Redefinition of Heart Disease and Specialty Formation in Early Twentieth-century Great Britain', in W. F. Bynum, C. J. Lawrence and V. Nutton (eds), *The Emergence of Modern Cardiology, Medical History*, supplement no. 5 (1985), 34–51.

38. Weymss Reid, *Memoirs and Correspondance of Lyon Playfair* (1899), pp. 159–60.

39. Steve Sturdy, 'From the Trenches to the Hospitals at Home: Physiologists, Clinicians and Oxygen Therapy, 1914–30', in John Pickstone (ed.), *Medical Innovations in Historical Perspective* (Basingstoke, 1992), pp. 104–23.

40. Lucy Bland, '"Cleansing the Portals of Life": The Venereal Disease Campaign in the Early Twentieth Century', in Mary Langan and Bill Schwartz (eds), *Crises in the British State 1880–1930* (1985), pp. 192–208.

41. John M. Eyler, *Sir Arthur Newsholme and State Medicine, 1885–1935* (Cambridge, 1997), p. 277. Eyler offfers the best general account of the wartime civilian actions against venereal disease, see pp. 277–94.

42. David Evans, 'Tackling the "Hideous Scourge": The Creation of the Venereal Disease Treatment Centres in Early Twentieth-century Britain', *Social History of Medicine*, 5 (1992), 413–33.

43. Mark Harrison, 'The British Army and the Problem of Venereal Disease in France and Egypt during the First World War', *Medical History*, 39 (1995), 133–58.

44. Michael Robson, 'The British Pharmaceutical Industry and the First World War', in Jonathan Liebenau (ed.), *The Challenge of the New Technology* (Aldershot, 1988), pp. 83–105; Judy Slinn, 'Research and Development in the UK Pharmaceutical Industry from the Late Nineteenth Century to the 1960s', in Roy Porter and Mikŭlas Teich (eds), *Drugs and Narcotics in History* (Cambridge, 1995).

45. Elaine Showalter, *The Female Malady. Women and Madness in English Culture 1830–1980* (1985), p. 3. See Andrew Scull, *The Most Solitary of Afflictions. Madness and Society in Britain 1700–1900* (New Haven and London, 1993); Andrew Scull, Charlotte Mackenzie and Nicholas Hervey, *Masters of Bedlam. The Transformation of the Mad-doctoring Trade* (New Jersey, 1996).

46. Martin Stone, 'Shellshock and the Psychologists', in W.F.Bynum, R. Porter, and M. Shepherd (eds),*The Anatomy of Madness*, (1985), vol. 2, pp. 242–71. See also Paul Frederick Lerner, 'Hysterical Men: War, Neurosis and German Mental Medicine, 1914–1921', unpublished PhD thesis, Columbia University, 1996 (Wellcome Library for the History and Understanding of Medicine).

47. Quoted in John Ellis, *Eye-deep in Hell* (1976), p. 118.

48. For the historical context of attitudes to hysteria, see Elaine Showalter, 'Hysteria, Feminism and Gender', in Sander Gilman *et al.*, *Hysteria Beyond Freud* (Berkeley and London, 1993).

49. Ibid., pp. 246–9.

50. Winter, *Great War*, Chapter 9.

51. Showalter, *Female Malady*, Chapter 7; Ted Bogacz, 'War Neurosis and Cultural Change in England, 1914–1922: The Work of the War Office Committee of Enquiry into "Shell Shock"', *Journal of Contemporary History*, 24 (1989), 227–56.

52. Harold Mersky, 'Shell-shock', in German Berrios and Hugh Freeman (eds), *150 Years of British Psychiatry, 1841–1991* (1991), pp. 245–67.

53. Showalter, 'Hysteria, Feminism and Gender'.

54. Alfred Crosby, *America's Forgotten Pandemic: The Influenza of 1918* (Cambridge, 1989), p. xiv. See also, David K. Patterson and Gerald F. Pyle, 'The Geography and Mortality of the 1918 Influenza Pandemic', *Bulletin of the History of Medicine*, 65 (1991), 4–21.

55. Sandra Tomkins, 'The Failure of Expertise: Public Health Policy in Britain During the 1918–19 Influenza Epidemic', *Social History of Medicine*, 5 (1992), 437–40.

Notes

Chapter 3

1. Steve Sturdy, 'Hippocrates and State Medicine: George Newman Outlines the Founding Policy of the Ministry of Health', in Christopher Lawrence and George Weisz (eds), *Greater Than the Parts. Holism in Biomedicine 1920–1950* (Oxford, 1998), pp. 112–34.
2. Christopher Lawrence, *Medicine in the Making of Modern Britain* (1994), pp. 81–2.
3. E. P. Hennock, *British Social Reform and German Precedents: The Case of Social Insurance, 1880–1914* (Oxford, 1987).
4. Brian Abel Smith, *The Hospitals* (London, 1967), p. 247.
5. Anne Digby and Nick Bosanquet, 'Doctors and Patients in an Era of National Health Insurance and Private Practice, 1913–1938', *Economic History Review*, 2nd series, **XLI** (1988), 86–7.
6. Ibid., p. 91.
7. Anne Digby, *The Evolution of British General Practice 1850–1948* (Oxford, 1999), p. 322. Digby discusses the question of standards of general 'panel' practice on pp. 318–22.
8. Ibid., p. 90.
9. Abel-Smith, *The Hospitals*, p. 404; Steven Cherry, 'Beyond National Health Insurance: The Voluntary Hospitals and Hospital Contribution Schemes: A Regional Study', *Social History of Medicine*, **5** (1992), 455–81; Martin Powell, 'Hospital Provision before the National Health Service Act. A Geographical Study of the 1943 Hospital Survey', ibid., pp. 483–504.
10. Martin Powell, 'An Expanding Service: Municipal Acute Medicine in the 1930s', *Twentieth Century British History*, **8** (1997), 334–57.
11. Abel Smith, *The Hospitals*, pp. 244–51.
12. For a graphic evocation of such tragedies, see Thomas Dormandy, *The White Death: A History of Tuberculosis* (1999). Subtler accounts of the patient experience may be found in Sheila Rothman, *Living in the Shadow of Death* (Baltimore, 1995), and Katharine Ott, *Fevered Lives* (Cambridge, MA, 1996).
13. Thomas McKeown, *The Role of Medicine* (Oxford, 1976), p. 9.
14. F. B. Smith, *The Retreat of Tuberculosis 1850–1950* (1988), p. 239. See John M. Eyler, *Sir Arthur Newsholme and State Medicine, 1885–1935* (Cambridge, 1997), Chapters 6, 9.
15. Linda Bryder, *Below the Magic Mountain: A Social History of Tuberculosis in Twentieth-century Britain* (Oxford, 1988), Chapter 7.
16. Smith, *Retreat*, p. 239.
17. See Christopher Hamlin, *Public Health and Social Justice in the Age of Chadwick* (Cambridge, 1997), p. 12 *et seq.*
18. Margery Spring Rice, *Working Class Wives* (Harmondsworth, 1939), Chapter 3. See also Margaret Llwellyn Davies (ed.), *Maternity: Letters from Working Class Wives* (1915; Virago edn, 1978); Digby, *Evolution of General Practice*, Chapter 8.
19. The classic discussion of the subordination of women's health to the interests of the infant is that of Jane Lewis, *The Politics of Motherhood: Child and Maternal Welfare in England 1900–1939* (1980).
20. Lara Marks, *Metropolitan Maternity: Maternal and Infant Welfare Services in Early Twentieth Century London* (Amsterdam, 1996), pp. 119, 121.
21. See Margaret Mitchell, 'The Effects of Unemployment on the Social Condition of Women and Children in the 1930s', *History Workshop Journal*, **14** (1985), 115.

Notes

22. Irvine Loudon, *Death in Childbirth* (Oxford, 1992).

23. Marks, *Metropolitan Maternity*, pp. 124–5, 186–91.

24. On the work of the School Medical Service, see Bernard Harris, *The Health of the Schoolchild. A History of the School Medical Service in England and Wales* (Buckingham, 1995).

25. John Burnett, *A Social History of Housing 1815–1985* (2nd edn, 1986), pp. 219–20.

26. Mark Swenarton, *Homes Fit For Heroes. The Politics and Architecture of Early State Housing in Britain* (1981), Chapter 4.

27. Burnett, *A Social History of Housing*, pp. 336–7.

28. Chief Medical Officer's Annual Report, 1922, p. 23; 1931, p. 11; 1932, p. 74. On the history of accidents, see Roger Cooter and Bill Luckin (eds), *Accidents in History: Injuries, Fatalities and Social Relations* (Amsterdam, 1997).

29. John Stevenson and Chris Cook, *Britain in the Depression: Society and Politics 1929–39* (1994). For Webster see notes 33, 37, 44 below; for Mitchell note 19 above.

30. Keith Laybourn, *Britain on the Breadline. A Social and Political History of Britain between the Wars* (Gloucester, 1990), pp. 53–66.

31. Klim MacPherson and David Coleman, 'Health' in A. H. Halsey (ed.), *British Social Trends Since 1900* (Basingstoke, 1988), pp. 402–3, 406–7.

32. A. L. Bowley and M. Hogg, *Has Poverty Diminished?* (1925); B. Seebohm Rowntree, *Poverty and Progress: A Second Social Survey of York* (1941).

33. Charles Webster, 'Healthy or Hungry Thirties', *History Workshop Journal*, **13** (1982), 110 *et seq.*

34. Christopher Hamlin, *Public Health and Social Justice in the Age of Chadwick 1800–1854* (Cambridge, 1998).

35. See, for example, Medical Officer's Annual Report, Northampton, 1923, p. 5; Medical Officer's Annual Report, Birmingham, 1922, Medical Officer's letter to the Public Health Committee.

36. Burnett, *Social History of Housing*, Chapter 8.

37. Stevenson and Cook, *Britain in the Depression*, p. 89. For limitations and local variability of allowances, see Charles Webster, 'Health, Welfare and Unemployment During the Depression', *Past and Present*, **109** (1985), 208–9.

38. Laybourn, *Britain on the Breadline*, pp. 55, 60.

39. Noel Whiteside, 'Counting the Cost: Sickness and Disability Among Working People in an Era of Industrial Recession 1920–39', *Economic History Review*, 2nd series, **XL** (1987), 245.

40. Webster, 'Healthy or Hungry?', p. 116.

41. Mitchell, 'The Effects of Unemployment', p.107.

42. Mitchell, 'The Effects of Unemployment', p. 111. These patterns and their background are authoritatively analysed in Irvine Loudon, *Death in Childbirth. An International Study of Maternal Care and Maternal Mortality 1800–1950* (Oxford, 1992).

43. Ibid., Webster, 'Healthy or Hungry', p. 117.

44. Charles Webster, 'The Health of the School Child During the Depression', in Nicholas Parry and David MacNair (eds), *The Fitness of the Nation – Physical and Health Education in the Nineteenth and Twentieth Centuries* (1993), pp. 78–9.

45. For the impact of commercial ventures in popularising vitamin consciousness among the British people, see Sally M. Horrocks, 'Nutrition Science and the Food and Pharmaceutical Industries in Inter-war Britain', in David

F. Smith (ed.), *Nutrition in Britain. Science, Scientists and Politics in the Twentieth Century* (1997), pp. 53–74.

46. Celia Petty, 'Primary Research and Public Health: The Prioritization of Nutrition Research in Interwar Britain', in Joan Austoker and Linda Bryder (eds), *Historical Perspectives on the Role of the MRC* (Oxford, 1989), pp. 105–6.

47. On incomes in general in this period, see John Stevenson, *British Society 1914–1945* (1984), pp. 119–24.

48. Peter Bartrip, *Themselves Writ Large: A History of the British Medical Association* (1996), pp. 201–5; Webster, 'Health, Welfare and Unemployment during the Depression', pp. 211–12.

49. Petty, 'Primary Research and Public Health', p. 106.

50. Webster, 'Health, Welfare and Unemployment', p. 211.

51. John Walton, *Fish and Chips and the British Working Class, 1870–1940* (Leicester, 1992); Anna Davin, 'Loaves and Fishes: Food in Poor Households in Late Nineteenth-century London', *History Workshop Journal*, **41** (1996), 167–92.

52. See Petty, 'Primary Research and Public Health', pp. 89–102.

53. On the work of the MRC, see A. Landesborough Thomson, *Half a Century of Medical Research* (1973, 1975), 2 vols; Austoker and Bryder (eds), *Historical Perspectives on the Role of the MRC.* On Sir George Newman, see Sturdy, 'Hippocrates and State Medicine'. Useful sidelights on Newman may also be found in Eyler's study of his contemporary and rival, Arthur Newsholme, *Sir Arthur Newsholme and State Medicine, 1885–1935* (Cambridge, 1997).

54. Bryder, *Below the Magic Mountain*, pp. 138–42. See also *idem,* '"We Shall Not Find Salvation in Inoculation": BCG vaccination in Scandinavia, Britain and the USA, 1921–1960', *Social Science and Medicine*, **49** (1999), 1157–68.

55. For the story of the development of insulin, see Michael Bliss, *The Discovery of Insulin* (Edinburgh, 1983).

56. MRC Annual Report, 1929–30, pp. 22–4; see also Chief Medical Officer's Annual Report, 1932, pp. 72–7. Landesborough Thomson, Medical Research Council, pp. 38–41.

57. See M. W. Wintrobe, *Hematology: The Blossoming of a Science* (Philadelphia, 1985); *idem* (ed.), *Blood Pure and Eloquent* (New York, 1980).

58. David Cantor, 'The MRC's Support for Experimental Radiology in the Interwar Years', in Austoker and Bryder, *Perspectives*; Landesborough Thomson, *Medical Research Council,* pp. 58–62.

59. MRC Annual Report, 1920–21, p. 13.

60. Irvine Loudon, *The Tragedy of Childbed Fever* (Oxford, 2000), Chapter 11.

61. Idem, 'Puerperal Fever, the Streptococcus and the Sulphonamides 1911–1945', *British Medical Journal*, **ii** (1987), 485–9.

62. Lewis, *Politics of Motherhood,* Chapter 4.

63. Steve Sturdy, 'Hippocrates and State Medicine', p. 125.

64. MRC Annual Report, 1933, pp. 12–13. See also John Burnett, *Liquid Pleasures. A Social History of Drinks in Modern Britain* (1999), pp. 133, 172–5.

65. Julia Parker and Catriona Mirrless, 'Housing' in Halsey (ed.), *British Social Trends,* p. 365.

66. Helen Jones, *Health and Society in Twentieth Century Britain* (1994), p. 70.

67. Peter Bartrip, *Themselves Writ Large. The British Medical Association 1832–1966* (1996), p. 207–8.

68. Mariel Grant, 'The National Health Campaigns of 1937–1938', in Derek Fraser (ed.), *Cities, Class and Communication* (New York and London, 1990).

69. Nancy Tomes, *The Gospel of Germs. Men, Women and the Microbe in America* (Cambridge, MA and London, 1998); Horrocks, 'Nutrition Science', p. 57.
70. Anne Karpf, *Doctoring the Media* (1988), pp. 32–43.

Chapter 4

1. Chief Medical Officer's Report for 1939–45 (hereafter CMOR), pp. 169–70.
2. Richard Titmuss, *Problems of Social Policy* (1950).
3. See, for example, José Harris, 'War and Social History: Britain and the Home Front During the Second World War', *Journal of Contemporary History*, 1 (1992), 17–35; Philip Ziegler, *London at War. Britain 1939–1945* (1995), Chapter 10.
4. These aspects of civilian war experience are well detailed in Helen Jones, *Health and Society in the Twentieth Century* (1994), Chapter 5.
5. CMOR, p. 195.
6. V. Zachary Cope (ed.), *Medicine and Pathology* (1952), p. 447.
7. The best critical account of the evacuation is by John MacNicol, 'The Evacuation of Schoolchildren' in H. L. Smith (ed.) *War and Social Change. British Society in the Second World War* (Manchester, 1986). See also Travis L.Crosby, *The Impact of Civilian Evacuation in the Second World War* (Beckenham, 1986), and John Welshman, 'Evacuation and Social Policy during the Second World War: Myth and Reality', *Twentieth Century British History*, 9 (1998), 28–53.
8. The rural middle class perspective is well presented in the wartime novels of Angela Thirkell, notably in *Northbridge Rectory* (1941).
9. See MacNicol, 'Evacuation', p. 17.
10. MacNicol, 'Evacuation', pp. 24–6.
11. On the School Medical Service, see Bernard Harris, *The Health of the Schoolchild. A History of the School Medical Service in England and Wales* (Buckingham, 1995).
12. For child guidance clinics, see Kathleen Jones, *Mental Health and Social Policy 1845–1959* (1960), pp. 136, 165.
13. CMOR, p. 246.
14. CMOR, p. 35; Cope, *Medicine and Pathology*, pp. 170, 176.
15. Graphic descriptions may be found in Ziegler, *London at War*, pp. 115–16; Angus Calder, *The People's War. Britain 1939–1945* (1969), pp. 181–97.
16. CMOR, pp. 172–3.
17. CMOR, p. 186.
18. Ibid., p. 66.
19. Cope, *Medicine and Pathology*, p. 159.
20. Titmuss, *Social Policy*, p. 193. See also Robin Means and Randall Smith, *From Poor Law to Community Care. The Development of Welfare Services for Elderly People, 1939–1971* (Bristol, 2nd edn, 1998), Chapter 2.
21. See Titmuss, *Social Policy*, pp. 183–202, 442–505; CMOR, pp. 187–9.
22. R. J. Hammond, *Food*, 1 (1951), 77.
23. Ibid., p. 77.
24. Ibid., p. 219.
25. Ibid., pp. 218–21. Hammond's statements on the belated engagement of nutrition scientists in the planning of wartime food policy are quite unequivocal, and he indeed specifically attacks the veracity of one specialist

Notes

memorandum of 1944 to the Food and Agriculture Organisation that implied that food policy had been scientifically determined from the outbreak of war (pp. 218–19). The influence of science is implied in Anne Wilbraham's account of Second World War food policy, and by John Burnett. See Jack Drummond and Anne Wilbraham, *The Englishman's Food. Five Centuries of English Diet* (2nd edn, 1957), pp. 448–50; John Burnett, *Plenty and Want. A Social History of Food in England from 1815 to the Present Day* (3rd edn, 1989), p. 290.

26. Burnett, *Plenty and Want,* pp. 292–3.
27. CMOR, p. 2.
28. Postwar rationing included, for the first time, bread allowances. Rationing only came to an end in 1953. Again, the effects of postwar rationing, the sense that the government was deliberately keeping people under-nourished, and the fatigue of women are documented in Angela Thirkell's postwar novels, for example, *Private Enterprise* (1947) and *Love Among the Ruins* (1948).
29. R. J. Hammond, *Food,* vol. 2 (1956), Chapter 23, 'The British Restaurant Movement', p. 411.
30. A. J. P. Taylor, *English History 1914–1945* (Harmondsworth, 1970), pp. 576–68.
31. CMOR, p. 7.
32. Max Blythe, 'A Century of Health Education', *Health and Hygiene,* **7** (1986), 105–15.
33. CMOR, p. 248.
34. Jones, *Health and Society,* pp. 97–9.
35. Charles Webster, *The National Health Service. A Political History* (Oxford, 1998), pp. 6–7.
36. R. E. O. Williams, *Microbiology for the Public Health: The Evolution of the Public Health Laboratory Service 1939–1980* (1985), Chapter 1.
37. CMOR, p. 161–3; Janet M. Vaughn and Sir Philip N. Panton, 'The Civilian Blood Transfusion Service', in C. L. Dunn (ed.), *The Emergency Medical Services,* vol. 1 (1952), p, 355.
38. CMOR, p. 140; Means and Smith, *Poor Law to Community Care,* pp. 23–4.
39. Ibid., p. 140. For a graphic account of the experience and impact of bombing on London's hospitals, see Frank Prochaska, *Philanthropy and the Hospitals of London: The Kings Fund, 1899–1990* (Oxford, 1992), Chapter 6.
40. CMOR, p. 135.
41. CMOR, pp. 158–61.
42. A. S. Daly, 'Anaesthetics in the Army', in V. Zachary Cope (ed.), *Surgery* (1953), p. 222; A. E. Barclay, 'Radiology' in Dunn (ed.) *The Emergency Medical Services,* vol. 1, pp. 356–65; see also Jennifer Beinart, *A History of the Nuffield Department of Anaesthetics, Oxford 1837–1887* (Oxford, 1987), Chapters 1 and 2.
43. J. M. Winter, 'The Demographic Consequences of the War', in Smith (ed.), *War and Social Change. British Society in the Second World War,* p. 163.
44. Winter, 'Demographic Consequences', p. 163.
45. Roger Cooter, *Surgery and Society in Peace and War. Orthopaedics and the Reorganisation of Modern Medicine, 1880–1948* (Basingstoke, 1993), Chapter 11, p. 219.
46. A. Kate Khoo, 'The Treatment of Burns in the Second World War', unpublished BSc dissertation, University College London, 1998 (Wellcome Library for the History and Understanding of Medicine).

47. Ivy Teoh, 'Reconstructing the Faces of War', unpublished BSc dissertation, University College London, 1997 (Wellcome Library).
48. Sir W. H. Ogilvie, 'General Introduction', in Cope, *Surgery*, p. 6.
49. Ibid., p. 7.
50. Joanna Bourke, 'Disciplining the Emotions: Fear, Psychiatry and the Second World War', in Cooter, Harrison and Sturdy (eds), *War, Medicine and Modernity*, pp. 225–38.
51. Robert H. Ahrenfeldt, *Psychiatry in the British Army in the Second World War* (1958), pp. 16, 23.
52. See Nafsika Thalassis, 'Soldiers, Doctors, Analysts: Psychiatry and the Second World War', unpublished MSc dissertation, Imperial College/University College London, 1998. For the impact of war on child psychiatry, see Thea Vidnes, 'Progress, Diffusion and Loss. A Study of the Psychological Effects of Child Evacuation from the Second World War to the Early Years of the NHS', unpublished BSc dissertation, University College London, 1998 (Wellcome Library).
53. For the deep symbolic importance of penicillin to the British, both during and after the war, see Robert Bud, 'Penicillin and the New Elizabethans', *British Journal for the History of Science*, **31** (1998), 305–33.
54. For the differences in the American and British approaches to the manufacture of penicillin on a large scale, see Jonathan Liebenau, 'The British Success with Penicillin', *Social Studies of Science*, **17** (1987), 69–86.
55. Dunn, *The Emergency Medical Services*, vol. 1, p. 318.
56. Ibid., p. 313.

Chapter 5

1. An accessible account of postwar change, and of the history of the welfare state as a whole, is provided in Nicholas Timmins, *The Five Giants. A Biography of the Welfare State* (1995). For Sir William Beveridge himself, see José Harris, *William Beveridge. A Biography* (Oxford, revised edn, 1997).
2. For the negotiations surrounding the exact provisions of the National Health Service Act, see John Pater, *The Making of the NHS* (1981); Rudolf Klein, *The Politics of the NHS* (2nd edn, 1989); Frank Honigsbaum, *Health, Happiness and Security. The Creation of the National Health Service* (1989); Charles Webster, *The National Health Service. A Political History* (Oxford, 1998).
3. Charles Webster, *The Health Services Since the War*, i, *Problems of Care: The National Health Service before 1957* (1988), p. 262.
4. Idem, *The Health Services Since the War*, ii, *Government and Health Care: The British National Health Service 1958–1979* (1996), pp. 92–109.
5. David Morrell, 'Introduction and Overview', in Irvine Loudon, John Horder and Charles Webster (eds), *The General Practitioner Under the National Health Service, 1948–1997* (Oxford, 1998), pp. 3–4.
6. See John Howie, 'Research in General Practice: Perspectives and Themes', in Loudon *et al.* (eds), *General Practice*, pp. 146–64; David Hannay, 'Undergraduate Medical Education and General Practice', ibid., pp. 165–81.
7. Charles Webster, 'Doctors, Public Service and Profit: General Practitioners and the National Health Service', *Transactions of the Royal Historical Society*, **40** (1970), pp. 197–8.

8. Webster, *The Health Services*, i, pp. 369, 370.
9. Webster, 'Doctors, Public Service and Profit', p. 216.
10. Drug expenditure had reached £114 million by 1963–64: Webster, *The Health Services*, ii, p. 138.
11. For a critique of NHS provision as regards women, see Lesley Doyal, 'Women and the National Health Service: the Carers and the Careless', in Ellen Lewin and Virginia Oleson (eds), *Women, Health and Healing. Towards a New Perspective* (New York, 1985), pp. 236–69.
12. Medical Officer's Annual Report for Birmingham, 1948, p. 14.
13. Charles Webster, 'The Elderly and the Early National Health Service', in Margaret Pelling and Richard Smith (eds), *Life, Death and the Elderly. Historical Perspectives* (1991), pp. 165–93.
14. For the evolution of the concept of community care, see Joan Busfield, *Managing Madness. Changing Ideas and Practice* (2nd edn, 1989), Chapter 10. For the emerging speciality of geriatrics, Moira Martin, 'Medical Knowledge and Medical Practice: Geriatric Medicine in the 1950s', *Social History of Medicine*, **8** (1995), 443–61; Geoffrey Rivett, *From Cradle to Grave. Fifty Years of the NHS* (1998), pp. 75–6.
15. Howard Glennerster, *British Social Policy Since 1945* (Oxford, 1995), pp. 208–9.
16. Webster, *The Health Services*, ii, p. 328.
17. For the background, origins and modern development of community care for those with learning disabilities and the mentally ill, see Peter Bartlett and David Wright (eds), *Outside the Walls of the Asylum. The History of Care in the Community 1750–2000* (1999), especially Jan Walmsley *et al.*, 'Community Care and Mental Deficiency 1913 to 1945'; John Welshman, 'Rhetoric and Reality: Community Care in England and Wales, 1948–74'; Sarah Payne, 'Outside the Walls of the Asylum? Psychiatric Treatment in the 1980s and 1990s'.
18. Busfield, *Managing Madness*, p. 350.
19. See Margaret Whitehead, 'The Health Divide', in Peter Townsend, Nick Davidson and Margaret Whitehead (eds), *Inequalities in Health* (Harmondsworth, 1988), pp. 248–54. There were, however, significant exceptions to this rule: see Lara Marks and Lisa Hilder, 'Ethnic Advantage: Infant Survival among Jewish and Bengali Immigrants in East London 1870–1990', in Lara Marks and Michael Worboys (eds), *Migrants, Minorities and Health. Historical and Contemporary Studies* (1997).
20. Klim McPherson and David Colemen, 'Health' in A. H. Halsey (ed.), *British Social Trends Since 1900* (Basingstoke, 1988), pp. 402–3, Table 11.2.
21. Jane Lewis, *What Price Community Medicine. The Philosophy, Practice and Politics of Public Health since 1919* (Brighton, 1986); John Welshman, 'The Medical Officer of Health in England and Wales, 1900–1974: Watchdog or Lapdog?', *Journal of Public Health Medicine*, **19** (1997), 443–50.
22. Mervyn Susser, 'Epidemiology in the United States after World War II: The Evolution of Technique', *Epidemiologic Reviews*, **7** (1985), 147–77; Lise Wilkinson, 'Sir Austin Bradford Hill: Medical Statistics and the Quantitative Approach to Prevention of Disease', *Addiction*, **92** (1997), 657–66.
23. See Richard Doll, 'The First Reports on Smoking and Lung Cancer', in Stephen Lock, L. H. Reynolds and E. M. Tansey (eds), *Ashes to Ashes. The History of Smoking and Health* (Amsterdam, 1998), pp. 130–82.
24. In the opening pages of *Bleak House*, first published in 1853 (Harmondsworth, 1971), pp. 49–50.

25. Anthony Wohl, *Endangered Lives. Public Health in Victorian Britain* (1983) pp. 219, 231–2.
26. Leonard Hill and Argyll Campbell, *Health and Environment* (1925), pp. 2–3.
27. Roy Parker, 'The Struggle for Clean Air', in Phoebe Hall, H. Land, R. Parker and A. Webb (eds), *Change, Choice and Conflict in Social Policy* (Aldershot, 1986), pp. 371–87.
28. Harvey M. Sapolsky, 'Science, Voters and the Fluoridation Controversy', *Science,* **162** (1968), 427–33.
29. Webster, *The Health Services,* ii, pp. 131–3, 241–2, 662–5.
30. Sir Richard Doll, 'Major Epidemics of the 20th Century: from Coronary Thrombosis to AIDS', *Journal of the Royal Statistical Society* Series A, **150** (1987), 377.
31. Peter Taylor, *Smoke Ring. The Politics of Tobacco* (1984), p. xix. See also Charles Webster, 'Tobacco Smoking Addiction: A Challenge to the National Health Service', *British Journal of Addiction,* **79** (1984), 7–16; *idem,* vol. 2, pp. 133–5, 242–5, 424–6, 665–9.
32. See Whitehead, *The Health Divide,* pp. 290–2 for differential smoking habits by social class and economic status in the years 1972–84.
33. Rob Baggott, *Alcohol, Politics and Social Policy* (Aldershot, 1990).
34. Anne Murcott, 'Food and Nutrition in Post-war Britain', in James Obelkevich and Peter Catterall (eds), *Understanding Post-war British Society* (1994), p. 161; see also Whitehead, *The Health Divide,* pp. 292–4; Baggott, *Alcohol, Politics and Social Policy.*
35. See, for example, Joshua Lederberg, Robert E. Sharpe and Stanley C. Oaks Jr (eds), *Emerging Infections. Microbial Threats to Health in the United States* (Washington, 1992); Richard Preston, *The Hot Zone* (1994).
36. K. Dunnell, 'Are We Healthier?', in John Charlton and Mike Murphy (eds), *The Health of Adult Britain 1841–1994* (1997), vol. 2, p. 180.
37. For a reasoned assessment of the significance of the health survey, see Mildred Blaxter, 'Health Surveys: What Do They Mean?', in Ghislaine Lawrence (ed.), *Technologies of Modern Medicine* (1994), pp. 88–94.
38. McPherson and Coleman, 'Health', pp. 402–3, 406–7.
39. See Milton Wainwright, *Miracle Cure* (Oxford, 1990).
40. Ibid., pp. 86–7.
41. On the worrying resurgence of Group A streptococcal disease since 1980, see Irvine Loudon, *The Tragedy of Childbed Fever* (Oxford, 2000), pp. 198–200.
42. For the experience of polio and its wider history, see Tony Gould, *A Summer Plague. Polio and its Survivors* (1995).
43. Rivett, *From Cradle to Grave,* pp. 56, 216.
44. James Le Fanu, *The Rise and Fall of Modern Medicine* (1999), pp. 23–6.
45. Edward Shorter, *A History of Psychiatry. From the Era of the Asylum to the Age of Prozac* (New York and Chichester, 1997), Chapter 6; Jack D. Pressman, *The Last Resort. Psychosurgery and the Limits of Medicine* (Cambridge, 1998); Eliot S. Valenstein, *The Psychosurgry Debate: Scientific, Legal, and Ethical Perspectives* (San Franscisco, 1980).
46. Shorter, *History of Psychiatry,* pp. 248–50.
47. Ibid., Chapter 8.
48. The best general account of new developments in the drug treatment of disease is given in Rivett, *From Cradle to Grave,* pp. 55–7, 138–40, 215–17, 301–3, 385–8.
49. Le Fanu, *Rise and Fall,* p. 102.

Notes

50. See William R. Clark, *At War Within: The Double-Edged Sword of Immunity* (Oxford, 1995).
51. Rivett, *From Cradle to Grave*, p. 66.
52. Le Fanu, *Rise and Fall*, pp. 126–7.
53. Rivett, *From Cradle to Grave*, pp. 147–9, 224.
54. Stephen Lock, 'Medicine in the Second Half of the Twentieth Century', in I. S. L. Loudon *et al.*, *The Oxford Illustrated History of Western Medicine* (Oxford, 1997), p. 133.
55. Elizabeth S. Watkins, *On The Pill. A Social History of Oral Contraceptives, 1950–1970* (Baltimore, 1998), pp. 50–1.
56. Audrey Leathard, *The Fight for Family Planning. The Development of Family Planning Services in Britain 1921–1974* (1980), pp. 2, 5. On the monitoring of pill safety, see Lara Marks, '"Not Just a Statistic": the History of USA and UK Policy over Thrombotic Disease and the Oral Contraceptive Pill, 1960s–1970s', *Social Science and Medicine*, **49** (1999), 1139–55.
57. John Keown, *Abortion, Doctors and the Law. Some Aspects of the Legal Regulation of Abortion in England and Wales from 1803 to 1982* (Cambridge, 1988), pp. 84–5. See also Rivett, *From Cradle to Grave*, pp. 155, 227, 404.
58. Naomi Pfeffer, *The Stork and the Syringe. A Political History of Reproductive Medicine* (Cambridge, 1993).
59. Le Fanu, *Rise and Fall*, p. 176.
60. Rivett, *From Cradle to Grave*, p. 405.
61. Rivett, *From Cradle to Grave*, pp. 69, 150–3, 225–6, 317–18; 400–2.
62. For the development of successful treatment for acute lymphoblastic leukaemia, see Le Fanu, *Rise and Fall*, Chapter 10.
63. Rivett, *From Cradle to Grave*, pp. 400, 402.
64. Irvine Loudon and Mark Drury, 'Some Aspects of Clinical Care in General Practice', in Loudon *et al.* (eds), *General Practice*, pp. 96–8.
65. Le Fanu, *Rise and Fall*, p. 176.
66. On the new genetics, see Tom Wilkie, *Perilous Knowledge. The Human Genome Project and its Implications* (1993).
67. For the background to the legislation on animal experimentation, see Richard French, *Antivivisection and Medical Science in Victorian Society* (Princeton, 1975); Nicholaas Rupke (ed.), *Vivisection in Historical Perspective* (1987); for the GMC, Margaret Stacey, *Regulating British Medicine* (Chichester, 1992).
68. For Bradford Hill's influence, see the essays collected in the special issue of *Statistics in Medicine*, **1** (1982).
69. H. Sjøstrom and R. Nilsson, *Thalidomide and the Power of the Drug Companies* (Harmondsworth, 1972).
70. John Abraham, *Science, Politics and the Pharmaceutical Industry. Controversy and Bias in Drug Regulation* (1995), pp. 66–77.
71. Lock, 'Medicine in the Second Half of the Twentieth Century', p. 138.
72. For the struggle to gain compensation for thalidomide victims and their families, see Phillip Knightley *et al.*, *Suffer the Children. The Story of Thalidomide* (1979).
73. Archibald Cochrane, *Effectiveness and Efficiency* (1972); Thomas McKeown, *The Rise of Modern Population* (1976).
74. Ivan Illich, *The Limits to Medicine* (1976); Ian Kennedy, *The Unmasking of Medicine* (1981).
75. Horizon, 'Hospital 1922' (1972), Wellcome Trust Film Library.
76. Rivett, *From Cradle to Grave*, p. 296.

77. Sir Bryan Thwaites, *The NHS: The End of the Rainbow?* (Southampton, 1987), pp. 12–15.
78. Edward Shorter, *Doctors and Patients. A Social History* (New Brunswick and London, 1991), p. 12; Rivett, *From Cradle to Grave*, p. 381.
79. See *The Black Report*, Chapter 9, in Townsend *et al.*, *Inequalities in Health*, p. 169.
80. Rivett, *From Cradle to Grave*, pp. 379–80.
81. Richard G. Wilkinson, *Unhealthy Societies. The Afflictions of Inequality* (1996).
82. BMA, *Growing Up in Britain* (1999).
83. Mary Shaw, Danny Dorling and Nic Brimblecombe, 'Changing the Map: Health in Britain 1951–91', *Sociology of Health and Illness*, **20** (1998), 694–709, pp. 702, 705.

Conclusion

1. J. M. Winter, 'The Decline of Mortality in Britain 1700–1950', in Theo Barker and Michael Drake (eds), *Population and Society* (1982), p. 100.

BIBLIOGRAPHY

This is a selected bibliography. Further references will be found in the footnotes to individual chapters. The place of publication is London unless otherwise indicated.

Abel Smith, Brian, *The Hospitals 1800–1948. A Study in Social Administration in England and Wales* (1964).

Abraham, John, *Science, Politics and the Pharmaceutical Industry. Controversy and Bias in Drug Regulation* (1995).

Ahrenfeldt, Robert H., *Psychiatry in the British Army in the Second World War* (1958).

Allsop, Judith, 'Health: From Seamless Service to Patchwork Quilt', in David Gladstone (ed.), *British Social Welfare: Past, Present and Future* (1995).

Austoker, Joan and Bryder, Linda, *Historical Perspectives on the Role of the MRC* (Oxford, 1989).

Baggott, Rob, *Alcohol, Politics and Social Policy* (Aldershot, 1990).

Bartlett, Peter and Wright, David (eds), *Outside the Walls of the Asylum. The History of Care in the Community 1750–2000* (1999).

Bartrip, Peter, *Themselves Writ Large. The British Medical Association 1832–1966* (1996).

Behlmer, George K., *Friends of the Family. The English Home and its Guardians, 1850–1940* (Stanford, CA, 1998).

Berridge, Virginia, *Health and Society in Britain Since 1939* (1999).

Bland, Lucy, '"Cleansing the Portals of Life": The Venereal Disease Campaign in the Early Twentieth Century', in Mary Langan and Bill Schwarz (eds), *Crises in the British State 1880–1930* (1985).

Bogacz, Ted, 'War Neurosis and Cultural Change in England, 1914–22: the Work of the War Office Committee of Enquiry into "Shell-Shock"', *Journal of Contemporary History*, **24** (1989), 227–56.

Bonner, Thomas, *To The Ends of the Earth. Women's Search for Education in Medicine* (Cambridge, MA, 1992).

Bonner, Thomas, *Becoming a Physician: Medical Education in Great Britain, France, Germany and the United States 1750–1945* (Oxford, 1995).

Brand, Jeanne L., *Doctors and the State: The British Medical Profession and Government Action in Public Health, 1870–1912* (Baltimore, 1965).

Braybon, Gail, *Women Workers in the First World War* (1981).

Brookes, Barbara, *Abortion in England 1900–1967* (1988).

Bryder, Linda, 'The First World War: Healthy or Hungry?', *History Workshop Journal*, **24** (1987), 141–57.

Bryder, Linda, *Below the Magic Mountain. A Social History of Tuberculosis in Twentieth-century Britain* (Oxford, 1988).

Buckley, Suzanne, 'The Failure to Resolve the Problem of Venereal Disease among the Troops in Britain during World War I', in Brian Bond and Ian Roy (eds), *War and Society*, **2** (1977), 65–85.

Bibliography

Bud, Robert, 'Penicillin and the New Elizabethans', *British Journal for the History of Science*, **31** (1998), 305–33.

Burnett, John, *A Social History of Housing 1815–1985* (2nd edn, 1986).

Burnett, John, *Plenty and Want. A Social History of Food in England from 1815 to the Present Day* (3rd edn, 1989).

Burnett, John, *Liquid Pleasures. A Social History of Drinks in Modern Britain* (1999).

Busfield, Joan, *Managing Madness. Changing Ideas and Practice* (2nd edn, 1989).

Bynum, William, *Science and the Practice of Medicine in the Nineteenth Century* (Cambridge, 1994).

Cartwright, Frederick D., *The Development of Modern Surgery* (1967).

Charlton, John and Murphy, Mike, *The Health of Adult Britain 1841–1994*, 2 vols (1997).

Cherry, Steven, *Medical Services and the Hospitals in Britain, 1860–1939* (Cambridge, 1996).

Cooter, Roger, *Surgery and Society in Peace and War. Orthopaedics and the Organisation of Modern Medicine 1880–1948* (Basingstoke, 1993).

Cooter, Roger, 'War and Modern Medicine', in W. F. Bynum and Roy Porter (eds), *Encyclopaedia of the History of Medicine* (1993), vol. 2.

Cooter, Roger and Pickstone, John (eds), *Medicine in the Twentieth Century* (Amsterdam, 2000).

Cooter, Roger *et al.* (eds), *War, Medicine and Modernity* (Gloucester, 1998).

Digby, Anne, *Making a Medical Living. Doctors and Patients in the English Market for Medicine, 1720–1911* (Cambridge, 1994).

Digby, Anne, *The Evolution of British General Practice 1850–1948* (Oxford, 1999).

Digby, Anne and Bosanquet, Nick, 'Doctors and Patients in an Era of National Health Insurance and Private Practice', *Economic History Review*, 2nd series, **xli** (1988), 74–94.

Doll, Sir Richard, 'Major Epidemics of the 20th Century: From Coronary Thrombosis to AIDS', *Journal of the Royal Statistical Society* Series A, **150** (1987), 373–95.

Drummond, Jack C. and Wilbraham, Anne, *The Englishman's Food. Five Centuries of English Diet* (revised edn, 1957).

Dwork, Deborah, *War is Good for Babies and Other Young Children. A History of the Infant and Child Welfare Movement in England, 1898–1918* (1987).

Evans, David, '"Tackling the Hideous Scourge": The Creation of the Venereal Disease Treatment Centres in Early Twentieth-century Britain', *Social History of Medicine*, **5** (1992), 413–33.

Eyler, John M., *Victorian Social Medicine. The Ideas and Methods of William Farr* (Baltimore, 1979).

Eyler, John M., *Sir Arthur Newsholme and State Medicine, 1885–1935* (Cambridge, 1998).

Flinn, Michael, *Scottish Population History from the 17th Century to the 1930s* (Cambridge, 1977).

Floud, Roderick, Wachter, Kenneth and Gregory, Annabel, *Height, Health and History. Nutritional Status in the United Kingdom, 1750–1980* (Cambridge, 1990).

Fox, Daniel M., *Health Policies, Health Politics. The British and American Experience 1911–1965* (Princeton, 1986).

Fraser, Derek, *The Evolution of the British Welfare State* (2nd edn, 1984).

Gilbert, Bentley, *The Evolution of National Insurance in Great Britain* (1966).

Glennerster, Howard, *British Social Policy Since 1945* (Oxford, 1995).

Gould, Tony, *A Summer Plague. Polio and its Survivors* (New Haven, 1995).

Bibliography

Granshaw, Lindsay, 'Stepping to Fame and Fortune by Means of Bricks and Mortar', in Lindsay Granshaw and Roy Porter (eds), *The Hospital in History* (1989).

Granshaw, Lindsay, 'The Rise of the Modern Hospital in Britain', in Andrew Wear (ed.), *Medicine and Society* (Cambridge, 1992).

Granshaw, Lindsay, 'On This Principle I Have Made Practice', in John Pickstone (ed.) *Medical Innovation in Historical Perspective* (Basingstoke, 1992).

Grant, Mariel, 'The National Health Campaigns of 1937–1938', in Derek Fraser (ed.), *Cities, Class and Communication* (1990).

Haley, Bruce, *The Healthy Body and Victorian Culture* (Cambridge, MA and London, 1978).

Halsey, A. H. (ed.), *British Social Trends Since 1900. A Guide to the Changing Social Structure of Britain* (2nd edn, Basingstoke, 1988).

Hamlin, Christopher, *A Science of Impurity. Water Analysis in Nineteenth-century Britain* (Bristol, 1990).

Hamlin, Christopher, *Public Health and Social Justice in the Age of Chadwick* (Cambridge, 1998).

Hammond, R. J., *Food* (1951), 3 vols.

Hardy, Anne, 'Urban Famine or Urban Crisis? Typhus in the Victorian City', *Medical History*, **32** (1988) 401–25.

Hardy, Anne, *The Epidemic Streets. Infectious Disease and the Rise of Preventive Medicine 1856–1900* (Oxford, 1993).

Hardy, Anne, 'Food, Hygiene and the Laboratory. A Short History of Food Poisoning in Britain, c. 1880–1950', *Social History of Medicine*, **12** (1999), 293–311.

Harris, Bernard, 'The Demographic Impact of the First World War: An Anthropometric Perspective', *Social History of Medicine*, **6** (1993), 343–66.

Harris, Bernard, *The Health of the School Child. A History of the School Medical Service in England and Wales* (Buckingham, 1995).

Harris, José, 'War and Social History: Britain and the Home Front during the Second World War', *Journal of Contemporary History*, **1** (1992), 17–35.

Hilton, Matthew, *Smoking in British Popular Culture* (Manchester, 2000).

Hodgkinson, Ruth, *The Origins of the National Health Service. The Medical Services of the New Poor Law 1834–1871* (1967).

Holloway, Sidney W. F., 'The Regulation of the Supply of Drugs in Britain before 1868', in Roy Porter and Mikúlas Teich (eds), *Drugs and Narcotics in History* (Cambridge, 1995).

Honigsbaum, Frank, *The Division in British Medicine: A History of the Separation of General Practice from Hospital Care, 1911–1968* (1979).

Honigsbaum, Frank, *Health, Happiness and Security: The Creation of the National Health Service* (1989).

Horrocks, Sally M., 'Nutrition Science and the Food and Pharmaceutical Industries in Inter-war Britain', in David F. Smith (ed.), *Nutrition in Britain. Science, Scientists and Politics in the Twentieth Century* (1997).

Howell, Joel D., '"Soldier's Heart": The Redefinition of Heart Disease and Specialty Formation in Early Twentieth-century Great Britain', in W. F. Bynum *et al.* (eds), *The Emergence of Modern Cardiology*, *Medical History* supplement No. 5 (1985).

Jay, Mike and Neve, Michael, *1900* (1999).

Jewson, Nick D., 'The Disappearance of the Sick-man from Medical Cosmology, 1770–1870', *Sociology*, **10** (1976), 225–44.

Jones, Greta, *Tuberculosis in Ireland* (Amsterdam, 2000).

Jones, Helen, 'An Inspector Calls: Health and Safety at Work in Interwar Britain', in Paul Weindling (ed.), *The Social History of Occupational Health* (1985).

Jones, Helen, *Health and Society in Twentieth Century Britain* (1994).

Karpf, Anne, *Doctoring the Media* (1988).

Keown, John, *Abortion, Doctors and the Law. Some Aspects of the Legal Regulation of Abortion in England from 1803 to 1982* (Cambridge, 1988).

Kevles, Daniel J., *In the Name of Eugenics. Genetics and the Uses of Human Heredity* (Harmondsworth, 1985).

Kunitz, Stephen, 'The Personal Physician and the Decline of Mortality', in Roger Schofield, D. Reher and A. Bideau (eds), *The Decline of Mortality in Europe* (Oxford, 1991).

Landesborough Thompson, A., *Half a Century of Medical Research* (1975).

Lawrence, Christopher, 'Incommunicable Knowledge: Science, Technology and the Clinical Art in Britain, 1850–1914', *Journal of Contemporary History*, **14** (1985), 503–20.

Lawrence, Christopher, *Medicine in the Making of Modern Britain* (1994).

Lawrence, Christopher and Dixey, Richard, 'Practising on Principle: Joseph Lister and Germ Theories of Disease', in Christopher Lawrence (ed.), *Medical Theory, Surgical Practice* (1992).

Lawrence, Ghislaine (ed.), *Technologies of Modern Medicine* (1994).

Laybourn, Keith, *Britain on the Breadline. A Social and Political History of Britain between the Wars* (Gloucester, 1990).

Leathard, Audrey, *The Fight for Family Planning. The Development of Family Planning Services in Britain 1921–74* (Basingstoke, 1980).

Le Fanu, James, *The Rise and Fall of Modern Medicine* (1999).

Lewis, Jane, *The Politics of Motherhood. Child and Maternal Welfare in England, 1900–1939* (1980).

Lewis, Jane, *What Price Community Medicine: The Philosophy, Practice and Politics of Public Health in Britain Since 1919* (Brighton, 1986).

Liebenau, Jonathan, 'The British Success with Penicillin', *Social Studies of Science*, **17** (1987), 69–86.

Lock, Stephen, 'Medicine in the Second Half of the Twentieth Century', in Irvine Loudon (ed.), *The Oxford Illustrated History of Western Medicine* (Oxford, 1997).

Loudon, Irvine, *Medical Care and the General Practitioner 1750–1850* (Oxford, 1986).

Loudon, Irvine, *Death in Childbirth. An International Study of Maternal Care and Maternal Mortality 1800–1950* (Oxford, 1992).

Loudon, Irvine, *The Tragedy of Childbed Fever* (Oxford, 2000).

Loudon, Irvine *et al.* (eds), *General Practice Under the National Health Service 1948–1997* (Oxford, 1998).

McKeown, Thomas, *The Modern Rise of Population* (1976).

MacLeod, Roy, 'Law, Medicine and Public Opinion: The Resistence to Compulsory Health Legislation, 1870–1907', *Public Law* (Summer, Autumn 1967), 107–28, 189–211.

Macnicol, John, 'The Evacuation of Schoolchildren', in H. L. Smith (ed.), *War and Social Change. British Society and the Second World War* (Manchester, 1986).

McPherson, Klim and Coleman, David, 'Health' in A. H. Halsey (ed.), *British Social Trends Since 1900. A Guide to the Changing Social Structure of Britain* (2nd edn, Basingstoke, 1988).

Bibliography

Malcolm, Elizabeth and Jones, Greta, *Medicine, Disease and the State in Ireland, 1650–1940* (Cork, 1999).

Marks, Lara, *Metropolitan Maternity. Maternal and Infant Welfare Services in Early Twentieth Century London* (Amsterdam, 1996).

Marland, Hilary, *Medicine and Society in Wakefield and Huddersfield 1780–1870* (Cambridge, 1987).

Martin, Moira, 'Medical Knowledge and Medical Practice: Geriatric Medicine in the 1950s', *Social History of Medicine*, **8** (1995), 443–61.

Means, Robin and Smith, Randall, *From Poor Law to Community Care. The Development of Welfare Services for Elderly People 1939–1971* (2nd edn, Bristol, 1998).

Melling, Joseph and Forsyth, Bill (eds), *Insanity, Institutions and Society, 1800–1914* (1999).

Mersky, Harold, 'Shell-shock', in German E. Berrios and Hugh Freeman (eds), *150 Years of British Psychiatry, 1841–1991* (1991).

Mitchell, Margaret, 'The Effects of Unemployment on the Social Condition of Women and Children in the 1930s', *History Workshop Journal*, **15** (1985), 103–23.

Murcott, Anne, 'Food and Nutrition in Post-war Britain', in James Obelkevich and Peter Catterall (eds), *Understanding Post-war British Society* (1994).

Oddy, Derek J., 'The Health of the People', in Theo Barker and Michael Drake (eds), *Population and Society in Britain 1850–1980* (1982).

Oddy, Derek J., 'Food, Drink and Nutrition', in F. M. L. Thompson (ed.), *The Cambridge Social History of Britain* (Cambridge, 1990), vol. 2.

Offer, Avner, *The First World War: An Agrarian Interpretation* (Oxford, 1989).

Oppenheim, Janet, *Shattered Nerves. Doctors, Patients, and Depression in Victorian England* (Oxford, 1991).

Parker, Roy, 'The Struggle for Clean Air', in Phoebe Hall *et al.* (eds), *Change, Choice and Conflict in Social Policy* (Gower, 1986).

Patterson, David K., and Pyle, Gerald F., 'The Geography and Mortality of the 1918 Influenza Pandemic', *Bulletin of the History of Medicine*, **65** (1991), 4–21.

Pennington, T. H., 'Listerism, its Decline and its Persistence', *Medical History* **39** (1995), 35–60.

Peterson, Jeanne, *The Medical Profession in Mid-Victorian London* (Berkeley and London, 1978).

Pickstone, John, *Medicine and Industrial Society* (Manchester, 1985).

Pickstone, John (ed.), *Medical Innovations in Historical Perspective* (Basingstoke, 1992).

Phillips, Jim and French, Michael, 'Adulteration and Food Law, 1899–1939', *Twentieth Century British History*, **9** (1998), 350–69.

Porter, Dorothy, '"Enemies of Race": Biologism, Environmentalism, and Public Health in Edwardian England', *Victorian Studies*, **34** (1991), 160–77.

Porter, Dorothy, *Health, Civilisation and the State: A History of Public Health from Ancient to Modern Times* (1999).

Porter, Roy, *The Greatest Benefit to Mankind. A Medical History of Humanity from Antiquity to the Present* (1997).

Porter, Roy and Rousseau, G. S., *Gout. The Patrician Malady* (New Haven and London, 1998).

Powell, Martin, 'An Expanding Service: Municipal Acute Medicine in the 1930s', *Twentieth Century British History*, **8** (1997), 334–57.

Bibliography

Pressman, Jack D., *Last Resort. Psychosurgery and the Limits of Medicine* (Cambridge, 1998).

Reiser, Stanley J., *Medicine and the Reign of Technology* (Cambridge, 1978).

Riley, James, *Sick not Dead: Sickness Among British Working Men in the Later Nineteenth Century* (Baltimore, 1997).

Rivett, Geoffrey, *From Cradle to Grave. Fifty Years of the NHS* (1998).

Robson, Michael, 'The British Pharmaceutical Industry and the First World War', in Jonathan Liebenau (ed.), *The Challenge of the New Technology* (Aldershot, 1988).

Scull, Andrew, *The Most Solitary of Afflictions. Madness and Society in Britain 1700–1900* (New Haven and London, 1993).

Searle, Geoffrey, *The Quest for National Efficiency* (Oxford, 1971).

Searle, Geoffrey, *Eugenics and Politics in Britain 1900–1914* (Leyden, 1979).

Shapiro, Arthur K., and Shapiro, Elaine, *The Powerful Placebo. From Ancient Priest to Modern Physician* (Baltimore and London, 1997).

Shorter, Edward, *Doctors and their Patients. A Social History* (New Brunswick and London, 1991).

Shorter, Edward, *A History of Psychiatry* (Chichester and New York, 1997).

Showalter, Elaine, *The Female Malady. Women, Madness and English Culture, 1830–1980* (1987).

Showalter, Elaine, 'Hysteria, Feminism and Gender', in Sander Gilman *et al.*, *Hysteria Beyond Freud* (Berkeley and London, 1993).

Sjøstrom, Henning and Nilsson, R., *Thalidomide and the Power of the Drug Companies* (Harmondsworth, 1972).

Slinn, Judy, 'Research and Development in the UK Pharmacuetical Industry from the Nineteenth Century to the 1960s', in Roy Porter and Mikŭlas Teich (eds), *Drugs and Narcotics in History* (Cambridge, 1995).

Smith, Francis B., *The People's Health 1830–1914* (1979).

Smith, Francis B., *The Retreat of Tuberculosis 1850–1950* (1988).

Soloway, Richard, *Birth Control and the Population Question in England 1877–1930* (Chapel Hill, 1982).

Stone, Martin, 'Shellshock and the Psychologists', in W. F. Bynum *et al.* (eds), *The Anatomy of Madness* (1985), vol. 2.

Szreter, Simon, 'The Importance of Social Intervention in Britain's Nineteenth Century Mortality Decline', *Social History of Medicine*, **1** (1988) 1–18.

Szreter, Simon, *Fertility, Class and Gender in Britain, 1860–1940* (Cambridge, 1996).

Szreter, Simon and Mooney, Graham, 'Urbanisation, Mortality and the Standard of Living Debate: New Estimates of the Expectation of Life at Birth in Nineteenth-century British Cities', *Economic History Review*, **51** (1998), 84–112.

Tansey E. M. *et al.* (eds), *Ashes to Ashes. The History of Smoking and Health* (Amsterdam, 1998).

Taylor, Peter, *The Politics of Tobacco* (1984).

Timmins, Nicholas, *The Five Giants. A Biography of the Welfare State* (1995).

Titmuss, Richard M., *Problems of Social Policy* (1950).

Thomson, Mathew, *The Problem of Mental Deficiency. Deficiency, Eugenics, Democracy and Social Policy in Britain c. 1870–1939* (Oxford, 1998).

Wackers, Ger, 'Innovation in Artificial Respiration: How the "Iron Lung" Became a Museum Piece', in Ghislaine Lawrence (ed.), *Technologies of Modern Medicine* (1994).

Wainwright, Milton, *Miracle Cure* (Oxford, 1990).

Bibliography

Wall, Richard, 'English and German Families and the First World War, 1914–1918', in Richard Wall and Jay M. Winter (eds), *The Upheaval of War. Family, Work and Welfare in Europe, 1814–1918* (Cambridge, 1988).

Watkins, Elizabeth, *On The Pill. A Social History of Oral Contraceptives 1950–1970* (Baltimore and London, 1998).

Weatherall, Miles, *In Search of a Cure. A History of Pharmaceutical Discovery* (Oxford, 1990).

Webster, Charles, 'Doctors, Public Service and Profit: General Practitioners and the National Health Service', *Transactions of the Royal Historical Society*, **40** (1970), 197–216.

Webster, Charles, 'Healthy or Hungry Thirties?', *History Workshop Journal*, **13** (1982), 110–29.

Webster, Charles, 'Tobacco Smoking Addiction: A Challenge to the National Health Service', *British Journal of Addiction*, **79** (1984), 7–16.

Webster, Charles, 'Health, Welfare and Unemployment during the Depression', *Past and Present*, **109** (1985), 204–30.

Webster, Charles, 'Conflict and Consensus: Explaining the British Health Service', *Twentieth Century British History*, **1** (1990), 115–51.

Webster, Charles, 'The Elderly and the Early National Health Service', in Margaret Pelling and Richard Smith (eds), *Life, Death and the Elderly: Historical Perspectives* (1991).

Webster, Charles, *The Health Services since the War, 1. Problems of Health Care. The National Health Service Before 1957* (1994).

Webster, Charles, *The Health Services since the War, II. Government and Health Care – The British National Health Service, 1958–1979* (1996).

Webster, Charles, (ed.), *Caring for Health. History and Diversity* (Milton Keynes, 1996.

Webster, Charles, *The NHS: A Political History* (Oxford, 1998).

Welshman, John, 'Images of Youth: The Issue of Juvenile Smoking, 1880–1914', *Addiction*, **91** (1996), 1379–86.

Welshman, John, 'The Medical Officer of Health in England and Wales, 1900–1974: Watchdog or Lapdog?', *Journal of Public Health Medicine*, **19** (1997), 443–50.

Whiteside, Noel, 'Counting the Cost: Sickness and Disability among Working People in an Era of Industrial Recession, 1920–39', *Economic History Review*, 2nd series, **xl** (1987), 228–40.

Williams, Naomi and Mooney, Graham, 'Infant Mortality in an Age of Great Cities: London and the English Provincial Cities Compared, c. 1840–1910', *Continuity and Change*, **9** (1994) 185–213.

Winter, Jay M., 'Infant Mortality, Maternal Mortality, and Public Health in Britain in the 1930s', *Journal of European Economic History*, **8** (1979), 439–62.

Winter, Jay M., *The Great War and the British People* (Basingstoke, 1986).

Winter, Jay M., 'The Demographic Consequences of War', in H. L. Smith (ed.), *War and Social Change. British Society in the Second World War* (Manchester, 1986).

Winter, Jay M. and Robert, Jean-Louis (eds), *Capital Cities at War. Paris, London, Berlin 1914–1919* (Cambridge, 1997).

Wohl, Anthony, *Endangered Lives. Public Health in Victorian Britain* (1983).

Woods, Robert and Woodward, John, (eds), *Urban Disease and Mortality* (1984).

Woods, Robert and Shelton, Nicola, *An Atlas of Victorian Mortality* (Liverpool, 1998).

Wright, David and Digby, Anne (eds), *From Idiocy to Mental Deficiency* (1996).

INDEX

Barnaard, Christian, heart
    surgeon, 160
BCG vaccine, 101
benzyl benzoate, 117, 136
Bernard, Claude, experimental
    physiologist, 5, 25
Beveridge, Sir William, civil
    servant, 139
biomedicine, 4, 9
Birmingham, 30, 93
births, hospital, 105
birth-rates, 2, 39, 107
Black Country, 25
Black, Sir Douglas, scientist,
    170
Black Report, the, 2, 170–1
blackout, and meningitis, 118
bleeding, 27
blood transfusion, 64, 68, 129
Blood Transfusion Service,
    127, 128–9
Boer War, 40, 48–9, 60, 64, 175,
    177
Bolshevism, fear of, 78
bomb, the atom, 104
bomb damage to hospitals,
    World War II, 130
bombing, World War II,
    114–15, 133
Boot, Jesse, and Boots the
    Chemist, 21
Booth, Charles, ship owner and
    social investigator, 41
Bosanquet, Nick, historian, 82
Boston Women's Health
    Collective, 168
bovine spongiform
    encephalopathy, 165, 169
Bowley, Arthur, social
    investigator, 92
Boy Scouts, 48, 137
brain death, 168–9
brain function, 25
brain tumour, first removal of,
    25
Bretonneau, Pierre, physician,
    25
Bright, William, clinician, 25

Bristol Children's Hospital,
    170
Bristowe, John Syer, surgeon,
    26
British Broadcasting
    Corporation, 108, 168
British Expeditionary Force, 49
British Medical Association, 35,
    79, 98, 99, 108, 117, 175
British Restaurants, 124–5
Brompton Hospital, 170
bronchitis, 34, 165, 178
Brown, Louise, 163
Bryder, Linda, historian, 53
Budd, William, epidemiologist,
    25, 31
bulimia, 165
burns, treatment, 134, 154

C

Calmette, Louis, bacteriologist,
    101
cancer, 8, 13, 24, 91, 103–4,
    124, 163–4, 171–2, 179
    breast, 147
    lung, 103, 124, 148, 150–1
Cancer Act 1939, 79
canteens, World War II, 124–5
cardiology, 66, 68, 134
cardio-vascular disease: see
    heart disease
casualties
    civilian
        in World War I, 110
        in World War II, 110–11
    military
        in World War I, 49–50,
            133
        in World War II, 133
catering, mass, World War II,
    125
cattle plague, 6
Central Liquor Control Board,
    50
cervical cancer screening, 169
Chadwick, Edwin, civil servant,
    5
Charing Cross Hospital, 168

Index

Ferrier, David, experimental physiologist, 25
fertility treatment, 153, 161, 162–3
financial stringency
  during the nineteenth century, 19, 141
  from 1919 to 1939, 78, 91, 93
  and the NHS, 140–1, 142, 143–4, 145–6
First Aid Posts, World War II, 113, 127–8
fish and chips, 99
fitness
  mental, 73, 135
  physical, 108, 137
Flanders, 64
Fleming, Alexander, bacteriologist, 135
Fletcher, Walter Morley, MRC Secretary, 97, 99–100
flies, 12, 33–4
Florey, Howard, microbiologist, 135
fluoridation, 148, 149–50
fog, 12, 34, 149
food
  faecal contamination of, 33
  quality, 37–8, 165
  supplies in World War I, 51–2, 58
  supplies in World War II, 114, 122–5
Food, Drink and Drugs Acts 1872 and 1875, 37–8
fractures, 28
France, 47, 58, 64, 101, 105, 111
Franco-Prussian War, 60, 65
Freud, Sigmund, pioneer psychoanalyst, 74
Freudian analysis, 71, 157
friendly societies, 17–18, 29, 80

G

Galton, Sir Francis, scientist, 40
Garrison, Fielding, historian, 63

Garsington, Oxfordshire, 6
gas gangrene, 62
gas poisoning, 62, 67
gastroenteritis, 34, 124; *see also* diarrhoea
General Medical Council, 23, 166
general practitioners, 14, 16–17, 18, 82, 142–3, 177
General Register Office, 1, 6, 24
genetic modification, 165
Gerhard, William, physician, 25
geriatrics, 145
germ theory, 5,
German chemical industry, 26, 71
Germany, 40, 45, 48, 50–1, 80, 101, 108, 110, 166, 178
Glasgow, 39
gonorrhrea, 69, 104, 120–2, 135
gout, 37
government policy, 29–30, 37, 43, 77, 89, 91, 99–101, 104, 105–6, 110, 139–40, 166–7, 171–2
Great War, 47 et seq., 175, 177
  casualties, 49–50
  Eastern Front, 62
  Western Front, 59, 60
grenades, 64
Guerin, Camille, medical scientist, 101

H

Haldane, R. B., scientist, 40
Haley, Bruce, historian, 6, 7
Harley Street, 14
head lice, 116, 116–17
headaches, 18
health
  concept of, 7–8, 11, 92–3, 154, 161, 169, 173
  consciousness of, 6–7, 45, 106, 139, 169, 178
  education, 43–5, 125–6, 148–9

213

Index

Nicolle, Charles, bacteriologist, 61
night shelters, *see* shelters
Nightingale, Florence, social reformer, 45
nightsoil, 32–3
North/South divide, the, 2, 17, 172
Notification of Births Act, 43, 79
Nottingham, 33
nursing, 19
nursing homes, 122
nutrition, 9–10, 38–9, 41–2, 95–100, 176, 178
  science, 41, 97, 98
  standards, 98

O

obesity, 165, 170, 179
old people, *see* elderly, the
On the Origin of Species, 4
open heart surgery, 159
opticians, 143
oral contraception, 161–2, 163
organ transplants, 154, 159–60
organic foods, 169
Orr, John Boyd, nutrition scientist, 98–9, 178
orthopaedics, 65, 133–4
osteoporosis, 163
outdoor medical relief, 20
outpatients, in hospitals, 15–16
overcrowding
  domestic, 36
  in air raid shelters, 119
  urban, 12
oxygen therapy, 67–8

P

paediatrics, 29, 116
paediatric surgeons, 159
painkillers, 26
panel patients, 81
Panorama, 168–9
Parkinson, James, physician, 25
Parkinson's Disease, 153, 158

Pasteur, Louis, scientist, 5
pathology services, 131
patients, 14
pauperism, 19, 20
penicillin, 104, 135, 154, 177, 178
peptic ulcers, 158
pesticides, 151
pharmaceutical industry, 71, 166
pharmaceutical trade, 21
phenacetin, 22
phenazone, 22
physical fitness, 108
physicians, 14–5
physiology, 25
Pincus, Gergory, endocrinologist, 161
placebo effect, 3–4, 175
plants, wild, 137
plastic surgery, 134
poison gas, 67
poliomyelitis, 24, 155
Poor Law, 18, 19–21, 79
Poor Law doctors, 20
Poor Law hospitals, 19, 79
Poor Laws, Royal Commission on, 20–1
population, density, 12
Poubelle, Eugene, administrator, 34
poverty, 1–2, 41, 92–3, 173
prescription charges, 144
prescriptions, 14, 18, 82
pressure groups, 148–9
preventive medicine, *see* disease prevention
privies, 32–3
'problem family', the, 115
Prontosil, 105
Prozac, 158, 161
psychiatry
  in the nineteenth century, 71–2
  in World War I, 73–4
  in World War II, 134
psychoanalysis, 157
psychopharmacology, 158

Index

slum clearance, 36, 89
smallpox, 6, 26–7
Snow, John, epidemiologist, 25, 31, 35
social class, 14, 15, 17
  differentials in health between, 11, 170–2, 174
social insurance schemes, 20, 45
social investigators, 41–2, 170–1
'soldiers' heart', 66
soot, 149
special needs, 144, 146
specialism, medical, 16, 130–2, 138, 156
spectacles, 143
Spencer, Herbert, Victorian sociologist, 4
spina bifida, 165
sport, 108, 169
standards of living, 5, 9, 92, 106–7, 109, 139–40, 179
staphylococcus aureus, 154
state medicine, 30
statistical epidemiology, 148, 166
STDs, 6, 68–71, 120–2, 135, 171
Steptoe, Patrick, pioneer of infertility treatment, 163
steroids, 153, 156, 160, 178
stethoscope, 23
Stevenson, John, historian, 91
stillbirth, 165
streptomycin, 154
stress, civilian
  in World War I, 53–4, 176
  in World War II, 112
stroke, 171
suicide, 165, 172
sulphonamides, 104–5, 118, 121, 177
surgeons, 15
surgeries, general practice, 142, 143, 177, 178
surgery, 5, 9, 28
  for cancer, 103–4
Sweden, 58
syphilis, 26, 69, 120–1

Szasz, Thomas, medical critic, 168
Szreter, Simon, historian, 10

T

Tatham, John, supervisor of statistics, 24
Teesside, 35
tetanus, 65, 114
textbooks, medical, 24
thalidomide, 166–8
therapeutic revolution, 11, 139, 153–4
thermometry, 5, 23
Titmuss, Richard, sociologist, 111, 115
tobacco, 150–1
Tomes, Nancy, historian, 108
Topley, W. W. C., bacteriologist, 63, 116, 128
Torrens and Cross Acts, 36
trench fever, 62
trench foot, 62
Treves, Sir Frederick, surgeon, 28
trinitrotoluene (TNT), 57
tuberculin, 85
tuberculosis, 10, 24, 25, 44–5, 100–1, 165, 176, 177
  in World War I, 53–4, 56, 176
  in World War II, 112–13
  sanatoria, 45, 58, 80, 85–6
  vaccine, *see* BCG vaccine
tuberculosis service, national, 84–6
Turrill, Joseph, diarist, 6–7, 27
Tyneside, 35
typhoid, 5, 9, 25, 31, 33, 60–1
  vaccine, 26, 60–1
typhus, 5, 25, 61–2

U

unemployment, 93–4, 96, 177
unhealthy trades, 36–7
urban growth, 1, 12
urban health, 12–13, 172, 174